ROBERT WANG CENTER
FOR INTERNATIONAL BUSINESS
FOGEMAN COLLEGE OF BUSINESS & ECONOMICS
THE UNIVERSITY OF MEMPHIS

MOVING OUT TO MEET THE WORLD

25 YEARS OF
INTERNATIONALIZING STUDENTS,
FACULTY AND EXECUTIVES

DAVID YAWN

David Yawn
Corporate Chronicles
1082 Kings Park
Memphis, Tennessee 38117
USA

ISBN: 978-0-615-63166-0

9 8 7 6 5 4 3 2 1

Table of Contents

Figures

Appendices

Acknowledgements

The author wishes to acknowledge Robert and Susie Wang and Ben Kedia for their visionary roles in launching the Wang Center for International Business. Following Mayor William Morris' invitation, Robert Wang provided the necessary springboard funding and encouragement to proceed and Ben Kedia faithfully carried out the vision into commendable, real-life applications year after year as director of the center and progenitor of the International MBA program. Jeanne Tutor, who served as the program coordinator and office manager at the center, was a vital contributor in sharing her own memories and viewpoints throughout this process. She compiled and organized all information for the appendices, formatted the book, and inserted graphics. Interns involved for some stages of this book included Jacklyn Carroll, Deepali Devanur, and Michael Fisher. Rebekah Yearout, Jocelyn Regenwether, Barbara Stevenson, Pat Taylor and Jack Clampit played central roles as proofreaders. Charlie Spencer provided his professional guidance in preparing the book according to industry printing requirements. His photography work and expertise brought significant value to this process.

Preface

Today's businesses compete in a highly charged atmosphere with instant communication, rapidly changing commercial environments, and complex sets of relationships. American businesses are facing global competition as never before while other nations become industrial strongholds in their own rights and increase their market shares across a more interdependent world economy. Industries now deliver to a multicultural customer base across an increasingly aware international marketplace.

Though Memphis has been fortunate to have international corporations such as FedEx, International Paper, Holiday Inns, and more, the city would not have seen the degree of applicable global learning without the existence and expertise of the Robert Wang Center for International Business. In fact, such corporations benefit from international specialty seminars the Wang Center conducts in order to augment their own working knowledge of global business practices.

The center has successfully endeavored to serve colleges and broad community educational bases throughout the Delta region. Thus its motto stands as decidedly appropriate: "Moving forward, building on the past: Proven results for underserved constituencies." To accomplish this goal, the center keeps these priorities in mutual focus: international education, international research, international outreach and international development.

Without argument, this center's close-knit team has carved out a sterling reputation both internally and across many academic communities for its leading-edge program designs, competitive curriculum, CIBER status, excellence of instruction, country-focused conferences and in general, the plenary way in which it prepares graduates to substantially contribute to today's global business marketplace. Many hard-won federal grants gave the center an early credibility.

It was apparent from the beginning that two Chairs of Excellence housed at the Wang Center (such chairs are created by the Tennessee General Assembly to attract distinguished professors at state universities) were more than just research chairs – they truly embodied the spirit of "entrepreneurial" Chairs of Excellence in International Business and International Economics. As a global portal during the years, the full efficacy of the Wang Center had yet to be presented in a permanent form to the broader marketplace of students, professionals, educators and business communities until the creation of this volume. The center's 25-year milestone also coincides with the centennial observance of the University of Memphis, the institution from which the center was born and where it now continues to grow.

Notably, the Memphis CIBER (Center for International Business Education and Research) has received over $8 million in grant awards from the U.S. Department of Education, which has been leveraged to raise about an additional $2 million to carry out the CIBER legislative mandates over the quarter century.

Chief among the gemstone programs at the center are the well-established and thriving International MBA (IMBA), the mentoring of Ph.D. graduates, the continued outreach to the business community, faculty development in international business seminar outreaches to the academic community as a whole and Historically Black Colleges and Universities (HBCUs) in particular. To date, the center has produced more than 300 IMBA graduates and about a dozen Ph.D. graduates.

This multifaceted story covers successful, advanced programs of instruction, the proponents and professors who participate in these, and additionally, the students and companies that benefit from its advances. Clearly, the Robert Wang Center at the University of Memphis serves as a diadem of the larger institution, a type of beacon on the hill that elevates the reputation of the entire university. It achieves this status consistently, year after year, primarily by meeting the mandates of the CIBER program created by the Omnibus Trade and Competitiveness Act. The center was created to conceptualize, initiate and conduct a full lineup of international programs and activities. Extensive research went into optimal ways to create and structure these programs to the benefit of faculty, students and executives.

"The research that faculty and graduate students conduct is also part of the vitality of this university and helps us connect with business programs at universities around the world," said University of Memphis President Shirley Raines. "The overseas internships for students are also so valuable in this regard. Business executives who hire our students have often said in essence, 'They arrive with their briefcases packed.' They know about the business world and have had that intellectual stimulus, which includes the knowledge and skills to also start businesses and become entrepreneurs. It is important for the small-business entrepreneurial fever that has captured the imagination of the business world to be part of globalization and its issues. Meeting and seeing people working around the globe makes a real difference. The Wang Center and Ben Kedia have used interdisciplinary teams of professors who all work together to help students understand countries, cultures and their unique business practices. They don't just theorize; faculty and students meet real people engaged in the business."

The group of institutions that have been accorded CIBER status by the U.S. Department of Education is an enviable circle (which includes schools such as Wharton, Columbia and Michigan State) and the Wang Center stands firmly among those ranks. Its edges of distinctiveness and various educational strong suits are elucidated across the course of this book. The passion for internationalization led to innovative programs initiated and directed by Kedia. This center encompasses the spirit of transformative persistence and a quest for excellence.

Robert and Susie Wang's own good-faith investment to launch the center a quarter-century ago became the bedrock and beachhead for international resources that have significantly grown and flourished. The philosophy of the center displays how it has been able to set itself apart as a top-tier academic showplace. To crown the work, successful graduates of the IMBA program, university faculty program participants, and executives provide testimonials. The process and curriculum are completely outlined in this account, even though it will inevitably continue to evolve over future years.

Dr. Tamer Cavusgil, who headed the Michigan State University CIBER program for 22 years and who is now Callaway Professor of International Business and Executive Director of CIBER at Georgia State University, has an informed perspective. "I have visited the Wang Center for at least 20 years, back when it was Memphis State University (MSU)," Cavusgil noted. "I followed the internationalization of the business program for some time at MSU and have always been impressed. Memphis was one of the earlier CIBER programs.

"I think it is one of the most prolific CIBERs in the country," Cavusgil elaborated. "They have a wide range of activities, including study abroad programs and faculty development, research and outreach programs. These are some of the most important contributions CIBERs can make, along with their business language curriculum.

"In order to carry on such a great agenda, these centers need a good team and the group in Memphis has always been accomplished and hardworking," the educational figure noted. "It requires leadership and structure in order to orchestrate such a program."

The Memphis CIBER also took the leadership in terms of bringing together a number of Historically Black Colleges and Universities (HBCUs) in order to infuse international education into their programs, and preparing their faculty to do so, he noted. "They also assisted in helping these schools prepare grant proposals for proper funding which has constituted an important contribution," added Cavusgil. Memphis is home to one of the most admired, respected and recognized programs by the U.S. Department of Education because of its value-added dimension in terms of reaching out to underserved universities.

"What began as a nice vision has become a living, breathing organism," said Mike Ducker, chief operating officer and president of the International Division at FedEx Express, in speaking of the Wang Center. "It is dynamic in terms of the experience that it gives students, the community and business leaders. From my personal perspective, it provides much greater exposure to international business than other programs in the area. The Memphis CIBER brings a high level of educational awareness combined with a practical approach to doing business. This is highly valuable to our city, state and individual companies such as ours at FedEx."

"Increasingly, as we are competing across the global marketplace, businesses are thinking about how to become more effective because of this present world of new markets, customers and innovative ideas," the senior FedEx executive added. "The center brings a different, practical perspective. With the kind of graduate program like the International MBA, you not only gain more technical skills, but also learn to think differently about complex problems. Moreover, it creates networks of people with whom you potentially can be in contact with for life."

This quarter-century time period provides the perfect juncture to take a close look at how the center has become an exemplary template for global learning.

–David Yawn

Establishment of the Robert Wang Center for
International Business at Memphis State University
1988

(Left) Dean Taylor Sims, President Thomas Carpenter,
Mayor William Morris, Robert Wang and Susie Wang

Foreword

An Inside Perspective from a University President

Dr. V. Lane Rawlins, former president of the University of Memphis (1991-2000), recalls in detail the early growth of the center. The Wang Center had just been established when he arrived in Memphis. "One of my early dinners was with Robert and Susie Wang, and I remember our conversations about their desire, and mine, to make the Wang Center something special for both international connections and broadening the education of business students from the U.S. and around the world. The University of Memphis is fortunate to have alumni and supporters as visionary and generous as the Wangs," said Rawlins, who is now president of the University of North Texas.

"I remember clearly the decision to go ahead with the IMBA under Ben's leadership and the high standards that were set," Rawlins said. "I also know the important part that the Wangs played helping with support, internships, and other matters. Ben Kedia's success at getting support for international business education is phenomenal and his record with CIBER grants is extremely impressive. I always tried to support his initiatives because they were winners for the students and the university. As my wife, Mary Jo, and I visited many overseas universities and internship sites together, our respect and affection grew for the Kedias. I traveled with Dr. Kedia to several countries and was always amazed that he knew people, had connections, and was revered by his colleagues. I learned from Ben and marveled that he was at home in London, Munich, Tokyo, Beijing, Hong Kong, or wherever business and education had a relationship."

"During my tenure at the University of Memphis, I saw the Wang Center and its programs go far beyond the scope of international business and become the central driver for our international programs across the campus," Rawlins continued.

"Dozens of faculty from many areas were supported in international experiences and students were given a chance to be involved in a way that is the equal of the great universities in the nation."

"The day Robert and Susie Wang became associated with the university was one of our brightest days, although no one could have known it at the time," the longtime collegiate administrator noted. "But the hopes and dreams of even the most generous and visionary are all for naught if they do not lead to plans and action. Kedia made the most of every opportunity and has made the Wang Center a jewel in the crown of the university and the envy of many other aspiring institutions. It is a great thing to celebrate these accomplishments."

Celebrating the Tenth Anniversary of the Robert Wang Center
September 8, 1999

(Left) Dr. Ben L. Kedia, President V. Lane Rawlins, Dr. Liliana Van Hoof
(University of Antwerpen), Mr. Robert Wang

Introduction

CIBER Program Specialist
U.S. Department of Education

Centers for International Business Education and Research (CIBERs) were created by Congress under the Omnibus Trade and Competitiveness Act of 1988 and are administered by the U. S. Department of Education as part of Title VI of the Higher Education Act. The purpose of the CIBER program is to link the manpower and informational needs of U.S. business to improve international competitiveness through global business education, training, research and outreach.

After decades of resting comfortably at the top of the global marketplace, American companies have awakened to fierce competition from businesses operating in developed and developing nations. As more countries become industrial powerhouses and their companies seek larger marketplaces, competition will continue to rise. U.S. supremacy is being challenged as the powerful force of technology and transportation drives the world toward a more integrated and interdependent global marketplace.

Doing business in a global economy requires a lot of new learning, including a heightened understanding of diverse cultures; broad knowledge of global economies, geography, history and politics; greater appreciation of business functions as they span organizational and national boundaries; enhanced competitive challenges both at home and abroad; utilization of productive resources and innovative research regardless of locations; dealing with new and unfamiliar stakeholders; grasping increasing ambiguity surrounding decisions and outcomes; and addressing different ethical dilemmas across nations.

Since the first six CIBERs were established in 1989, the program has not only grown dramatically to include 33 centers nationwide today, but has also broadened its overall programmatic scope. In the beginning years, CIBER programs focused primarily on curriculum development; however, this focus broadened subsequently to include research on global competitiveness, faculty development in international business (both in the U.S. and abroad), learning of foreign languages and cultures, and outreach to businesses and other academic institutions. The University of Memphis' Robert Wang Center for International Business was designated as a CIBER by the Department of Education in 1990. This book provides the details of the Wang Center's accomplishments over the past 25 years and the impact it has had in terms of curricula, faculty development in international business, research, and outreach to the regional business community and other academic communities. Memphis CIBER has also partnered with 46 Historically Black Colleges and Universities (HBCUs) over a period of 10 years (which will be continued to 2014) to assist them in their internationalization endeavors by sharing its experience and expertise.

More specifically, over the past 25 years, the Memphis CIBER has:

- Established the International MBA (IMBA) Program with a focus on Germany, France, Japan, China, Mexico, South Asia, the British Isles and the United States. *303 students have graduated from the IMBA Program.*

- Advised and supported the undergraduate International Business Program (INBS), including study abroad and internships. *Currently, 157 undergraduate students are participating in this program*

- Provided research support focusing on international competitiveness for faculty and doctoral students and accorded them opportunities to present papers at national and international conferences, plus provided summer international business research support for selected business faculty and doctoral students. *The Memphis CIBER has supported more than 240 faculty and students in over 520 research presentations and other activities.*

- Organized an annual Faculty Study Abroad Program in Europe (Lille, France; Antwerp, Belgium; Strasbourg, France; or Brussels, Belgium). *313 faculty members from 140 institutions in 45 states have attended these programs.*

- Sponsored annual Globalization Seminars offered to U.S. business faculty. Currently, six seminars are available: Introduction to International Business, International Accounting, International Finance, International Management, International Marketing, and Global Supply Chain Management. *1,020 faculty members from 318 institutions have participated in this training, representing 48 states.*

• Created a consortium to support a four-year, lockstep program promoting the internationalization of business education on the campuses of HBCUs in partnership with other CIBERs and the United Negro College Fund's Institute for International Public Policy (IIPP). *Twelve (12) HBCU schools completed the 2002-2006 program; 14 HBCUs and 14 CIBERs partnered in the 2006-2010 program; currently, 20 HBCUs and 20 CIBERs are participating in the 2010-2014 program.*

• Conducted the annual Business Language Workshops for Spanish, French, German and Japanese foreign language faculty. *711 language faculty members from 360 institutions have participated in these workshops, representing 48 states.*

• Organized presentations to administrators, faculty and students, as well as provided consultation for adding international focus to business schools at over 90 U.S. academic institutions.

• Established Global Executive Network, International Business Breakfast Forum, and numerous international business seminars offered for business executives. *Over 6,500 participants from the business community have attended these programs.*

• Organized and delivered Global Business, Culture, and Leadership Seminars focusing on three regions: Asia, Latin America, and Europe. *More than 550 business executives have participated in this program.*

In summation, over the past 25 years, the Memphis CIBER has played a key role in internationalizing business education at the University of Memphis and other institutions in the region and the country. Through vision, creative thinking and judicious use of limited resources, the Memphis CIBER has emerged as an exemplary national resource center of global expertise. Students in the program have been able to develop global mindsets and build the confidence to effectively compete in the global marketplace. Faculty members have been funded to internationalize their courses and carry out research in keeping with the changing world, resulting in increasingly developed global mindsets through focused travel abroad programs. Furthermore, businesses have gained insights and training to help them export and succeed in international markets. Memphis CIBER's most significant contribution has been — and will continue to be — helping current managers and younger, emerging leaders develop the optimal capabilities for competing in the global marketplace.

Twenty-five years since the first six CIBERs were established, we certainly live in a different business world today. We have witnessed the power surge of regions beyond the U. S. and Western Europe. There is a growing need to deal with the rising prominence of China, India, Brazil and Russia. Rising tensions and diversities within the Middle East and the complexities of Africa and Latin America create new challenges and exciting opportunities. Multiple initiatives — from continuing professional education for faculty (and subsequent curriculum reforms and research opportunities) to forging alliances with other business schools overseas — will continue to challenge the Memphis CIBER to help key stakeholders address these new realities of globalization.

– Susanna Easton, CIBER Program Specialist,
U.S. Department of Education

Chapter One

❧

Global Macro Economic Changes
of the 1980s and 1990s

Before documenting the activities and accomplishments of the Wang Center, we feel that it is worthwhile to review the global economic changes of the 1980s and 1990s that served as the impetus for the founding of the CIBER program (Chapter 1), the city of Memphis' role as an international community (Chapter 2), the specific mission and vision of the Wang Center (Chapter 3), and explicit linkages between the University of Memphis and CIBER grant mandates (Chapter 4). This macro to micro approach provides a foundational background that should help readers better understand the Wang Center's purpose and accomplishments.

We begin by reviewing the changing global economic arena from 1980-1995, which serves as a parenthetical window framing the formative years of the Wang Center. It is through this contextual backdrop that the Wang Center formulated its international educational programs. Across the span of the 1980s, the world encountered a juncture of tectonic-scale changes in commerce. These rapid-fire transformations were being produced against a backdrop that displayed a wholesale migration of key nations into an unprecedented push toward more free-market economies.

Traditionally, three distinct types of modern-era economies existed across the world: planned economies, free market economies, and hybrid structures. During this significant decade, we saw a full-scale rolling back of the Cold War, new regional trade alliance formations, a weakening of the Japanese economy and the opening up of China to a new form of free-market commerce. It was in the midst of this economic structural reshuffling that the Robert Wang Center for International Business was born and formed. One might easily classify these waves of parallel global political and economic system transformations as almost unprecedented since the Industrial Revolution. See Figure 1 displaying this sea-change shift titled "Changing Political and Economic Systems 1985-2014." Figure 1 displays a strong, almost magnetic, trend line of shifts of most of the nations into a more free market, democratic quadrant from planned or mixed economic control structures. The following pages briefly describe some of these transformations whereby nation by nation discovered that planned economies were not the pathways to build wealth.

Soviet military buildup at the expense of domestic development kept the USSR's GDP at the same level during the first half of the 1980s. The Soviet-planned economy didn't respond adequately to the demands of a complex modern economic superstructure. Massive production often did not meet consumer needs. Decisions facing Moscow became overwhelming. When in 1985 Mikhail Gorbachev assumed power, a determined assault on the economic crisis was undertaken. It was a time of Perestroika (economic restructuring) and Glasnost (openness) across the former Soviet empire. The Soviet GDP rose sharply from $900

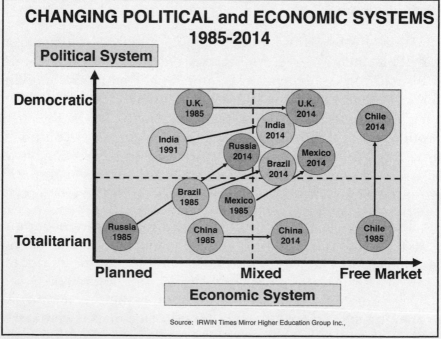

Figure 1. Changing Political and Economic Systems (1985-2014)

billion to $1.5 trillion in a period of five years: in 1989, the Soviet economy was one-third to one-half that of the U.S.

In 1991, Boris Yeltsin announced that Russia would proceed with radical market-oriented reforms along the lines of Poland's "big bang," also known as shock therapy. A conversion of the world's largest state-controlled economy into a market-oriented one would have been extraordinarily difficult regardless of directions selected. Russia embarked on liberalization, stabilization, and privatization. Eventually, the markets would determine prices, product mixes, and output levels. Efficiency was to be rewarded and waste punished. Only by stabilizing the national budget could the government dismantle the old planned economy and usher in capitalism, a position reformers held. Fixing a double-barreled combination of political and economic structures was a painful transition. At the same time, Russia had to deal with the larger disintegration of the union, all unique challenges. Former Soviet state enterprise managers were skilled at coping with old demands on them under the Soviet system of planned production targets, but the new incentive system of market capitalism mystified many. They knew how to meet old output targets but profitability was not as much part of the equation. New approaches would take years to master.

It was also a period during which **China** was exploring the potential of engaging in a free-market experiment, and then through for-profit joint ventures with worldwide entities. China's economy grew at an average rate of 10 percent per year during 1990–2004, the highest growth rate in the world at that time. Despite China's impressive economic development, reforming the state sector and modernizing the banking system remained major hurdles. Half of China's state-owned enterprises (SOEs) were inefficient and reporting losses. In 1997, President Jiang Zemin announced plans to sell, merge, or close most SOEs in a call for increased non-public ownership or privatization. In 2000, China claimed success in a three-year effort to make the majority of large state-owned enterprises profitable.

China serves as a prime example of a country maintaining a one-party political system while experimenting and undergoing tremendous institutional change. As a result, that nation has joined the global supply chain with a vengeance and is in the process of creating formidable multinational corporations itself. Thus China is not important merely due to its abundant and inexpensive labor supply, but it is also an increasingly important consumer market.

Indian economic policy, even after independence in 1947, was influenced by the colonial experience and became somewhat akin to a form of democratic socialism. Domestic policy tended to be protectionist with a strong emphasis on economic interventionism, a large public sector, business regulation, and central planning. It was a market-oriented, mixed economy. The state basically led economic development through nationalization, subsidization of vital industries, increased taxation, and highly protectionist trade policies. Steel, mining, telecommunications, insurance, and power plants, for instance, were effectively nationalized. However, trade and foreign investment policies were somewhat liberal. India's rate of growth in the first four decades after the 1947 independence was not favorable when compared, for instance, with growth rates in other Asian countries.

The collapse of the Soviet Union, India's former major trading partner, resulted in a balance-of-payments crisis. India asked for a $1.8 billion bailout loan from the International Monetary Fund (IMF), which in turn demanded reforms. In response, India initiated the economic liberalization of 1991. The reforms did away with the elaborate red tape required to set up and run businesses. Changes also called for reduced tariffs and interest rates as well as the end to many public monopolies. At last, foreign direct investment in many sectors gained an expressway-style approval system. India has progressed toward a free-market economy with a substantial reduction in state control of the economy and increased financial liberties.

Mexico's economy became highly vulnerable due to state-controlled economic policies of the 1970s. These turned sharply against Mexico in the following decade and delivered the worst recession in the country since the Great Depression. By 1981, Mexico was facing sloping oil prices, higher world interest rates, rising inflation, a highly overvalued peso, and a crippled balance of payments that caused the flight of capital. Mexico's GDP grew at a rate of just 0.1 percent per year between 1983 and 1988, while inflation rose to an average of 100 percent. Consumption was highly restrained.

Pressure of rapidly accelerating inflation finally jolted the Mexican government into action and a high-level governmental team developed a stabilization plan. The stabilization program introduced an equilibrium budget and introduced a new currency pegged to the dollar. Once this realignment was achieved, the new currency would be introduced, accompanied by liberalization of trade to increase competition. Finally, in 1994 as fiscal and monetary policies were relaxed and foreign investment bolstered by ratification of NAFTA, the situation started turning the corner in terms of consumption and investments. Inflation was brought down to single-digit annual figures.

For **Brazil** during the second half of the 1980s, sweeping fiscal reform that enabled noninflationary financing of the public sector was needed to control inflation and restore the capacity to invest. Political obstacles prevented the reform from materializing. Between 1980 and 1985, the rise in the CPI (consumer price index) had escalated from 86 percent to 248 percent annually. In 1986, the situation became desperate. Brazil instituted a general price freeze, wage readjustment and freeze, and a freeze on rents and mortgage payments and on the exchange rate.

Fernando Collor de Mello was sworn in as president, facing imminent hyperinflation and a virtually bankrupt public sector. His administration introduced a stabilization plan aimed at removing restrictions on free enterprise, increasing competition, privatizing public enterprises, and boosting productivity. However, management errors and affected societal sectors pushed back earlier accomplishments. A new and determined minister of finance, Fernando Henrique Cardoso, led a sophisticated team to develop a new stabilization plan. That plan, launched in 1994, met little resistance because it was discussed widely and avoided price freezes.

Inflation was brought down to single-digit annual figures, but not fast enough. Brazilian goods became more expensive compared with goods from other countries, leading to account deficits. On a good note, interest was renewed in Brazilian markets as inflation rates stabilized. The Real Plan eliminated inflation after many failed attempts to control it. Millions of citizens turned into consumers.

Chile, around the time of the coup in 1973, experienced hyperinflation that reached 700 percent at a juncture when the nation with high protectionist barriers had no foreign reserves. GDP was falling. Expropriations, price controls, and protectionism led to the problems. Economic reforms were originally drafted by Chilean economists known as the "Chicago Boys" because many had studied at the University of Chicago. These were economists who mostly had opposed Salvador Allende's government. The plan had three aims: economic liberalization, privatization of state-owned companies, and stabilization of inflation. The reforms were implemented beginning in 1974 and continued through the early 1990s.

The international competitiveness of Chilean exports increased by a real exchange-rate depreciation of about 90 percent. This policy generated a boom in exports, led to reasonable interest-rate levels and helped prevent capital flight. This initiative also sought to consolidate market-oriented reforms of the 1970s and 1980s, including the privatization process, the opening of the economy, and development of new capital markets. It devised a plan to reduce import tariffs below the 35 percent level reached earlier to a lower uniform level along with the promotion of exporting by fiscal incentives and a competitive exchange rate. During 1974 and 1990, more than 500 companies were privatized. Economist Milton Friedman called this process "The Miracle of Chile" to describe liberal and free market reorientation.

Even the **U.K.**, which was heralded for a long time as Europe's premier example of a democratic, free market economy, in the two-decade foundational change period threw off many of the shackles of its Labor Party-controlled, state-owned industrial superstructure whose tentacles particularly spread across transportation and energy industries. The election of Margaret Thatcher in Great Britain in 1979 marked the end of the post-war consensus – a mixed economy with nationalization of major industries. It brought forth a new approach to economic policy with privatization, deregulation, and tax structures.

Major state-controlled firms were privatized in the 1980s, including British Aerospace, British Telecom, British Leyland, Rolls-Royce, and British Steel. The English electricity, gas and water industries were divided and sold. Currency exchange controls were abolished. The Single European Act allowed for the free movement of goods within the European Union. The subsequent recovery, which saw growth of over 4 percent late in the decade, led to claims of a British "Economic Miracle." By the end of 1986, Britain was enjoying an economic boom, and the area saw unemployment drop substantially by the end of the decade. The British economy continued to grow well into 1990.

Due to these transformations, the high-flying growth rates in various countries of the developing world were still playing catch-up with mature industrial markets. The Group of Seven (G7) agreed to open their telecommunications markets and define policies. The group is comprised of seven of the world's leading countries that meet periodically to achieve a cooperative effort on international economic and monetary issues. The G7 began in 1975 as the Group of Six and included the countries of France, Germany, Italy, Japan, United Kingdom, and United States, and was joined by Canada the following year. Collectively, the G7 nations comprise about half of global GDP.

China, with one billion potential customers, continued to represent a fertile ground for business. The U.S. National Intelligence Council has said that the likely emergence of China and India as new major global players – similar to the advent of a united Germany in the 19th century and a powerful United States in the early 20th century – will transform the geopolitical landscape with impacts substantially as dramatic as those in the previous two centuries. That would produce four major economic blocks by 2050: China, India, the United States and the EU.

In essence, nations around the world were finally coming to the pragmatic realization that state enterprises have not and do not work well as wealth creators. If this root realization had arrived earlier, the European Union member nations might not be facing the degree of austerity measures they put in place in 2012. In essence, the world was greatly transforming in a relatively short time frame. These changes have not come about easily. Countries have gone through trials and errors, advances and regresses and often one step forward and two steps backward through political and economic experimentations over many years. Perhaps, these trials and errors will likely continue, but progress will continue to march forward as well.

Basically, emerging nations were all at once coming to the forefront of commerce. These countries included China, India, Brazil, Russia, Indonesia, Mexico and Turkey – all members of what was termed the E7, denoting the emerging economy nation state grouping. Meanwhile, the traditional G7 which constitutes the traditional advanced economics (including the U.S., Japan, and the U.K.) were experiencing external challenges to their longtime preeminent status. See Figure 2 titled "Relative Size of G7 and E7 Economies" showing that in 1990 the E7 (in terms of purchasing power parity) constituted 37 percent of the G7's GDP; in 2010 it was 57 percent; and it is projected to leapfrog to 145 percent in 2030, and 199 percent by 2050, according to World Bank, IMF, and Price-Waterhouse Cooper.

"What has happened in the past 25 years, no one could have even imagined then," said Ben Kedia, longtime director of the Wang CIBER at the University of Memphis, his tenure spanning the entire focal period of this book's coverage. Factors that led to the unprecedented changes include the fact that the G7 are mostly mature economies now with solidified and heightened wage rates, burdened by rising health costs, not to mention the

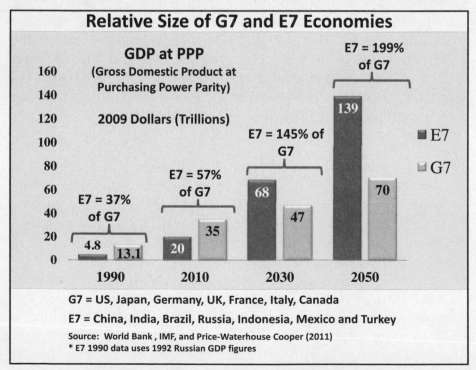

Figure 2. Relative Size of G7 and E7 Economies

retirement and pension commitments, particularly exercised de rigeur by European nations.

"The U.S. economy produced half of the world production with only five percent of the world's population in 1950 and today, produces about twenty percent of world production," Kedia said. "American managers increasingly face international competition from U.S. and especially from non-U.S. companies at home and abroad. These competitive pressures require firms to have globally competent managers with greater knowledge and skills to navigate organizations and to compete effectively both at home and abroad."

"It can hardly be expected that American businesses will continue to lead and compete in the world they don't sufficiently understand," Kedia said. "Therefore, it is an essential job of business schools to train their students in international environments, cross-cultural management, global financial markets, international marketing, and different business practices – especially as these relate to the fast-growing emerging markets of Asia, Africa, Eastern Europe, Latin America, and the Middle East."

Increased economic interdependence among nations is a key motivating reality behind the drive to internationalize business programs at all levels. Policies linking economies have thus redefined the contexts in which businesses operate. International trade, global capital investment and cooperative business ventures each require different types of understanding to function effectively.

Chapter Two

❧

Memphis as an International Community During the Wang Center's Startup Period

Memphis itself in the 1980s – the municipal home base of the Wang Center – has grown in successive waves to become an inland center of international commerce. Front Street cotton merchants were among the first in the city to build the bridge to overseas business, paving a trail for others to follow. The agribusiness industry helped generate what was for a long time the largest private company in Memphis, cotton merchant Dunavant Enterprises, which commonly brought in yearly revenues of over $1 billion. Cook Industries, a major commodities firm, Plough Inc., and Holiday Inns, an international hospitality enterprise, were other examples of Memphis-grown international ventures. All were very industrially vibrant when the Wang Center launched operations.

At the time of the Wang Center's formation in the 1980s, a study by the U.S. Department of Commerce ranked Memphis as the 38th largest exporting metro area and the 17th largest in terms of dollar volume increases. The Memphis Metro Area exported more than $3 billion annually, mostly in the form of commodities. An estimated 40 to 45 percent of the rice grown in the region and one-fifth of the Mid-South's cotton traditionally has been exported, so these commodities had long-standing overseas interfaces. In the agricultural arena, the city logically is the headquarters of the National Cotton Council, National Hardwood Lumber Association and Agricenter International, all of which have enjoyed exchanges with overseas companies and institutions.

Sharp Manufacturing Co. of America became the first major Japanese capital investment in Tennessee when in 1979 it opened a $20 million plant. Sharp in 1992 built an additional

140,000-square-foot, $16 million plant to make components for microwave ovens. Brother Industries USA, owned by Brother Industries Ltd. of Nagoya, Japan, employed about 600 people in the Bartlett area at the time, where it built an $8 million plant on 20 acres in 1987. Brother made a subsequent $4.9 million expansion and added shifts in 1990 – serving as a trend line then for Japanese companies both planting and growing in the city.

The U.K. also had a particular interest in the city on the Mississippi River. The following British companies had acquired parts of all of these large companies, most of which were founded in Memphis: Bass PLC ($2.3 billion in 1990 for Holiday Inns), GKN ($30 million in 1979 for Parts Industries Corp.), Sedgwick James ($307 million in 1986 for Crump Cos. Inc.) and Smith & Nephew ($283 million in 1987 for Richards Medical Co.) Smith & Nephew Richards Inc. in 1989 completed a $6 million addition to its administrative and research complex. Smith & Nephew since then opened a $5 million, 56,000-square-foot addition to its headquarters in a move that allowed the company to expand its staff.

Since 1947, the Memphis World Trade Club had assembled those involved in international trade, and the Mid-South Exporters Roundtable grew as another trade group for those engaged in overseas business. The Memphis International Council acted as a clearinghouse for many of the organizations. The U.S. Department of Commerce International Trade Administration also established a presence in the city and in 1996, the office became an Export Assistance Center, part of a national and regional network of export experts. Moreover, the Memphis 2005 strategic initiative had, as one of its many goals, the enlargement of the international trade and investment index for the Memphis MSA.

On the cultural/business side, the Memphis in May International Festival celebrates a different country each year. Now attracting over one million celebrants to its month-long series of programs, the festival has long been recognized as a centerpiece of the city's annual event calendar.

Distribution centers and warehouses were at the top of relocating industries' site selection criteria lists. At the time the Wang Center opened, Memphis sported some 105 million square feet of industrial space, most of it geared toward warehousing. Several common elements determined the interest of the larger firms relocating to Memphis. These included ease of distribution throughout the U.S. with a particular focus on Southern market access, the airport, location on the river, dual interstate connections, a conducive climate, several Class I railroads, scores of motor carriers, reasonable taxes, good labor market, drop-off shipping advantages afforded by the FedEx SuperHub's proximity, and a cooperative government.

In addition to multiple professional trade associations in Memphis, the city over time established chapters of several cultural organizations geared toward foreign visitors and commerce, such as the World Affairs Council, Memphis International Council, Friendship Force, and the Memphis Council for International Visitors. As spread out as international firms are on the globe, they nevertheless made Memphis one of their points of connection as they shifted their attention from the coastlines more into the heartland of Middle America.

About 50 international firms conduct regular business in metropolitan Memphis, representing more than a dozen foreign nations and providing thousands of jobs. The city has moved out of its regional sphere and into more of an international orbit. The new world citizenship that has been imposed upon the region also carries with it a responsibility for active participation on the world stage.

A Snapshot of the University at the Time the Wang Center Opened

The 1980s at the University of Memphis (then Memphis State University) could be thought of as the "Dr. Tom Carpenter" era, as he was hired in 1980 to become the university's ninth president. MSU was growing increasingly into a refined identity in that decade as witnessed in part by several milestones. *The Helmsman* grew into a daily newspaper, the Communications and Fine Arts Complex was completed, the university celebrated its golden anniversary, an early scholars program was introduced to attract high school seniors with high GPAs, and the state General Assembly created Chairs of Excellence with a $44 million appropriation that could be matched by private funds, among other major strides. This funding was significant as eminent scholars and research initiatives could be attracted even more to the state's public institutions. The first Chair of Excellence at Memphis State University, one in molecular biology, was established through a matching gift. Overall, the university funding formula was revised to help bring funding to parity with other comparable regional universities.

The university's state-of-the-art Fogelman Executive Conference Center opened in 1986, complete with dining facilities, a multi-level lodging complex, a couple of presentation theaters, meeting rooms for breakout sessions and most importantly in this regard, the housing of the Wang Center and also the Bureau of Business and Economic Research. The School of Accountancy, meanwhile, was established during that same year at Fogelman College.

Milestone after milestone was being marked campus wide across the landscape of the 1980s. University administrators saw that the Marcus W. Orr Center for the Humanities was formed to encourage interdisciplinary research and teaching, and the Center for Research Initiatives and Strategies for the Communicatively Impaired was launched as a Center for Excellence in the School of Audiology and Speech Language Pathology.

Dr. James Muskelley, the university's then-director of international studies, found it was remarkable that only a few years prior, there were few opportunities for Memphis State's students to study abroad. There was no formal exchange program at all, Muskelley noted at the time. Few students would sign up for foreign study programs sponsored by other universities and participation was sporadic. When Memphis State University became a member of the International Student Exchange Program (ISEP), it helped arrange one-to-one exchanges between foreign institutions, beginning in 1988. More than 200 universities and 35 nations were then members of ISEP. Muskelley noted in the *Memphis State Magazine* that language barriers, high tuition costs and confusing procedures often prevented students from arranging foreign study programs on their own. An early international stride was accomplished in 1985 when MSU signed an exchange agreement with Huazhong Normal University in China, laying early groundwork in this regard.

The Commercial Appeal in July of 1991 published a full exposition of the Fogelman College of Business through an article penned by staff reporter Lisa Jennings. She described how former Memphis State University President Carpenter wanted the university to become the flagship institution for business and the Fogelman College of Business and Economics to be a flagship college of the university. Not only that, but he wanted the College of Business to play a key role in the city's economic development as a whole. The business college at that time had drawn national attention, particularly for recruiting widely recognized faculty. Fogelman College was then one of about 280 business schools in the nation accredited by the American Assembly of Collegiate Schools of Business, the only recognized accrediting agency for such schools. The college at that time held nine of the university's Chairs of Excellence, designed as funded faculty positions created with outside donations matched by the state. The business school also was cited for distinguished professorships, which are positions similar to Chairs of Excellence, though funded by the university.

The article additionally described how the Wang Center was striving to encourage international business by establishing faculty and student exchange programs overseas and forging ties with foreign business communities. Kedia mentioned how the goal even then was to closely link liberal arts and business faculty members to offer a more holistic education. Instead of learning just about business in other countries, students would be taught about culture, language, and geography as well as business practices. It is notable that the Wang Center's own internal strategies for internationalizing business school components were affecting various departments effectively as early as 1991. More faculty members were involved in developing international emphases in their own disciplines. They started participating in summer course programs and spent time as visiting professors at overseas universities. Moreover, they partnered with faculty members from other institutions to initiate and promote cross-disciplinary dialogues. Some invited foreign dignitaries to speak. Functional areas of business such as accounting, finance, marketing, and management began to be taught within a global context or with an international dimension.

Near the same time (1991), Dr. V. Lane Rawlins replaced Dr. Tom Carpenter as president of the university. Rawlins was previously vice chancellor for academic affairs for the University of Alabama system. As an administrator, he oversaw more than a thousand faculty members. Even in his earliest remarks upon arriving at his new position in 1991, President Rawlins said, "There are going to be some research areas that clearly are going to be international, including a growing emphasis on research in the field of molecular biology. I would like for Memphis State to take its place as a major urban research center, particularly in research applied to problems of modern society."

Working then as dean of Fogelman College, J. Taylor Sims was involved with the center during its first couple of years, so he was engaged in its earliest stages of development. "The timing back in 1988 was appropriate as part of the funding opportunities to develop an excellent faculty and enhance our programs. It was literally the most excellent opportunity in the college's history to develop an international center with assistance from private, state and federal funding. This was the time matching funds were available from the state for Centers of Excellence and endowed faculty," said Sims.

During his five-year tenure as dean, Sims helped develop endowed professorships in every academic area including two for the Wang Center which provided necessary steps to, among other things, develop an excellent doctoral program.

"My practice was to hire the best people available, even some advanced associate professors, promote them to tenured full professors with an endowed chair, upon their entry into the college," Sims said. "Ben Kedia was a professor at LSU whose dean, Jim Henry, a friend of mine, was sorry to lose him, but could not compete with me in terms of an offer. I must say that Kedia was and is my superstar. Upon arrival, he immediately went to work on a U.S. Department of Education CIBER grant in a joint effort with Southern Illinois University (SIU) focusing on the Delta Region. SIU later dropped out because of lack of funding. The project was Ben's. He has held the endowed Chair for the balance of his career and the directorship of the center with rave reviews." Sims now has a leadership role in his work at Old Dominion University.

In 1991, MSU named Otis W. Baskin as the new dean of the Fogelman College of Business and Economics. He filled the vacancy created the prior June when Sims left to become vice president and provost at Cleveland State University in Ohio. Baskin had headed development of a new business school at Arizona State University West. The Fogelman College of Business even at the time was the largest college on the MSU campus. Nearly one of every four declared majors at the university was at that time seeking a business degree. The college then had about 3,200 undergraduate students and 900 graduate students seeking master's degrees and about 100 others working toward doctorates. Baskin was a believer in cultivating useful ties among business schools, local companies and promoters of economic development.

The University of Memphis (which changed its name in 1994) in February of 1998 established its 24th Chair of Excellence and was seeking a top-ranked scholar in international business to fill the new professorship. The Sparks Family Chair of Excellence in International Business was established with a gift from Memphis businessman Willard R. Sparks and his wife, Rita T. Sparks. The state provided matching funding for the $1 million endowment. The Sparks Chair was the tenth Chair of Excellence for the Fogelman College of Business and Economics. By the close of the year, the University of Memphis was the proud repository of two major building facility additions: the $26 million McWherter Library and also the $6 million Michael D. Rose Theater.

Dr. Rawlins left the university in 2000 to become president of Washington State University. Dr. Ralph Faudree, dean of the College of Arts and Sciences, became interim president. He now serves as provost. "The Wang Center has had a substantial impact on all of the international programs at the University of Memphis, and not just those associated with the Fogelman College of Business and Economics," notes Provost Faudree. "Dr. Kedia reached out to other colleges, such as the College of Arts and Sciences, to involve both faculty and students from these disciplines. Consequences of this were an increased flow of international visitors and students, additional international experiences and study abroad opportunities for U of M students, in addition to an internationalization of the curriculum. Dr. Kedia is a person who is comfortable in such a wide range of environments and he effectively used this to actively promote the Wang CIBER in particular and internationalization in general." Faudree noted that, surprisingly, the first time that they met was in Budapest, Hungary, in 1990 after Kedia took the Chair of Excellence position at the University of Memphis. "I was there on an academic leave and he was attending the Association of Universities for Democracy Conference promoting international programs for the U of M."

Dr. Shirley C. Raines became the 11th president of the university in 2001 and also the first woman to hold that position. "During these 25 years, we have seen the kernel of an idea with the emphasis on international business grow substantially among our students and faculty as we bring our students to the world and the world to our campus," President Raines recently said during an interview. "Having working alliances with other international business educational institutions allow us to keep in touch with international business education and research strides. Like all good sustainable initiatives, it started with a very good sound idea at its core and expanded in meaningful ways to represent various entities at the University of Memphis and what it should stand for as a metropolitan research university."

Soon after President Raines' appointment, the Kemmons Wilson School of Hospitality and Resort Management, a $15 million facility, opened as a combined hotel and school. Two other major facilities joined the main campus map in 2003: the John Wilder Tower, a multi-use administrative student services building (representing a full-scale renovation of the former library) and the FedEx Institute of Technology, situated next to Fogelman College of Business and Economics. U of M broke ground on the three-year construction on a $46 million, 170,000–square-foot replacement University Center, the largest building on campus since the new library, in 2007. The same year, the Confucius Institute opened in partnership with Hubei University in Wuhan, China. The institute promotes the understanding of Chinese language and culture.

Fogelman College of Business began an online master's in business administration degree in 2009, requiring two on-campus residence sessions. The university also launched its School of Public Health that year, offering a Ph.D. track in social and behavioral sciences the following year. The Cecil C. Humphreys School of Law reopened in the heart of Downtown in the renovated space of the former Front Street Post Office to be closer to the courts district. The university launched its year-long Centennial Celebration in 2011.

Chapter Three

❧

The Formative Mission
and Vision of the Wang Center

Now that the discussion has progressed from the big picture of the world and its regions, then to the city of Memphis and an overview of the University of Memphis, it is logical now to bring the focal point to the Robert Wang Center itself and its benefactors.

"Without Memphis State, I would not be here," said an appreciative Robert Wang near the time of the center's dedication.

"The university gave me a $2,200 graduate assistantship. It is time to pay back," Robert Wang said again during his acceptance speech of the Distinguished Alumni Award. He viewed the center as responding to a need he saw in the Memphis business community to expand from a regional hub to a strong international one. He declared, "I feel that in an urban university such as Memphis State, the obligation is to mix the existing business community with the academic world and then, both would benefit."

A Chair of Excellence is a trust funded by three sources. A private donor's funds are matched by financing from the university. In turn, the State of Tennessee appropriates funds equal to that of the private and university contributions. Robert Wang's benevolent gift to help launch the center's foundational beachhead was matched by the university and then by the state for a total of $1.25 million. Through the interest and efforts of William Morris, then mayor of Shelby County, the county government provided the initial funds to endow the Shelby County Chair of Excellence in International Economics. This effort was a first-case scenario locally in the matching of funds from a local government to produce such an endowment. Mayor Morris relayed his sentiments regarding the university's interest and concern for the global arena during a December 1997 commencement address to

Memphis State University graduates: "The economic interests of Memphis and our strategies to expand those interests span from the Pacific Rim to Western Europe and the Middle East." He was a longstanding advocate of growing international ties between the city and the world and also augmenting the university's own strong suits in the global arena.

Mr. Robert Wang
Benefactor and Namesake

Robert Wang

Robert Wang was born in China in 1948 and emigrated to Taiwan, where he completed his college education. Sociology, which he studied there, taught him to respect the relationship between cultures and values. While in college, he worked part-time jobs tutoring during the evenings and translating books from English to Chinese. This experience further enhanced his ability to study human behavior, culture, and psychology along with the basic business fundamentals necessary to be most successful.

"Learning is not just about school; it's about life," Wang once said in a booklet prepared for a program during his early years in business. "The more you learn, the more you realize how much there is to be gained, not only from everything you read, but also from every person you meet and every place you go. Learning from others' experiences leads to a willingness to share their knowledge and enriches life."

Robert Wang came to the United States in 1973 in a quest to learn more. After paying for his dormitory fee, he had only about $10 left. However, he was thirsty for this knowledge that would lead toward his goal, and he knew he could make it. "You have to believe in yourself, stay focused on what you want in life and go in that direction."

He received his master's degree in sociology with a good blend of business management courses. "My major helped me enormously in business by studying human behavior, culture and psychology along with the basic business fundamentals," Wang said.

In Memphis, Robert Wang not only studied different cultures, he actually experienced them too. "I was living a life thousands of miles from my Eastern upbringing, both literally and figuratively. And again, I was using this experience to learn about life in another country – a country founded on diversity and one that continues to grow with a unique blend of cultures and talents. We all have an opportunity here. We just have to set our sights on our own American dream and then work toward that with all of our energy and enthusiasm in order to prepare ourselves properly for success."

We have heard about starting a business on a shoestring, but how about macramé string? The only financial-related credit that Robert and Susie, his wife, had at the beginning of their business career was a credit card, so they invested in a van and a shipment of macramé cord, metal rings and wooden beads. Their apartment unit became their office where Susie maintained the daily operations while Robert was on the road selling the specialty home decor crafts. (Susie earned her MA from Memphis State University.) The early days were fraught with meeting a daily cash flow, the changes in the market, and high interest rates. All in all, the Wangs held steadfast to their business ethics of determination, honesty, hard work and working smartly through innovative practices.

In 1976, he and his wife laid out a map of the Mid-South, charted potential customers within a 400-mile radius and set out to sell $10 worth of merchandise for every mile traveled. It was a seven-day-a-week job. "I usually left late Sunday afternoon and returned home early Saturday morning," he recalled. "And then on Sunday morning, I went to the warehouse to fill orders for next week. Sunday nights, I was back on the road again." That schedule and working atmosphere represented the early phase of the business.

Susie Wang

In business, as in life, one must select the right partner. If you are happy at work and happy at home, you can take anything life may deliver, he said. "I had the good sense and good fortune to pick someone who is my partner both at home and at work. I met and married Susie Lee while I was at Memphis State University. I still consider that to be the smartest decision I ever made. Our sons inherited our passion and work ethic. They continue to be a constant source of wonder, love and pride and we learn from each other," he stated in an archival booklet. "It is an amazing and rewarding experience for families to share their hopes and dreams and knowledge."

In January 1981, Robert Wang was voted the first Memphis Small Business Executive of the Year. The event was cited in *Mid-South Business* (later *Memphis Business Journal*) newspaper with the headline, "**Wang's Quick Growth Secures Award: Wang's Ideas, Good Timing – Take $10 to $10 Million**." By 1986, the burgeoning business operated in over 500,000 square feet across multiple distribution centers, wholesale warehouses, showrooms and retail stores throughout the nation.

Over time, the company became America's largest distributor of craft, decor and specialty home items. Much of this success was generated by the innovative approach of the Wang couple and their dedicated employee team. Susie Wang's practical business acumen has served to forward the business at many junctures along the way.

Among awards and distinctions that Robert Wang has received include: the Master of Free Enterprise Award (1993 by Junior Achievement), the Memphis Small Business Executive of the Year plaque, the Memphis State Alumni of the Year Award, the Memphis Society of Entrepreneurs, the Cook Halle Award, and the International Business Person of the Year, presented by the Academy of International Business. Notable dignitaries who also received the Master of Free Enterprise Award, for instance, have also included: Frederick W. Smith, Abe Plough, Kemmons Wilson, Joseph R. "Pitt" Hyde and Michael Rose.

Success has been both exciting and rewarding. That being said, the Wang family has taken enormous pleasure in being able to give back to their community as well. "I know how hard it is to start with nothing and have to work and go to school at the same time," the company founder and center's namesake said. "I also know how important my education has been to me, so I've tried to help others share that experience." The endowment that established the Wang Chair of Excellence and the center with the support of others was Robert and Susie Wang's way of giving back to the institution which enabled them an opportunity to learn their trade. "My background in education helps me understand global business and cross-cultural differences and I want to promote and encourage this exchange of ideas and interaction around the world."

"I've always thought Memphis needed a more global view of what is going on," he continued. "We have good examples of that in the city, such as with FedEx, but some companies in Memphis limit their business to this region of the country. Memphis needed to expand its boundaries and explore the wealth of knowledge that is out there. The center has done a tremendous job of teaching that and brings a great deal to the area."

The entrepreneur uses the metaphor of climbing a mountain to describe the life of business. Thus, it is a journey whose steps count every bit as much as the destination. It also is the journey which provides not only the results, but the satisfaction as well.

Dr. Ben L. Kedia
Wang Center Director

While he was still at Louisiana State University – before he officially took his present position in Memphis – Kedia made the

Ben L. Kedia

strategic decision to visit the University of Memphis one day each month for a year. These key visits included meetings arranged by Thomas Miller, then chairman of the Department of Management. Kedia met with administrators, faculty and staff in departments campus wide, enabling him to gain a true framework and snapshot of potential collaborations and resources for the Wang Center activities.

Kedia, the holder of the Wang Chair of Excellence in International Business and director of the center, earned his Ph.D. from Case Western Reserve University in 1976, his MBA from Clark Atlanta University, his LLB (Bachelor of Laws) from the University of Bombay, and his B. Com (Bachelor of Commerce) from University of Rajasthan (India). His most long-term teaching and research interests include: cross-cultural and comparative management, international strategic management and business policy, and industrial organizational structure. Prior to his appointment to the Wang Chair, Kedia had served as a professor of management and chairman of the Department of Management at LSU.

He already had built up an distinctive record of research with numerous publications in nationally and internationally refereed journals. In addition, Kedia had many contract research grants at LSU ranging upwards of $96,000. He was able to obtain initial Business and International Education (BIE) grant seed money of $161,000 for a period of two years on behalf of the center at Memphis State University. During the twilight, or interim, hiring period, Kedia wrote the center's first CIBER grant proposal which was due in 1989 – all while he was still occupying his position at LSU. It was submitted by the University of Memphis. He supervised every successive grant application. The Wang Center now is the recipient of millions of dollars in grants and contracts, including the major grants from the U.S. Department of Education designating the University of Memphis as a national resource Center for International Business Education and Research (CIBER).

Over time, Kedia has directed multinational management courses in England, West Germany, Japan, France, Belgium, the Netherlands, Sweden, Denmark, Norway, the Soviet Union, and the People's Republic of China and Hong Kong, among other locations. In addition, he has traveled to Brazil, Argentina, Chile, Mexico, Austria, Hungary, Poland, Singapore, Thailand, Malaysia and Australia to present papers and seminars. He was a visiting scholar at the University of Strasbourg (France), Indian Institute of Foreign Trade (India), Nankai University (China), University of Dortmund (Germany), and Czech Management Center (Czech Republic).

The director has served as division chair, program chair and doctoral consortium chair of the International Management

Division of the Academy of Management. He also served as program chair, vice president and president of the Academy of International Business – U.S. Southeast and as president and member of the Executive Committee of the CIBER Association. His professional memberships have included the Academy of Management, Academy of International Business, Decision Sciences Institute, and the Southern Management Association.

Kedia brought a global view to the prestigious new center. Soon after his appointment in Memphis, Kedia spoke to various representative key organizations, including: the World Affairs Council, the World Trade Club of Memphis, the Mid-South Exporters Roundtable, the U.S. Department of Commerce-Export Office, the Memphis Area Chamber of Commerce, the International Business Council, the Tennessee Economic and Community Development, the World Trade Center of Chattanooga, Memphis Sales and Marketing Executives and Rotary Club, and other constituent groups. He has spoken on such topics as the European Union, complexities in managing international business, understanding cultural and organizational factors in international business, multicultural business negotiations, region-specific case studies of business blunders, traditions and transformations in Third World societies, and problem areas for exporters. The professor realized that almost every business starts as a small, fledgling operation. Kedia sometimes illustrated this through citing Mattel Corporation, which was born in a garage with a few dolls and then blossomed into a global industry. "The important thing is that someone has to have a dream and follow that dream," he said. Furthermore, he stated, "That's what makes small businesses into larger business. As areas of the world achieve more efficiency, they look for other companies for strategic alliances for production, marketing methods and managerial techniques."

During this time period of intense travel and commitment to the center and its initiatives, Kedia noted that he derived his most profound, long-term inspiration and encouragement from his wife, Asha, who patiently, competently and lovingly took care of the home front and their three children, Sanjay, Namita and Seema, who are all a constant source of joy and pride. He also equally cherishes his international daughter-in-law, Oksana, and two grandaughters, Alina and Maya.

University's Support of the Center's Missions

The university provided a foundation for the Wang Center – an incubator for addressing the need for building international alliances and global-oriented educational programs that were concurrently growing at the university. An early agreement with a French university permitted students from Memphis to spend a year studying in France. Dr. Victor Feisal, who was the university's vice president for academic affairs, stated in a university magazine in the spring of 1990, "Today's transportation and communication systems make it necessary for American students to know and understand other people and other cultures if they are to succeed in the modern world."

Kedia expressed early on his desire to create a new degree – a master's degree in international business which would require students to have foreign language skills and enhance those skills by spending six months working and/or studying overseas. It was necessary to develop 14 new international business courses, which Kedia hoped to be incorporated into the bachelor's and master's business administration degrees. Fortunately, that intention became a reality and the IMBA (established with the help of the aforementioned BIE grant and CIBER grants) came to fruition and stands as a core component of the center's programs.

"What comes to mind as a hallmark first and foremost with the Wang Center is its motivating and sustaining work with its IMBA program," said U of M President Shirley Raines. "The Memphis CIBER established the International MBA and made it work in ways that are significant. It has made sure it is translatable and transferable in different settings around the world."

Memphis Business Journal reporters in January 2006 asked administrators and faculty from area colleges to answer the following question: How would tomorrow's workers and business leaders benefit from participation in a study abroad program? Kedia replied that there is hardly any question that the pace of globalization is increasing, and to succeed in this environment, businesses will need managers who understand international markets, know a foreign language, and appreciate global cultures and their effects on business practices. Study abroad programs are one of the most effective ways to inculcate these global skills.

"Our educational institutions need to prepare global citizens who will be comfortable visiting, working and living in different countries," said Kedia. He touted the International Master of Business Administration program as a way to best prepare this new kind of global leader. The two-year program by that time required five years of foreign language classes – including three years at the undergraduate level – as well as a semester of study abroad and a semester-long business internship in the country of the student's language focus.

Indeed, studies show that students want to acquire foreign knowledge and experience to provide them with an advantage in their careers, which remains the strongest motive for going abroad. They want to improve their skills in business applications of a selected foreign language and gain better understanding of a different culture. Not only that, most seek adventure in the freedom that comes with being away from their home country. Some students who travel overseas for academic reasons also believe that the experiences will earn them recognition at home in addition to improving their employment possibilities. Traditionally, though, motivating students to participate in study abroad experiences has been a challenging task in American higher education. Using what he had learned in his studies, Kedia cited in 2001 that about one percent of students in American colleges and universities traditionally had participated in study abroad experiences. "American students need to be exposed to different cultures and approaches because they affect the way people think, solve problems, negotiate, value work, and reward achievement."

Chapter Four

❧

Positioning the Wang Center to Align with University and CIBER Grant Missions

The Robert Wang Center for International Business traces its inception from the initial funds made available by Robert Wang for a Chair of Excellence and its expansion to the congressionally mandated Omnibus Trade and Competitiveness Act of 1988 in which the U.S. government embarked upon a bold plan to significantly enrich the working knowledge that American business students would require to do business with the rest of the world. Thus, the U.S. Department of Education offered grant opportunities to establish Centers for International Business Education and Research (CIBERs). Furthermore, just prior to this legislation, Tennessee Gov. Lamar Alexander had created academic Chairs of Excellence and Centers of Excellence programs across the state. The programs established more than 20 chairs at Memphis State University, including 11 chairs in the Fogelman College of Business. This key move through Gov. Alexander's initiative placed on the blackboard for the Tennessee Board of Regents an opportunity to approve a measure that resulted in the establishment of the Robert Wang Center for International Business in 1988. What has followed in the path of these early seeds has grown into a robust program that amounts to a quarter century of progress.

CIBERs would become the regional and national repositories for teaching improved business methods, emphasizing the international contexts in which business is transacted. They were created to provide instruction in critical foreign languages and customs and offer research and training in international aspects of trade. Improving education in all of these areas would better prepare business people to engage with trading partners worldwide.

The Center's Mission and Vision Defined

The State Board of Regents intended for the Wang Center for International Business to serve as a focal point for learning, research and outreach. The Wang Center was established to complement other ongoing activities at the university, including multidisciplinary program development activities at the College of Arts and Sciences, and chiefly, at the Fogelman College of Business and Economics.

Months after the center opened its doors in 1988, a formal dedication ceremony was held on July 12, 1989 in its Fogelman Executive Center quarters near Central and DeLoach – now appropriately named Innovation Drive. A simple black-and-white invitation drew attendees. Once they arrived, they received a full-fledged program of dedication where there was a full slate of prominent keynote speakers.

Dedication of Robert Wang Center for International Business
July 12, 1989

Participating in Dedication Ceremonies for the Robert
Wang Center for International Business were (left to right)
Susie Wang, Robert Wang, Dr. Kanji Haitani, Dr. Ben L. Kedia,
Mayor Bill Morris and President Thomas G. Carpenter.

Fogelman College Dean Dr. J. Taylor Sims led the remarks with the assistance of Dr. Thomas Carpenter, president of the university. Shelby County Mayor William Morris and Wang Center chair holders Kedia and Dr. Kanji Haitani spoke to the audience, followed by benefactor Robert Wang. "The capability to compete in world markets must be founded upon an understanding of other cultures and the university's function is to enrich that understanding," Carpenter said in his speech.

"Our local economy is not local anymore," Mayor Morris added. "It is global, and if we are to be competitive in the future world economy, our businesspeople must have the skills, knowledge and academic backgrounds for this sophisticated international business world." Together, these remarks serve as an introduction and as a definition of the initial purpose and springboard role of the Robert Wang Center as it applied to the university and the community. Everyone – even initially – began to use the center as a benchmark in the community's quest to become an arena for international business learning.

The center was inaugurated, as well, to initiate regional, national and international undergraduate and graduate recruitment programs with the mission of solidifying interaction with local, regional, national and international business communities and organizations. The idea was to create an awareness of world-scale markets and the potential involvement of American business in those markets. The initial anchors of the center were the two endowed chairs: the Robert Wang Chair of Excellence in International Business and the Shelby County Chair of Excellence in International Economics.

Mayor Morris remarked further at the time, "I challenged my alma mater to set international affairs as a top priority. The creation of this center clearly demonstrates that Memphis State not only accepted the challenge, but responded with vision and energy. In so doing, it is establishing itself as a center of international learning." Continuing, Morris added that as the march of technology continued to shrink the "business time" that once separated us from other cultures and nations, the interconnectedness of the global economy was pounding at our proverbial trade gates .

In the *Memphis State University Magazine* article penned by reporter Susan Akers, university President Carpenter is quoted as describing the nascent center in this form: "Even though Memphis is an inland city, it is capable of being just as much an international trade center as a coastal city on either the West Coast or the East Coast. The establishment of the Wang Center is tangible evidence of our commitment to move in that direction. Our future as a society and as a nation depends on our ability to operate in a global society."

Furthermore, as Robert Wang himself stated at the time of its launch, "I feel that in an urban university such as this, the obligation is to mix the existing business community with the academic world – then both would benefit."

Dr. Sims, in a *Commercial Appeal* guest editorial column in 1989, postulated that the greater Memphis area was then in an ideal position for international business development and had the talent and economic attractiveness to move forward. He noted how Memphis already was following the international development plan of many forward-thinking local economies. A template that some business leaders in Memphis were following at the time was predicated on the National League of Cities' groundbreaking report titled *International Trade: A New City Economic Development Strategy*. This work provided a policy checklist for formulating strategies in the global marketplace.

Dean Sims discussed what he called five diverse policies for effective planning and action at the time: local government officials leading politically, educational institutions providing knowledge-based technical assistance to business, the chamber providing a marketing role, business leaders engaging in company formation and expansion, and community leaders developing an understanding of the need and importance of international development goals. The challenge – then as now – was to get every player to pull in the same direction at the same time without shifting the responsibility for arriving at solutions. "The goal," said Sims, "was to attract new business, expand existing companies, encourage capital formation and promote economic diversification."

The Center's Mission Tied to the Greater Mississippi Delta Region

The Memphis CIBER's story cannot be separated from the institutional, local, and regional contexts in which it operates.

Assets, challenges, and opportunities have all shaped the CIBER's focus and provided a framework for future plans. The Memphis CIBER operates amid surroundings defined by widespread poverty, lack of economic resources, and a stunted awareness of the rest of the world. At the same time, the region is characterized by tremendous natural resources, raw human capital, vital transportation routes, entrepreneurial spirit, and a willingness to collaborate through trade and commerce.

Memphis is positioned in the Mississippi Delta at the junction of Tennessee, Arkansas, and Mississippi, and serves as the geographic center and transportation hub for an eight-state region. The Delta must leverage its natural resources, develop the human resource base, capitalize on its transportation advantages, and continue to expand its businesses to compete efficiently. The Memphis CIBER has thus tailored many of its program priorities while developing partnerships with Historically Black Colleges and Universities and with multiple regional businesses and academic programs at the University of Memphis. Various partnerships have produced model programs that serve as the inspiration for other CIBERs. Moreover, it has influenced the curriculum at the University of Memphis, higher education in the state of Tennessee, and other institutions elsewhere in the U.S. and the world.

Throughout the process and from early onward, Susanna Easton, CIBER Program Specialist at the U.S. Department of Education, was very helpful to all CIBERs in interpreting the law and advising appropriately about the true meaning and expectations that were intended to guide the CIBER grant phase process, Kedia noted.

Business Models are Informed by Practical Research

"Research is an important part of what we do," Kedia said. "We examine prevailing social, cultural, political, technical and economic situations in foreign countries and look at their implications for international business in general, and American business in particular. All of those things can and do affect business." As an educator, he said he and his staff were tasked with the need to remove some of the psychological and attitudinal barriers for international business and provide knowledge, expertise and skills to succeed in the global marketplace.

Building upon this concept further, he believes that although larger companies are generally familiar with what it takes to establish business overseas, many have not made all the right calculations. When speaking of smaller business as a whole, he said there also needs to be a widespread change in managerial philosophy and orientation. "First of all, they must believe opportunity exists overseas and then take advantage of these opportunities," Kedia said. Many small Mid-South companies with quality products and competitive prices have not intensely explored opportunities abroad. To do so, they need to develop nurturing relationships with overseas representatives and clients. "It is not a quick-return scheme," Kedia cautioned.

Even though small American companies may find it difficult to break into foreign markets on their own because of lack of capital or depth of management, they can form strategic partnerships or alliances with overseas companies looking for partners wanting to enhance their own businesses.

Early Ventures for Institutional Collaborations

Beginning in the summer of 1990, Memphis State students started attending classes in Spain and England. Meanwhile, MSU professors were teaching at universities in Hong Kong and Czechoslovakia. The Wang Center already was working with the Memphis Area Chamber of Commerce and the Tennessee Department of Economic and Community Development (DECD) office to help identify and encourage export markets for state products. The center also had started working with state and federal agencies to attract foreign investors to Tennessee.

The Memphis CIBER center staff hit the ground running at the onset and over time continued to work toward creating potential collaborations with other universities. Kedia initially partnered with Southern Illinois in making application for a federal grant to establish a Center for International Business Education and Research. He also traveled overseas to discuss program funding mechanisms that would link Memphis State University and the University of Tennessee with counterparts in Eastern Europe. He and President Carpenter attended the founding conference of the Alliance of Universities for Democracy in Budapest, which was a group of independent universities formed to help

Eastern European educational institutions in their transition to democracy after the Cold War's aftermath. That gathering resulted in the decision by Memphis State and UT-Knoxville and others to apply for a grant from the U.S. Agency for International Development. The plan was developed to help those who taught under a communist system to inform their college students about mechanisms necessary for use in a market economy.

As early as 1989, Fogelman College of Business Dean Sims went on a 10-day trip to Japan to build ties between the college and several Japanese universities. The trip had grown out of talks that two professors in Memphis had with their counterparts in Japan and Europe. These conversations also became part of a plan to launch the new master's of business administration degree in international business. Professor Kanji Haitani at the time noted that such cooperation was essential in the increasingly global economy. He emphasized that American businesses must be adept in competing in such a climate, and furthermore, that business schools must internationalize their curricula and encourage the same in the business community. Kedia provided a major bulwark for this program, saying at the time that the budding International MBA program then being developed would require students to gain a working knowledge of international business. It was to include a foreign language requirement and a mandatory semester overseas.

The growth of the center coincided with many inroads the city and development officials were making overseas at the time. For instance, in October of 1999, a foreign trade mission on which former Governor Ned McWherter took 15 businessmen and officials to Japan, covered much ground in terms of creating stronger ties. While there, they participated in a joint meeting of the Southeast U.S. and Japan Association in Tokyo and in a seminar in Nagoya about online industry advantages for industries within Tennessee. They were part of a larger delegation of 70 Tennessee business, educational and local representatives on the mission. A Brother Industries representative went along to present a strong case of why it located in Bartlett (a Memphis suburb). The delegation also visited with senior executives of Sharp Electronics in Osaka. See Figure 3 depicting linkages of the Memphis CIBER with other institutions worldwide. Appendix C provides an overview of the institutions.

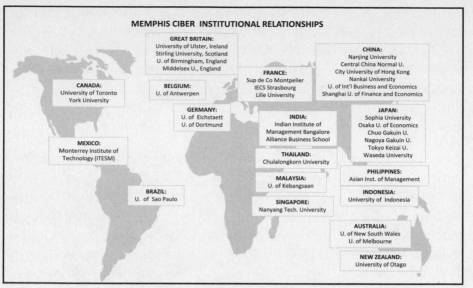

Figure 3. Memphis CIBER Institutional Relationships

The Vital Seeds of Early Grant Funding

As alluded to, seeds first had been planted for Memphis State University to work in conjunction with Southern Illinois University to submit a joint grant proposal to the U.S. Department of Education on a $1 million project in hopes of establishing a Center for International Business Education. Kedia took Sims, the dean of the College of Business, and Jack Carpenter, dean of the College of Arts and Sciences, to meet with their SIU counterparts and the quest was to become one of the few chosen CIBER centers. He was told by the powers in the Department of Education that it would not be an easy task, and Kedia knew well that Memphis would be competing with the best-resourced universities and faculties in the nation. Nevertheless, he was determined and believed that it would surpass the proverbial "little engine that could."

Except for the determination and vision by Kedia and his team, it would not have gained the momentum which it did and would not have sustained itself. The USDOE awarded MSU and SIU grant funding of $1 million in 1990. Over time, the center staff team became known internally as the "Wang Gang." See Appendix A for a listing of all Wang Center staff.

The concept included the creation of a nexus for increased international business expertise in the Mississippi River Delta region. The main goal was to give students the knowledge of how to do business in other countries; for executives, the center would accomplish the same through workshops, seminars and conferences about business techniques in other countries.

Coinciding with these aims was Memphis State University's application for a federal grant of up to $200,000 to establish an interdisciplinary program of language and culture in the departments of international studies and foreign language, and in relationship with international business at both bachelors' and masters' levels.

The next boost to the still-new Wang Center came in that summer of 1990 when MSU used a previously awarded federal Business and International Education (BIE) grant to expand its programs. The project included new courses at the Fogelman College of Business and Economics and a series of seminars for Mid-South business representatives. The U.S. Department of Education had approved a $161,000 grant for the project in April 1990 for a two-year period. Another $10,000 came from the Tennessee Department of Economic and Community Development. New international business courses provided a concentration for students pursuing bachelor's and specialized master's degrees in business administration. These classes later led to the basis for a master's degree in international business at the university.

Additional Early Successes in CIBER Granting

In a 1994 article in the *World Business Review* periodical, Kedia explained how the CIBER centers have four main objectives: curriculum development, faculty development, international business research, and outreach to business and academic communities. Fulfilling these goals was central to attainment of grants in their every phase, though various cycles were assigned new and specialized emphasis themes. See Figure 4 titled "Performance Measurement Framework: Integrated Outcomes" which highlights key goals and strategies of the University of Memphis related to U.S. competitiveness in four key categories that also align with CIBER mandates: Education, Development, Research and Outreach.

Through the many center activities, the center was striving to not only ensure American participation in the international arena through fulfilling its mission, but also to produce through its key IMBA program a generation of American business leaders dedicated to an appreciation of other cultures, international competitiveness, and service and product excellence, along with ethical international business practices.

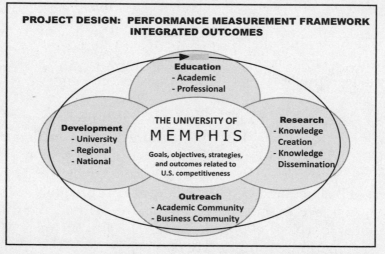

Figure 4. Project Design: Performance Measurement Framework

Interim Dean Ferrell noted in 1994 that the university was in a good position to take advantage of increased opportunities in international business. "With the CIBER, we are able to train faculty members at other schools to improve the teaching of international business throughout the region."

Continued successes resulted in the U.S. Department of Education renewing the CIBER with a new three-year grant to Memphis State to fund the center through 1996, which amounted to a total of more than $1.7 million the Education Department had awarded Memphis State University for international business education. Among the center's activities was the new master's degree program in international business designed to prepare graduates to function in a global business environment and provide them with language and cultural training, geographical study and international work experience. Alongside this plan, and most certainly part of the attraction that funded the grant, was a growing list of seminars conferences and assistance opportunities for Mid-South businesses entering the international marketplace. All were structured to address relevant world occurrences of the time. (The International Business Education Center project had begun three years prior when MSU and SIU-Carbondale joined to win one of about 17 federal grants to establish education and research centers).

Over time, Memphis State came to operate the program alone. Among universities that had won the international business education grants at that time were Duke, Columbia, Illinois, Michigan State, Indiana, Michigan, Pittsburgh, Purdue, Southern California, South Carolina, Texas A&M, and UCLA. This illustrious roster placed the Memphis CIBER in excellent company.

By September of 1999, the Wang Center had celebrated its 10th anniversary. To help celebrate the 10th anniversary, the Wang Center invited key professors from international institutions who coordinated and supported IMBA students on their study abroad and internship activities (see photo below).

At this time, the center had more than just a birthday to celebrate. The Memphis CIBER announced it had been awarded a $900,000 grant by the U.S. Department of Education to support

International Guests Help Celebrate the Tenth Anniversary of the
Robert Wang Center for International Business
September 8, 1999

(Back row, left) Prof. J. D. Agarwal (Indian Institute of Finance); Professor Bernhard Schipp (Dresden, Germany); Dr. Ben L. Kedia (Wang Center, Univ. of Memphis); Prof. Dr. Hans Tummers (IECS Strasbourg, France); Prof. Dr. Martin K. Welge (University of Dortmund, Germany); Prof. Johannes Schneider (Catholic University of Eichstatt, Germany); (Front row, left) Mrs. Ben (Asha) Kedia; Jayme Vita, (Office of Secretaria de Industia, Brazil); Prof. Dr. Liliane Van Hoof (University of Antwerpen, Belgium); Prof. Dr. Nicolas Hendrichs (ITESM, Monterrey, Mexico) its ongoing work. Those funds also marked the fourth grant award the center had received from the DOE. The Wang Center was at the time one of 28 CIBERs the Education Department established throughout the country, said Judy Scales, then associate director. "We're very proud because we're the only CIBER in the seven states that surround us," Scales noted in a newspaper article at the time. She said the center would use the grant for outreach to businesses and to the academic community, with a focus on colleges and universities in the Lower Mississippi Delta Region. See Figure 5 that displays the current 33 Centers for International Business Education and Research.

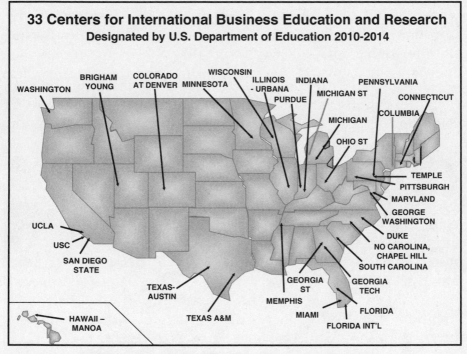

Figure 5. 33 CIBERs Established by the U.S.
Department of Education (2010-2014)

The Core of the Center's Platforms Strengthens

"Dr. Kedia's framework for developing global competency really formed the basis for all aspects of Wang Center programming," said former associate director Deborah Hernandez. She is now director of research development at the University of Memphis.

"The framework is rooted in stages along a competency continuum with specific exposures, skills, and behaviors tied to each stage of development. Wang Center programs were methodically developed to move students, faculty, businesses, and academic institutions along the continuum from initial exposure to awareness, understanding, and full competency. Importantly, the need to ensure cross-pollination among experts in business, language, and cultural studies to produce competency is reflected in the range of programs offered by the Wang Center. As a result, programs were designed to expose foreign language faculty to business terminology and to provide incentives for these faculty to incorporate business language and customs into their existing courses."

Business faculty were introduced to the business customs and cultures of various parts of the world through domestic and international faculty development programs designed to help them globalize their courses and to develop new courses and new research in international business. University administrators were supported to participate in these programs, as well, in order to build ties between the University of Memphis and international universities and help eliminate barriers to cross-disciplinary curricular and research on campus, Hernandez noted. Such research included everything from offshore outsourcing, global leadership mindsets, and emerging market studies to technology and knowledge management topics. "Intensive programs for business executives employed hands-on activities to teach language, culture, and customs in a context of negotiating and managing international business relationships," she said. "The design of the International MBA program, with its intensive international work and study abroad experience, and support for undergraduate study abroad also align with this framework. I believe this very systematic approach, tied to Dr. Kedia's well-researched framework, positioned the Wang Center as a results-oriented leader among its peer CIBERs."

Conferences Mount in Number and Complexities

Over time, seminars and workshops offered to the business community abounded. Here is an illustrative sampling with details provided in a subsequent section of this volume. A global cyber security conference brought together some of the nation's leading cyber security professionals for dynamic presentations on identity theft rings, software security, human trafficking, and organized cybercrime. The Center for Cyber Security and FBI helped begin this program.

A business seminar focused on export opportunities in Asia linked export officials with Memphis-area businesses. At this event, participants received updates on current events, market prospects and economic situations of the region. Through this seminar, participants learn how to successfully navigate the business cultures of these markets and gain knowledge of available resources and marketing activities. Furthermore, they are able to meet one-on-one with senior commercial officers of the U.S. Commercial Service – trade experts who are on the ground in key markets around the world.

A Global Green Initiative Conference in 2009 wrapped together discussions on the transformation of transportation and how we invest in and use energy, infrastructure and technology. Subtopics included the greening of the global supply chain, global green logistics standards, transport carrier responses to energy realities, biofuels, pollution and public policy, hybrid electric vehicle advancements, and alternative fuels, among other topics. Meanwhile, other seminars were concerned with doing business in India, Chile and other focused areas of the world.

The Seven Distinct Grant Cycles Reviewed

Seven distinct grant cycles evolved over the landscape of the Wang Center since the first cycle commenced in 1990. This first cycle, extending from 1990 until 1993, was titled "Institutional Change." It built upon the foundations of institutional collaboration, resources, and strategies for the internationalization of the university curriculum and also witnessed the formation of the international MBA program. The second cycle (1993 to 1996) named, "Outreach," dealt with faculty development in international business (FDIB), faculty study abroad in Europe, business foreign language faculty workshops, and on-site foreign language instruction for business firms. The third cycle (1996 to 1999) carried the title of "New World Regions and Languages." It focused upon faculty study abroad exchanges in South America, introduced Chinese and Japanese languages into the curriculum, and expanded international university linkages.

Since its inception, the Wang CIBER has developed programs and activities that firmly established the center as a regional and national resource center. In doing so, it has developed institutional and university linkages for program support, adopting new technology to gear programs and share results. This involves leveraging best practices with partner institutions for maximum benefit.

The fourth cycle (1999 to 2002) highlighted "Information Technology" as its core theme. During this period, the center's emphasis also involved leveraging energy and resources of the broader university community to promote and support information technology training and experiences. "Underserved Constituencies" served as the appropriate format for the fifth cycle (2002 to 2006). In this phase, the center embarked intently on underserved institutions and regions of the lower Mississippi Delta to build a regional educational and training pipeline for international business. The sixth cycle (2006 to 2010), named "Extending Reach and Impact," placed an increased international focus at all levels of curriculum and encouraged more study abroad opportunities, along with increased faculty training in international education.

In 2011, summer faculty study abroad options included the following selections: EU, Latin America/Caribbean, Mercosur, European Economies in Transition, Africa and Russia. All were in coordination with various universities. Recent winter study abroad programs offered umbrella options in India, China or Southeast Asia.

The seventh and current cycle (2010 to 2014) is quite robust and carries the title of "Meeting the Challenges of Globalization." This phase encompasses integration of the IMBA and CD MBA (Customer Driven MBA) programs for global corporations, a partnership with Bioworks, collaborations with the Confucius

Institute, international experiential learning, more faculty study abroad, an international business network, and a cyber security symposium series. All of these together adhere to the umbrella theme of "Moving Forward, Building on the Past: Proven Results for Underserved Constituencies." See a graphic exposition of the seven CIBER grant cycles in the accompanying Figure 6. The University of Memphis awarded Kedia a "Millionaire PI (Principal Investigator)" award for his success in grant awards.

Dr. Ben L. Kedia
received a
"Millionaire PI"
(Principal Investigator)
Award"

Spring 2012

Moving Forward, Building on the Past: Proven Results for Underserved Constituencies

1st Cycle - 1990-1993: Institutional Change

- Building the foundations of institutional collaboration, resources, and strategies for internationalization of University curriculum
- International MBA

2nd Cycle - 1993-1996: Outreach

- Faculty Development (FDIB)
- Faculty Study Abroad in Europe
- Business Language Workshops (Spanish, German, French)
- On-site foreign language instruction for business firms

3rd Cycle - 1996-1999: New World Regions and Languages

- Faculty Study Abroad in South America
- Introduce Chinese and Japanese Languages into the curriculum
- Expand International University Linkages

4th Cycle - 1999-2002: Information Technology

- Leveraging energy and resources of the broader University and community to promote and support information technology training and experiences

5th Cycle - 2002-2006: Underserved Constituencies

- Focus on underserved institutions and regions of the Lower Mississippi Delta to build a regional educational and training pipeline for international business

6th Cycle - 2006-2010: Extending Reach and Impact

- Increased international focus at all levels of curriculum
- Additional Study abroad opportunities
- Increased faculty training in international education

7th Cycle - 2010-2014: Meeting the Challenges of Globalization

- International Experiential Learning
- Faculty Study Abroad
- International Business Network
- Cyber Security
- Outreach to HBCUs

Figure 6. Memphis CIBER Grant Cycles (1990-2014)

THE
International
MBA

EDUCATION FOR GLOBAL BUSINESS SUCCESS

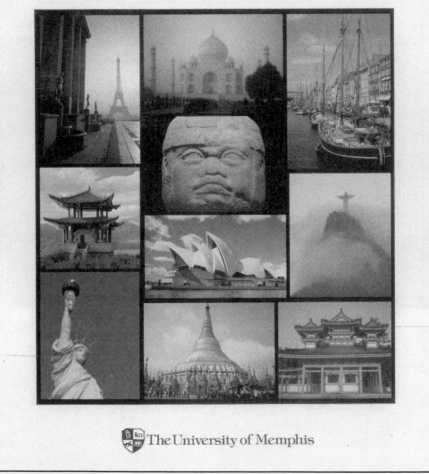

The University of Memphis

Chapter Five

∾

Students
Moving Out to Meet the World

The center's director has written extensively over the years in various scholarly journals about the rationale for formalized global business programs in higher educational institutions. In one such white paper titled, "Transforming Business Education to Produce Global Managers," Kedia provides a scenario of how small the world is that we live in. "Just two decades ago, the term globalization was seldom used beyond the economists concerned with the transformation of the worldwide economy," he said. "Today, however, that term is used to emphasize the increasing integration of and interdependence among diverse nations."

"To emphasize this notion, we generally tell our students that the business world is embedded in a global economy; as proof, they need to look no further than their own experiences of eating a pollo campero (a Guatemalan fast food chain that has expanded rapidly across America), driving a Toyota, or using a Nokia cell phone. We also talk about the sale of American products abroad and the rise of global brands that are the same throughout the world. Such war stories are one way business faculty members internationalize the business curriculum."

This internationalization of curriculum also has been affected by not only the changing economic landscape but also pressures from business school accreditation associations. In addition to grounding the students in global awareness, advanced programs take a specialization approach to create deeper international understanding of socio-political contexts for conducting business.

The International MBA Program (IMBA)

Preparing students to be effective in the global arena was a matter of not only providing substantive academic programs, but also infusing an understanding of context, people and cultures and how to relate to them. This program is geared to deliver that kind of exposure and approaches in terms of differences in ways businesses in other nations affect the way people think, solve problems, negotiate, respond to authority, value work, set work norms and reward achievement. Its combination of academic programs and exposure to foreign cultures enhances students' awareness and sensitivity to cross-country differences in managerial applications, while developing skills to operate effectively in a variety of environments.

It is interesting to intricately sketch the actual build-up to the program's realization, along with the underlying thought processes. Kedia had prepared his case well, and the University of Memphis agreed with his goals. It stepped up the momentum a full notch when in response to Kedia's plans, it fast-tracked its own plans to convert the first master's degree in international business administration. To accomplish this, associate deans from the Fogelman College, the Wang Center, and the College of Arts and Sciences set the new IMBA for a scheduled fall of 1993 launch. Students would complete this new full-time program within two years as it was then designed. All but two of the classes were selected for the students and the same students would be in the same classes together each semester. The five-semester, 54-credit hour program would require students to take three semesters of one advanced foreign-language, along with designated accounting, economics, finance, management and marketing classes.

This was the first full-time master's program in the Fogelman College at Memphis State University that had a global focus and which dealt with economic issues, management issues and cultural issues of the international economy, stated David Ciscel, then associate dean for graduate programs in the Fogelman College of Business. The fourth semester would be the international semester. Students would either intern at an international company arranged by the Wang Center or they would complete graduate courses in business at an approved institution overseas.

By the time the International MBA was launched that fall, 21 students were enrolled (see photo). "This program was started with the realization that there was a lack of international expertise among existing managerial cadre," Kedia said. "The basic idea was that the business school had been teaching expertise in business, whereas the College of the Arts and Sciences has been teaching about the rest of the world." The IMBA program sought to link the two disciplines together.

To emphasize the language component, only students with three years of language study in German, French and Spanish at the undergraduate level were admitted to the program. This level of expertise in a foreign language was further advanced with the requirement of additional language courses and was combined with the knowledge of the geographic area as well. Fluency in a foreign language was important, because nine of the 54 credit hours needed for completion of the International MBA program were in the overseas business internship. "We wanted students to work with the company so that they could polish their language skills and reinforce their cultural understanding," Kedia explained. International students admitted to the program brought their own home country languages and, of course, required level of English proficiency and added cross-national and cross-cultural flavor to IMBA classes.

The U of M soon expanded its IMBA program with an emphasis on a Chinese language track. A thorough understanding of Chinese culture and its effect on doing business in China was seen as an essential component of the established IMBA program.

IMBA Class of 1995: First Row: Stephen DiLossi, Heidi Wysong, Laurie McSwiggin, Karine Christin, Marion Sorrells, Yen-Chin Chu,Nicole Billeaud, and Pat Taylor (staff). Second Row: Mei-Ying Chuang, Linda Taneff, Jonathan Ballinger, Susanne Nilson, and Dr. Irene Duhaime. Third Row: Dr. Ben Kedia, Tonna Bruce, Ben Clark, Patrick Wilkerson, Roger Walters, Robert Bagby, John Bass, and Jeffrey Whitworth. Fourth Row: Todd Blowers, William White, Waiel Abukhaled, David Edwards, and Dr. Otis Baskin.

"The Chinese would not do business unless they trust the person they are doing business with," said Kedia in an article at the time. "They are really interested in seeing that the entity they do business with will do business on a long-term basis."

In fine-tuning this prospect, internship projects were identified for each participating student by the host companies and by utilizing each student's own analytical and problem-solving skills in finance, marketing or management on a given project. The IMBA program is designed to help students become future managers who can meet the challenges of global competition by expanding knowledge of the international business environment through foreign business language competency, specialized area studies, summer studies abroad and overseas internships. Thus, it combines a strong academic program with intensive exposure to other cultures and business practices.

Edge magazine, the economic development guide of the Tennessee Valley Authority, touted the IMBA program at the University of Memphis, describing it as "one of the first in the region to recognize the need for such a degree." It also stated that Kedia early on began organizing a demanding curriculum at the Wang Center to prepare graduates for management positions around the world. He launched the program in 1993 after securing a three-year, $1 million grant from the U.S. Department of Education for the Memphis CIBER. Kedia was quoted as saying, "I saw the need for this program years ago because I knew the economy was becoming much more interdependent and more global." He noted a definite shortage of international experience among present-day managers and designed the program to provide experience and expertise in all aspects of international business, from global financial management to production operations to advanced foreign language skills.

The IMBA now is the premier program developed and administered by the Memphis CIBER. The program has been successful, graduating more than 300 students with sophisticated business acumen, global mindsets and advanced understanding of language as well as global culture. In a testament to its success, IMBA alumnus and highly successful entrepreneur, Wei Chen, CEO and president of Sunshine Enterprises, provided $250,000 to enrich the student experience and expand the program during the next grant cycle. A model for other MBA programs at the U of M and nationwide, the IMBA emphasizes experiential learning and immersion. Designed for students entering into international business, or wishing to expand their international career opportunities, this five-semester, lockstep program features a rigorous core curriculum with a mandatory two semesters of international internship and study abroad components. Students hone their skills in the business practices, culture, and language of the host country. Current language tracks include Spanish, French and German as well as the less commonly taught Japanese and Chinese. For U.S. students without a second language competency, the program has been expanded to English speaking countries for study abroad and internship opportunities (i.e. India). Figure 7 graphically shows how international business courses, international learning and language and cultural skills grow together to build global competencies.

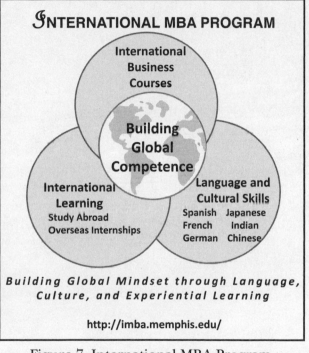

Figure 7. International MBA Program

Dr. Yuki Matsuda is associate professor of Japanese at the University of Memphis' Department of Foreign Languages and Literatures. "Over the years, the Wang Center gave me an opportunity to grow as a scholar and a business language educator," Matsuda said. "Dr. Kedia had a vision of what a successful program should be in this global age. The IMBA program has been very popular among foreign language majors who hope to use their language skills and cultural knowledge for their future careers."

Matsuda came to the University of Memphis as a coordinator of the Japanese program in 2000. At that time, the Japan track of the IMBA program had an exchange partner in Tokyo. While the

Japanese university had a very good business school, the exchange program did not meet the needs of our students. "For example, our IMBA students had to find internship positions by themselves, and during the internship, the students also needed to find an apartment in the Tokyo area and live away from the university," Matsuda said. "It is very difficult for a student to find an internship and a place to live in a foreign country, and we needed an alternative institution to send our students to. For this reason, Dr. Kedia and I decided to change our exchange partner in 2002. During the year, Dr. Iemoto from Osaka University of Economics was visiting the Memphis university for one year as a visiting scholar and proposed a new place of study and internship for the IMBA program. Dr. Kedia and I visited the university in Osaka, Japan, in June 2003 and started sending IMBA students there from that year."

Meanwhile, the undergraduate Japanese program had grown, and in 2008, the U of M started offering the major in Japanese within the Department of Foreign Languages and Literatures. As more students graduate as a Japanese major, more become interested in the International MBA program. They are hoping to keep studying Japanese language and culture while learning about international business. "I strongly hope that the IMBA program will keep attracting capable students who will be global leaders of the next generation," said Matsuda.

Ralph Albanese serves as professor and chair of Foreign Languages and Literatures at the University of Memphis. He also is a longtime partner with the annual Business Language Workshop. "The Department of Foreign Languages and Literatures had a very good working relationship with Fogelman College and particularly with the IMBA program since 1992. We offered a wide array of business language courses in Spanish, French, German, Japanese, and Chinese," Albanese said. "During the mid-1990s until 2005, our enrollment in these various language tracks was at times between 25 and 30 students. Our faculty was highly motivated and committed to providing their students with the most up-to-date and relevant information pertaining to business language and culture."

Memphis language professors Will Thompson (French), Monika Nenon (German), Felipe Lapuente (Spanish), Yuki Matsuda (Japanese) and De-An Swihart (Chinese) often presented papers at professional meetings, published articles, and attended pedagogical workshops. "They were all given financial support from the Wang CIBER to participate in national forums," Albanese said. "These faculty members understood that business is an integral part of culture and therefore, deserves a place in a foreign language curriculum. During this period, the IMBA program brought great credit to the University of Memphis and enhanced its reputation. It should also be noted many graduates of the IMBA have testified to the importance of their language skills in acquiring their position after graduation." See Appendix F for IMBA graduating class photos; see Appendix G for IMBA Internships and Sampling of Employment.

What Kedia envisioned was a thorough program to blend business courses with international content and coursework in cultural understanding and area studies, along with enrichment in language proficiency. Each of the business track programs would combine not only language enrichment, but would offer a focused business practicum so students could be exposed to and understand the context of conducting business in another country or region. In addition to traditional classroom settings, the program will emphasize guest lecturers, study abroad opportunities and hands-on experience through international internships with corporations.

Luke Perkins on IMBA internship at Schweppes in Paris, France (Class of 1999)

Overseas Experiences Viewed as the Heart of the IMBA Program

Being hands-on is the very reason why overseas study and interaction through internships were central to the IMBA program. Kedia, for instance, hoped that a visit by Wang Qui Sheng, president of Central China Normal University in Wuhan to the U of M would result in a stronger relationship that would include study abroad and internship opportunities for students in the Chinese component of the International MBA. The University of Memphis over time built a longstanding exchange program with the Chinese university. "Given that the Chinese respect people they have known longest, we think we will be able to work out a relationship with them that will be mutually helpful to each of us," Kedia said.

University of Memphis President Rawlins and Kedia embarked on a 17-day visit in 1996 to China, Hong Kong and Japan to sign faculty and student exchange agreements with six Asian universities. While in Beijing, President Rawlins served as a panelist during the first U.S.-China Conference on Business Management Training, sponsored by the U.S. Embassy, China's Ministry of Foreign Trade and Economic Cooperation and the U.S. Department of Commerce. The panel also discussed ways to build partnerships between universities and corporations.

The trip to Asia, chronicled in the *Memphis Business Journal,* was quite significant in many regards and took much groundwork ahead of time to make it into a success. The two academic entrepreneurs spent more than half of their stay in Asia visiting institutions in China. That portion of the trip served as a foray for two major initiatives, one of which was to launch a consortium of Tennessee institutions to provide management training for employees of the American joint venture companies in China. There was a tremendous need in China for management training because that type of training heretofore was not available there.

The first stop in Asia for the delegation was Beijing, home of China's University of International Business and Economics. Formally known as the Beijing Institute of Foreign Trade, it worked closely with international companies wanting to form joint ventures in China. Most of the companies involved are joint ventures in China that were then based in Hong Kong, Singapore and Japan.

Before leaving Beijing, Rawlins and Kedia were among those who took part in the first conference on international business sponsored by China's Ministry for Economic Cooperation. The university president talked about what he termed as "the triangle" that needed to exist in order to set up joint ventures. The triangle consisted of the Chinese university, the American university and the joint ventures themselves. Also before leaving Beijing, the two visited the United States Embassy where they met with Ambassador and fellow Tennessean James Sasser.

A tour of Nankai University, a comprehensive school about 75 miles southeast of Beijing, resulted in an exchange agreement with officials there. Nankai University has a strong Chinese language and cultural program, but the classes were in Chinese. From Beijing, they traveled to Wuhan where they visited the central China Normal University. They then traveled to Nanjing where they visited Nanjing University, which has a strong international business communications program. Another memorandum of understanding was signed at that location to set the stage for faculty and student exchanges. The idea was to send University of Memphis faculty there for six weeks where they could teach a short course and learn about the Chinese culture.

The trip next took them to Hong Kong, where they visited with officials from the City University of Hong Kong and the Hong Kong Polytechnic University. Hong Kong, which for a century had been a British colony, came under Chinese mainland rule the following summer. Afterward, the two traveled to Japan where they attended the 30th anniversary celebration of the establishment of Chuo Gakuin University. Rawlins and Kedia planted two tulip poplar trees there to commemorate the occasion and the relationship between Chuo Gakuin University and the University of Memphis. To intensify the relationships between overseas universities and the U of M, the center invited many scholars to visit Memphis to discuss the exchange program and to meet with students and administrators. See Appendix D for a listing of Visiting Scholars.

The IMBA program expanded to add a Chinese track in 1997. The original components were European studies for students with French or German proficiency and Latin American studies for those who speak Spanish. The program by then had graduated about 80 students, some of whom earned jobs at international companies including FedEx, International Paper, and Medtronic.

"The Asian expansion and the Latin American expansion are both very important," Kedia explained. "That is where the economies are growing very fast. Half of the population of the world is in Asia." The economy in China, which has a population of more than 1.2 billion, was growing at 9 percent per year, so fast that it is projected to be larger than the United States economy by 2030. China's economy was then already about half the size of the American economy. Kedia also planned to add Japanese as a component of the International MBA in 1998 and a Portuguese/ Brazilian component by the turn of the millennium.

Pat Taylor, as IMBA coordinator at the Wang Center, was centrally involved in the admission process for the IMBA program and recruitment of the first and successive classes for the graduate program, personally orienting some of the incoming foreign students into the Memphis and university culture. Many students had meals at her home. Taylor would speak with applicants many times before and after their arrival to the university. Her work extended from 1992 to 2011. "I remember funny times, too. There was one instance when we went to the airport to pick up a Chinese girl in the midst of Elvis Week. Seeing her quizzical expressions in the sea of Elvis look-alikes was priceless."

Today's IMBA Program Enhancements

Today, the IMBA has three main sections or components: the specialized master's program itself, the study abroad emphasis, and internships abroad with extended exposure opportunities in the foreign country. Foreign students coming to the University of Memphis IMBA program study here and work at companies in Memphis, while American students enrolled in the program study and intern overseas. The IMBA focuses on a number of countries: Germany, France, Japan, China, Mexico, Great Britain, India, and the United States. Assistantships are available for highly qualified students. Overseas experience is gained through study abroad programs and/or internships. The Country Business Track is for American students with three years of foreign language training. It concentrates on business practices, culture and languages of Germany, France, Japan, China, Mexico or Peru. The World Region Business Track specializes in the practice of business and geographical regions where English is the accepted business language. The U.S. Business Track is reserved for international students

Karen Starkey (right) on IMBA internship at Audi in Ingolstadt, Germany (Class of 1999)

and provides in-depth exposure to American business practices and culture.

These cornerstones have resulted in a premier program for international business education in the Mid-South. The program is congruent with the highest caliber peer universities throughout the U.S.; companies spanning the globe allow such students to experience overseas internships and cultural studies unmatched by other programs in the region. Specific internship assignments are determined by the host companies.

Host companies continue to play an important role in internships. They accept interns for full-time assignments, which typically take place from September through December during a student's fourth semester in Fogelman College's IMBA program. Students from the United States are placed with firms abroad, based on the students' foreign-language skills. Internship assignments are centered on issues that will most affect their host companies. Assignments can range from market research to departmental reorganizations to the development of information systems. Compensation for interns is determined by the host company.

Truly, the IMBA classroom is unlike any most have encountered before. The environment is engaging and the discussions are eye-opening. These aspects of the program are due to the fact that the IMBA faculty members are not only experts in their respective fields, but also have international experience themselves.

Testimonials of the Efficacy of the IMBA Program

Positive student testimonials abound, even from the early period. "I pursued an IMBA rather than an MBA for two reasons," said IMBA Class of 1996 graduate Frank Holloman. "First, the successful business of the future will not be confined or defined by national borders. Second, I feel it's important that business school graduates understand and know how to work effectively with different people and in different cultures."

"Deciding to enter this program was one of the best decisions I've made for my career," said IMBA Class of 1999 graduate

Anurag Babbar of Saharanpur, India. "The teachers are experts in their fields. They've been in the industry and also have a global perspective. We learned to appreciate the differences in cultures and how to adjust to those differences."

The Wang Center in May of 1998 was not only sending 12-15 students abroad each year, but also receiving about 10 students from other countries, who were placed in Memphis internship positions in such companies as Dobbs International, FedEx, Smith & Nephew and Sofamor Danek Group. Companies liked the work ethics of these students and the contributions they made to the businesses. The program helped the companies and the students took the internship assignments seriously. Although it was not the only goal of the program, the center enjoyed a 25 to 33 percent success rate of internships resulting in career positions. Often, students serving an internship in a foreign country were placed in an American affiliate office which improved their chances of landing a stateside job with that company after graduation.

"The International MBA program is clearly the crowning achievement of the Memphis CIBER," said José de la Torre, Dean and Byron Harless Eminent Scholar at the Graduate School of Business at Florida International University, in a formal 2005 peer review. "Starting with the class of 1993, it has attracted a large share of the university's and the CIBER's resources. The university's commitment to this program is exemplary. While it is an expensive program to run in terms of faculty commitment and attention, it clearly provides U of M a distinctive competence in a crowded market populated by many undifferentiated MBA programs. This is an intensive and comprehensive program that produces extraordinarily well-prepared students. I was impressed by the enthusiasm and dedication of the faculty teaching in the program, both from the business departments as well as from language and regional studies."

Companies involved as hosts in this program virtually change lives. Students leave their firms with a refined sense of business skills and significant on-the-job experience. As they interact with actual work teams, they gain important cross-cultural skills that they can apply throughout their careers. Formal reporting requirements, grading and evaluation procedures are part of the program as well. After a candidate's host firm talks with a program administrator to coordinate a potential internship position, they began interviewing pre-screened candidates and select students that best meet their needs. The host company also designates an on-site internship supervisor, who acts as a liaison with the IMBA program throughout the internship. The on-site supervisor provides a written evaluation of interns' performance both midway and at the conclusion of the internship.

"The center has provided important study to help local businesses and to educate students for an international experience," said Wei Chen, chief executive officer of Sunshine Enterprise, Inc. He is an IMBA graduate and also a member of the Wang CIBER Advisory Council. "In today's globalized world, it allows our city to compete worldwide and the corporations to recruit capable employees with this level of international experience." Chen is a strong advocate of the International MBA, saying that it offers students courses focusing on international study and internship abroad. The business members of the CIBER Advisory Council are one of the program's major assets. They constitute a tremendous expertise for the CIBER and for the university." See Appendix B for the CIBER Advisory Council business and academic members.

"CIBER has brought tremendous knowledge and competence to the local community," Chen added. "In the past 30 years, Memphis has evolved to become a global player due to the success of FedEx, AutoZone, Holiday Inn, etc. The center provides great resources for these companies to compete internationally.

"The IMBA provides a curriculum with international focus and internships abroad for hands-on experience," he continued. "I cannot think of any other MBA program that can provide this kind of unique experience. Many International MBA students end up finding a job opportunity abroad after their study and become truly global thinkers and players."

Chen in 2011 took a flight around the world to benefit St. Jude Children's Research Hospital, a journey he had started planning 22 years ago. He had lunch in Memphis with Robert Wang before his trip and was encouraged when the founder of Creative Co-op told him that there are many people who have dreams, but that he had the courage to act on those dreams. Chen said also that he wanted to highlight Memphis, and that giving back to the community was what the trip was all about. There were many risks in flying a single-engine airplane around the world, but in business, risks are taken every day, he said. Years ago, Chen came to Memphis without first knowing anyone, he took a risk himself to move to Memphis and study for the IMBA. When he started his company, he took a risk again. About a year and a half before his trip, Chen started planning and understanding the potential jeopardies involved. In making the trip, he became the first Chinese citizen to fly a single-engine airplane around the world. The trip took 69 days and he traveled 21,000 nautical miles to 21 countries and 41 cities. Chen took about 250 pictures each day.

Some of the interns in the IMBA program worked overseas conducting research to evaluate market potential for their host companies. They not only worked at a corporate headquarters, but even traveled abroad on behalf of their firms. They were able to use their language and cultural skills in performing the assigned tasks for their company. In other instances, they have helped identify and contact key players in the foreign market, business or government to assist in their firm's entry or expansion into that sought market. Moreover, they are able to use the latest information technology, both hardware and software.

Sarah Maurice (IMBA Class of 2009) recalls that she was well into her MBA education at another university when she learned of the International MBA program at the University of Memphis. After thorough research and a visit to the campus to meet with program staff, she made the decision to leave her current program in East Tennessee and move across the state to attend the University of Memphis IMBA program. "I was impressed with the curriculum, AACSB accreditation, and the required study abroad component. I also was intrigued with the idea of studying alongside students from this country and all over the world. I strongly desired a new experience and joined the world regions track, which was designed for English-speaking students who wanted to study in another English-speaking country. I had two choices based on the relationships the program had developed with other institutions. One was University College Dublin in Dublin, Ireland, and the other was the Indian Institute of Management in Bangalore, India."

She chose to attend summer classes in Bangalore, India, and hoped that her decision would lead to a culturally enriching experience. "I never could have imagined how that experience would change my life both professionally and personally," the 2009 IMBA grad expounded. "Upon arriving in India and experiencing several setbacks regarding housing and sickness, I immersed myself in the culture and adapted to my environment. I made friends immediately and worked on group projects in classes that challenged me. The students I studied with were some of the brightest, most intellectually curious and fun-loving people I have ever met. I still keep in touch with them today through Facebook."

The graduate student then traveled throughout the country with her new friends and said that she had the time of her life. "I learned a lot about myself and others, and came back to the United States with an entirely different perspective on life. Moreover, I witnessed firsthand not only cultural differences that make us unique, but the similarities among people from all over the world that draw us together. It sounds like such a cliché, but it was a life-changing experience for me and I wouldn't trade a single moment of it – not even the hardships in the beginning. It was so much more than a simple semester abroad."

Sarah Maurice recently accepted the position of chief operating officer at Campbell Clinic in Memphis where she works with a variety of personalities and positions within the healthcare community. In her previous position at Methodist Hospital, one of her primary responsibilities was to assist in the acquisition process of physician practices and she accomplished this by forming relationships with the physicians, their staff, and all of the members of the Methodist corporate team that welcome these practices into its family of business. "We have a large group of people that must work together to transition formerly small (many of them family-owned, physician clinics) into a larger corporate culture, while being sensitive to the needs of all parties involved," Maurice explained. "It requires much more than diplomacy or formalities, but rather a genuine desire to listen to and understand the needs of everyone. I work to facilitate harmonious relationships that allow us to learn to work with one another in a way that enhances patient care and associate commitment to our mission and values as a service organization."

"The lessons I learned about business and people during my study abroad in Bangalore, India, no doubt influence the way I work with fellow colleagues back here in Memphis. My thirst for new experiences has not ended, and is in fact stronger than ever, now that I realize how many more opportunities are out there to develop and grow in my personal and professional life. The decision to attend the University of Memphis IMBA program was one of the best decisions I have made and marked the beginning of an entirely new chapter in life. I'm grateful to the program staff, my fellow students who I now call my lifelong friends, and all who are a part of keeping this program around for future students to embark upon their own new experiences through culturally enriching opportunities."

Internship and Partner-Company Success Stories

In France, IMBA interns working for the company Millipore became involved in research, negotiation and implementation into European subsidiaries of that corporation regarding a credit card purchasing program for non-inventory acquisitions. For Georgia-Pacific, they assisted in locating and organizing information to support whether or not to launch a European request for proposal for plastic packaging materials. The request dealt specifically with plastic films and bags used in the packaging of Georgia-Pacific's European customer products such as paper towels and disposable tableware. For General Motors in France, they created parameters as to how transmissions, whether new, serviced or remanufactured, are priced. They also worked on designing procedures so that the prices would remain current while taking into account changing materials' costs. And for Altir Techologies in that same country, interns analyzed competitors and their websites. They also translated that company's website into English.

In Germany, for BDO Healthcare Consulting, interns found contacts, prepared presentations and performed all other tasks needed to keep a patient acquisition project running. They organized information, coordinated business functions and wrote a business plan. For Messe Munchen, they investigated the potential key accounts for trade fairs in Western Europe and the United States. Interns for this company acted as contact persons for the sales force in Germany and participated in key accounting customer acquisitions. They also played roles in the daily organization of a trade fair and maintenance of a website in both German and English. For Media Saturn, they worked in the finance department with various financial systems and also dealt with issues related to the switch from the Deutsche Mark to the Euro.

In Mexico, for Cemex, interns benchmarked the current commercial websites with other websites, both inside and outside the industry. They developed a marketing campaign for the cement and concrete products that focused on electronic sales business for the company. For Entertec, they worked on projects, which called for attaining a standardized price for all batteries. They helped develop the inventory payment procedures at Johnson Controls Industry and Entertec. And for Grupo IMSA, the interns assisted in the benefits and compensation department work, the planning and development department's strategies and the corporate image department. They researched the policies and procedures of that company's American subsidiaries and presented findings to consultants.

Brett Norman, now corporate controller at Kele, Inc., was a student in the IMBA Class of 2005. "Several components I gained through the IMBA program have helped me excel in my professional career. These include the following: a strong foreign language skill focus (Spanish was my track), a cohort environment with team-based learning, class diversity in terms of race, gender, and educational backgrounds; the exposure to different cultures with a good balance of business and social aspects from classes, classmates and internship/study abroad experiences. I studied at Tec de Monterrey in Monterrey, Mexico, and worked in Guadalajara, Mexico."

"For me, what stands out the most was my work-study experience in Monterrey, Mexico," said Ryan Gatgens, IMBA Class of 2006, and now director of portfolio management at Constellation Energy Resources. "The first term of the IMBA program prepared me with the foundational elements to live and work aboard, but the second term required me to put that knowledge into action every day as I went to work for a Fortune 500 company. Working in a foreign business environment was challenging, but it forced me to view the world from the perspective of someone outside the U.S. As a professional in a global commodities business, those experiences along with the international economics curriculum provided me with a great knowledge base to launch my career."

"My time at the University of Memphis IMBA Program was an incredible time of my life," noted Jesús Parrilla, IMBA Class of 2001 and now CEO of Explora Chile, S.A. "Not only the exchange with my professors was valuable and formative, but also with my classmates, most of whom were from overseas." He was impressed by the personalized attention of the professors toward the students. "The camaraderie among staff and students was fundamental in the academic success of all of us. Management principles instilled in the program and the mandatory internship marked my professional career the most. The quality of the partner companies that the university had was outstanding as was the relationship and coordination between both. I was blessed to land an internship program at Gate Gourmet and after that, my professional career took off."

Strategies for Facilitating Internships

The center initiated its internship programs in Europe, Mexico and the United States during the 1994-95 academic year in preparation for the first class of IMBA students. Europe was designated for the French and German speakers, and Mexico for the Spanish speakers. "In Europe, we started the program with the University of Dortmund with the help of Professor Martin Welge there and it lasted for several years," Kedia said. After some time, the German internship affiliation moved to the University of Ingolstadt where Professor Doctors Bernd Stauss (services marketing) and Johannes Schneider (economics) coordinated the program there.

"In France, the school we started originally was with Ecole Superieure de Commerce de Montpellier, one of the leading business schools in France. As was the case with other such universities, the local institutions introduced us to companies in their area with whom they had ongoing contacts. That helped a lot with internship placements."

In Mexico, the center began affiliations with Monterrey Tech, which was just a two-hour flight away from Memphis. The center staff traveled to Monterrey and talked with many companies in the area, particularly American companies operating there, but also some Mexican companies. This was easier to do directly because of the quick flight, relatively speaking.

"Over time, we also decided that students would study one semester before entering their internships," Kedia explained. The premise was that the student would acquire local knowledge and give time on the staffing side to actually identify and locate the internships. Meanwhile, the program at Montpelier migrated to the Ecole du Management in Strasbourg, France. Most such programs were reciprocal arrangements whereby their students came to Memphis in exchange for University of Memphis students going there. The reciprocity also extended to waivers of tuition both directions.

The center then introduced internship connections in Japan and China. In Japan, arrangements were made with Sophia University in Tokyo. There, however, the center had to stay on top of the internships more directly because the universities could not always assist in internship placements. Moreover, the long commutes for students were so involved in Tokyo that a decision was made to migrate to Osaka University of Economics in Osaka. That university was unique in that it had dormitories for foreign students in particular – which is very unusual in Japan. Professor Iemoto had tremendous business connections among companies across Osaka because of his various consulting roles and credibility and he was able to utilize those relationships for the benefit of Memphis students. In China, the center first connected with Nankai University outside Beijing, then moved to Nanjing University.

Then, the Wang Center introduced what became known as the World Region Track, Kedia said, after deciding that there are parts of the world where a second language was not necessarily required, chiefly because English was considered a primary business language. Such applicable locations were the United Kingdom, Ireland, Singapore, Hong Kong, India, Australia, and Holland. "They didn't have to have a second language, but they still had to go overseas," Kedia said. One such program under this track started out in Londonderry, Northern Ireland, at the

University of Ulster. The structure of that program was such that by the time they could send exchange students here, they would have already graduated. Therefore, center staff moved it for a few years to University College in Dublin. However, students there were not getting a different enough cultural exposure, so the center created a relationship in India at the Indian Institute of Management Bangalore. It created yet another linkage in that city, namely with Alliance University.

Meanwhile, around 2008, hostilities emerged at a precipitous pace along the U.S.-Mexican border, so the notion of sending students to Mexico was considered unsafe by all. Therefore, the Spanish language and Latin American cultural experience was transferred to ESAN in Lima, Peru.

The forging of a wide variety of international business school partnerships was always part of the IMBA program's goal, even from the early days. Generally, strategic alliances involve more than just an exchange of students and faculty members. Partners set up an ongoing structure that provides members of the alliance with network contacts and opportunities in regions far away. At the same time, strategic alliances provide student participants avenues to enhance their global competence by taking courses in different countries and regions. Finally, business school alliances supply students with access to more experiential international placements such as internships, study abroad programs, and exchange programs. Such alliances help business schools cope with increasing demand for, and challenges of, the internationalization of business programs.

Ph.D. Student Success with Graduate Assistantship Support

Original research plays a key role in meeting CIBER mandates and affects the current body of knowledge with regard to international business. Ph.D. students spread the impact of their international research across the world through their future roles as professors internationalizing their own classes. This plan proves to be a true connector-bridge leverage, both far and wide.

Doctoral-level education specifically targeted for international business is a relatively modern emphasis. Ph.D.-echelon education in this arena is viewed as an endeavor that most readily reproduces itself through generations of future faculty members and also in the development of practitioners.

As such, doctoral education of this kind must explore market relationships and environments in a more extensive way than ever before. As business faculty members, they make doctoral education more relevant and representative of the globalization of the economy. If they are to provide the teaching necessary to prepare future generations of business leaders and educators, they must increasingly fine-tune their own global competencies. Greater economic interdependence among nation-states is the motivating reality behind the drive to internationalize doctoral programs in business nationwide. This goal helps the graduates think and manage better cross-functionally.

A key provision of the Memphis CIBER's program is to provide research direction and financial support to doctoral students to facilitate their research and presentation of papers at conferences. One of the many initiatives achieved through the Wang Center over the years was to provide assistantships to doctoral students. Typically, their direct association and residency with the university extends from four to five years, and their roles in international research at the center were one of the mainstays which the CIBER program grants sought. The intention is to train future generations of academics who will teach courses from an international perspective. The AACSB previously noted that about 87 percent of Ph.D.'s in business remarkably had not had a single international course. The international level of education cannot normally be attained through conventional business courses. In the doctoral programs, there is much emphasis on research and presentation of papers within the disciplinary functional areas. At the Wang Center, the doctoral candidates perform original research under direction of Kedia. This effort provides yet another large impact in the internatioinal domain in Memphis because of this CIBER initiative.

This type of emphasis coalesced in the summer of 1996, when more than 100 educators from around the nation gathered at the University of Memphis to discuss ways to internationalize the business curricula at their schools. That conference attracted 40 business school deans and at least 60 faculty members. The conferees struggled with such questions as how to change curricula, faculty, programs and processes. Kedia said that a primary theme was that since students today must be adaptable and internationally mobile, there is a central need for these students to understand foreign languages along with the international sociopolitical environment – that the modern knowledge worker should have a worldview that incorporates these important elements.

The presence of the Memphis CIBER continues to attract internationally focused scholars to the Fogelman College of Business and Economics. In turn, these scholars recruit and train the next generation of internationally focused Ph.D. students. In the last decade alone, with assistance from the center, these scholars have helped Ph.D. students develop at least 20 internationally focused dissertations and 60 IB-themed papers, many of which were presented at international conferences and then developed and published in top journals. In fact, one of the former doctoral students is Dr. Tomas Hult, the Academy of International Business Executive Director and current CIBER Director at Michigan State University.

"It would be difficult to overstate the importance of Kedia and the Wang Center for our Management Doctoral Program," said David G. Allen, Ph.D., professor in the Department of Management at Fogelman College. "Through the center, Ben has provided our doctoral program an internationally recognized presence in the international business arena that has enabled us to attract high-quality doctoral students from around the world, provide them first-class training, and place them in prominent positions."

For example, alums of the programs supported by the center include a chairman of one of the most prominent corporate governance centers in Asia, as well as numerous successful award-winning research scholars at universities such as Clarkson, Texas A&M International, Berry College, the University of Mississippi, the University of Texas at Arlington, Illinois State, the University of Akron and the University of North Texas. This kind of pedigree supports and develops the next generation of international business scholars.

"Having served as the coordinator of the Management Ph.D. program, I know firsthand how important the support of the Wang Center has been," Allen continued. "Attracting and developing top-notch doctoral students is an expensive endeavor in both time and resources. Even in difficult financial times, we have been able to count on Ben and the Wang Center to fund and support doctoral students, enabling our program to maintain a critical mass of scholars. Through the Wang Center, Ben also supports the students to present their scholarly research at national and international conferences, an activity that is vital to their development and eventual success. In sum, I think Ben has been the most important individual, and the Wang Center the most important resource, in maintaining and growing our Ph.D. program."

Charles A. Pierce, Ph.D., interim chair, Department of Management at Fogelman College, formerly coordinated the Management Ph.D. program at U of M. As such, Pierce is acutely aware of contributions that both the Wang CIBER and Kedia made in enhancing the doctoral education in Management with emphasis on International Management/International Business. Doctoral students who were involved in the Wang Center curriculum received graduate assistantships through CIBER funding and were mentored by Kedia. Doctoral students also received CIBER support to present papers, attend conferences, purchase, collect and compile research data for dissertations.

"Through Dr. Kedia's research advising efforts, CIBER and the Wang Center have produced stellar Ph.D. graduates in the area of international business and management," Pierce noted. "These are some of the best Ph.D. student placements in the history of the Fogelman College's Department of Management at the University." Pierce believes that the Wang Center is a huge recruiting magnet for Ph.D. students, adding that, "Even students with research interests in areas other than international business still choose to study at the University of Memphis because we have a CIBER."

The ripple effect continues to echo far and wide. "I can fly across country to a national conference, bump into someone at the conference hotel, and as soon as they notice I'm from the University of Memphis, they know we have Dr. Kedia and CIBER," Pierce said. "Through Dr. Kedia's generous research and travel support, more than 60 Ph.D. students in the Fogelman College of

Business and Economics have been able to present their research papers at some 100 national and international conferences. The presentation of these papers is a key component to the students' international business and management education and vital for obtaining their initial academic job placements." See Appendix H for brief bios of the Ph.D. graduates and a summary of graduate students who presented international research.

The International Business Program for Undergraduates (INBS)

Bachelor-degree level students also have the opportunity to gain a good foundational understanding of foreign cultures and opportunities in the changing global economy. Firms in fields such as logistics, IT, marketing and management consulting are seeking graduates with an international orientation to their learning base. The INBS (International Business BBA) program also prepares students for graduate education.

The broad, interdisciplinary curriculum allows students to choose courses in business, foreign language and social studies that build on the foundations of general education and business core courses. They are able to concentrate on economics, finance, logistics/supply chain management, marketing management or a hybrid blend of these aspects. Foreign languages offered include French, Italian, Spanish, German, Russian, Japanese and Arabic. The Office of International Programs and Internships provides up to date information on study abroad programs designed for international business majors and also internship opportunities. Adding an internship to the coursework provides valuable hands-on training that complements the classroom learning. The students also are eligible for competitive scholarships.

The state of Tennessee requires two years of foreign language at the high school level and the University of Memphis requires two years of the same language at the undergraduate level. The Wang Center coordinates the historical, geographic, cultural and political aspects with the specific language. All of these disciplines reinforce each other in this type of concentration of curriculum. Students who participate in a study abroad program benefit in additional ways. They gain a deeper understanding of a foreign culture and region, improve their language skills through everyday activities, and gain insights into operations of foreign firms through site visits to businesses and institutions in the host country.

Epsilon Chi Omicron, an international business honor society, is open to international business majors who maintain certain GPAs as juniors and seniors. Adding an internship to their coursework provides valuable hands-on training that complements their classroom learning. Moreover, the INBS program can also prepare candidates for graduate-level education. See Appendix I for more information on the undergraduate INBS program. The Society of International Business Students is composed of both undergraduate INBS BBA students and graduate students in the IMBA program and is operated by and for the students. See Appendix J for a list of students who received Study Abroad scholarships.

GlobalEd

Executive Education for the Global Leader

A Leader's Guide to
Asian Cultures

Country
Profiles

Cultural
Insights

Behavioral
Patterns

Business
Practices

Global
Leadership

GlobalEd

Executive Education for the Global Leader

A Leader's Guide to
Latin American Cultures

Country
Profiles

Cultural
Insights

Behavioral
Patterns

Business
Practices

Global
Leadership

Chapter Six

∾

Bringing the World to Business Executives

Conferences, Workshops and Seminars for
Area Business Executives

In collaboration with national, regional and local organizations or agencies, as well as professional associations and businesses, the Wang Center organized many conferences and seminars in order to '"bring the world" to Memphis area business executives.

A prime example is the Wang Center's partnership with the Tennessee Foreign Language Institute (TFLI) – the U.S.'s only state-funded organization of its kind. The intent of this institute, created by the Tennessee Legislature, was to provide enhanced language skills to companies and citizens. Rick Marcus, who worked administratively at the headquarters in Nashville for the institute, started coordinating classes for the Memphis community in a satellite TFLI branch located in the Wang Center. A number of local companies which had frequent telephone dealings with their branch offices in another country also sent a number of their employees to this institute. Varco-Pruden, ALSAC-St. Jude, LeBonheur Children's Medical Center, Thomas & Betts, Helena Chemical, Sparks Companies, Cummins Engine Co. and APAC were among these examples. Applications of this conversational language learning were for emergency and medical personnel, human resource departments, and those wishing to travel abroad.

Under Marcus' leadership, about 10,000 hours of foreign language training was provided to about 900 participants in 50 companies. The training was offered in Arabic, Chinese, Italian, Portuguese, Russian and host of other languages. The center provided the institute with office space and monetary support. See

Appendix K for an overview of the company participants of the Memphis branch of the Tennessee Foreign Language Institute.

Key conferences earmarked for area industry practitioners became the hallmark of this emphasis as well. From the onset, the Wang Center staff proved it knew how to kick off what would become a whole series of symposia in grand style. As early as 1989, the then-new center was moderating conferences, such as one titled "The Challenge of Doing Business in the Soviet Market." How timely that was! The Berlin Wall had just been taken down and markets in both East and West had not yet engaged in a commercial flow of business that would follow. Nevertheless, the center was right on board with case studies of Memphis companies doing early work in Russia. Sessions included ways to facilitate U.S./U.S.S.R. business ventures, cultural considerations, legal perspectives and other matters. Sergey Shibaev, Soviet Minister of External Economic Relations, and Vladimir Checklin, U.S./U.S.S.R. Trade and Economic Council Representative, and Irina Savelyeva, legal scholar and law teacher with Moscow State University were among the presenters.

Dr. Henry Kissinger, former U.S. Secretary of State, was featured at the first Arthur Andersen International Business Symposium in 1990. The symposium, titled "Memphis: Seizing the Global Opportunity," was to be the first annual business conference held in Memphis and sponsored by one of the Big Five accounting firms in conjunction with the Chamber and the Wang Center. Secretary Kissinger was selected as the symposium's kickoff speaker because of his role in the world community and his stance amid governmental and foreign affairs. He also served as a consultant to major international corporations, domestic and foreign, and advised them how to do business and capitalize on interests throughout the world.

HENRY A. KISSINGER

Henry A. Kissinger, chairman of Kissinger Associates, an international consulting firm, served as Secretary of State and Assistant to the President for National Security Affairs under President Nixon. In 1983, he was appointed by President Reagan to chair the National Bipartisan Commission on Central America. Winner of the Nobel Peace Prize in 1973, Dr. Kissinger was also awarded the Presidential Medal of Freedom (the nation's highest civilian award) in 1988, and the Medal of Liberty in 1986. As a prime mover in international relations, he has a unique perspective on events in the world today. He has written numerous books and articles on United States foreign policy, international affairs, and diplomatic history. His syndicated column appears in leading U. S. newspapers and in over 40 foreign countries.

Keynote speaker Kissinger, during his address, suggested that the United States should not play a dominant role in the international reform of the Soviet Union. "If we get ourselves into the frame of mind that we have to fix every society around the world, we are going to exhaust ourselves. We don't have the resources to do it." At the time of his speech, America had about 22 percent of the world's gross national product, which was good, but not enough to dominate the scene anymore. Kissinger also discussed the relationship of the United States with Japan and China and also U.S. policy regarding the Middle East.

WILLIAM E. BROCK

William E. Brock, President of The Brock Group, a firm he started in 1989, was U.S. Secretary of Labor from 1985 to 1987, and served on the Economic Policy Council and the President's Task Force on Regulatory Relief. Brock served in the U. S. Senate from 1970 to 1977 and was named U. S. Trade Representative in 1981. In that capacity he was the President's chief trade advisor and international trade negotiator, and also chaired the cabinet-level Trade Policy Committee. Brock is active nationally and internationally on major forums dealing with 1992, European and Pacific Rim issues, and the politics of trade and infrastructure.

By the time the program arrived on the calendar, former U.S. Senator and Secretary of Labor William Brock was among the featured speakers at the symposium. Sen. Brock said that the race for preeminence among nations would be dominated by those whose industries can adapt to change while rapidly producing quality products. "The world is linked together now – and (to the extent none thought) possible even 15 to 20 years ago," noted Brock, who had served previously as both U.S. Labor Secretary and as a U.S. trade representative. "We're going to have to face much shorter product life cycles, much faster new product introductions and smaller production units."

Secretary Brock added that competition among nations will be based on what he called "systems capitalism," with many different kinds of capitalism unique to each country doing business among world markets. He found danger in taking nationalistic responses to an international economy. "What we face here is that economic and political issues will not be confined to national decisions only."

Several other key speakers made addresses. University Professor Haitani reminded his audience that Americans must understand the cultural differences in Asian countries before they can do business there. "In the United States, the basic unit of society is the individual. In Japan, the basic unit is the group, starting with the family and extending to the work team, the corporation and the country," the professor said. "While Americans work under individual contracts and according to job descriptions, Japanese workers' concept of responsibility is doing what is good for the group, covering for their colleagues' deficiencies," he added. In addition, the decision-making process in Japan is slower than Americans are accustomed to because the Japanese strive to avoid conflict. "Harmony at all cost is the implicit national motto."

Former Federal Express executive Jim Barksdale also addressed the international business symposium at the Peabody Hotel. "Companies using time-based competition offer more choices and lower costs," said Barksdale, who was Chief Operating Officer at FedEx at

JAMES L. BARKSDALE

James L. Barksdale, Executive Vice President and Chief Operations Officer for Federal Express Corporation, is responsible for the daily operations of the world's largest full-service all cargo airline. In the eight years since Barksdale assumed his current position, the company has grown from $1 billion to more than $7 billion in revenue and has expanded its operations to more than 119 countries in North and South America, Europe, Australia, the Middle East and the Far East.

the time. "You may choose not to operate globally, but you're competing globally," he added. He emphasized too, how innovation is increasingly important in global competition. "If you see an opportunity to fill a niche, you'd better fill it before your competition does. You're going to have to change. As more becomes possible, more is being demanded," he said. Barksdale offered several other key points including the fact that companies that manage time aggressively have these characteristics: they stay close to customers' desires, they bring in more attractive customers and leave the more price-sensitive ones to competitors. Furthermore, they set the pace for innovation and industries and they grow faster with higher profits.

In May of 1992, the second Arthur Andersen International Business Symposium featured the well-known co-author of the book "*In Search of Excellence.*" Tom Peters, in addition to Ben Wattenberg, radio/television commentator, columnist and author. The theme of the second annual conference was was "*Competing in the Global*

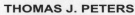

THOMAS J. PETERS

Tom Peters, founder of The Tom Peters Group, is recognized as one of the most incisive and thought-provoking business analysts of our time. As coauthor of *In Search of Excellence* and *A Passion for Excellence*, author of *Thriving on Chaos, Handbook for a Management Revolution*, and as a prolific contributor to the business press and broadcast media, Peters has virtually rewritten the basic principles of management practice and international market competition. Through his appearances before hundreds of public and private sector audiences, and through his collection of best-selling audiotapes, Mr. Peters has upended traditional thinking and turned his challenge of business orthodoxy into a worldwide revolution.

Marketplace." Peters also co-authored "*A Passion for Excellence*" and wrote "*Thriving on Chaos: A Handbook for Management Revolution.*" He was known as a guru for management and industrial dynamism and adaptability. Wattenberg was a senior fellow at the American Enterprise Institute, a think tank in Washington. He was a commentator on the weekly CBS radio network's Spectrum series, a contributing editor of *U.S. News & World Report*, a syndicated columnist and author of several books. Whattenburg also was senior editor of the *American Enterprise Magazine.*

By the time the May symposium kicked off, several speakers were added to the dais, including: John Robson, deputy secretary of the U.S. Treasury; David Kininmonth, New Zealand's top trade official in the United States; George T. Shaheen, managing partner of Andersen Consultants' worldwide operations; Brian Smith, partner in charge of Arthur Andersen's practice in Central and Eastern Europe and coordinator of the firm's audit and business advisory services in Europe, Africa and the Middle East; Jay Martin, president of Memphis-based National Safety Associates, then a leading marketer of home water filters; Richard Bell, former assistant Secretary of Agriculture and then president and chief executive officer of Riceland Foods Inc. of Stuttgart, Ark.; Nellie Fong, a partner in an Arthur Anderson's Hong Kong office and specialist in Far East investments; Sergei Gergan, a TV commentator, and Kedia.

"We saw the symposium series as a key element in creating an international business culture in the Mid-South region and supporting our international economic development efforts of the city and the state," Kedia explained. The Arthur Andersen Symposium was not the only venue for business seminars as the center increased its reach early on. For instance, in the spring of 1991, a Japanese diplomat spoke about business relationships between the United States and Japan. Yashuhiro Hamada, the consul general in New Orleans, spoke during a seminar on "Building Business Partnerships with Japan," sponsored by the Robert Wang Center. About 50 people attended the program. Participants included a representative of the Japan External Trade Organization assigned to the Tennessee DECD in Nashville and also a professor of management science at Tokyo Keizai University.

Just one month later, the director of the Canadian office of the U.S. Department of Commerce and the minister for congressional relations from Mexico visited the university in an effort to sell the idea of a free trade agreement across the nation. As chronicled by Amy Gillentine in *Update* newsletter, William Cavitt of the Department of Commerce's Canadian office remarked at the time that "The North American Free Trade Agreement offers an unparalleled opportunity to capture the energies of our three economies and propel us into the vanguard of global competitiveness."

Memphis State University became involved in a large-scale teleconference at the end of that month of October featuring Soviet Republic President Boris Yeltsin. This broadcast dealt with how to do business in the Soviet Union and featured 12 other Soviet government officials, bankers and legal experts on the panel, along with 10 American experts in Washington. The discussion was broadcast live at the Fogelman Executive Center. Several local experts helped lead a panel discussion after the telecast. The Wang Center sponsored the broadcast.

Continuing to build upon the momentum, the president of the Memphis surgical equipment firm of Smith & Nephew Richards was keynote speaker at a conference on U.S. competitiveness with a special focus on the service sector. Sessions focused on national cultures, human resource management, competition between America and the Far East, educational competitiveness and corporate restructuring in global markets. "The purpose of the conference was to reflect on strategies needed to improve the service sector's contribution to national competitiveness," Kedia said. More than 100 business people attended the conference.

Shortly before the early 1992 bilateral trade talks between the United States and Japan, Kenneth Holland, then chairman of Memphis State University's department of political science, and Kedia discussed U.S.–Japanese relations before the public. "We have to reinvest in the United States," Kedia noted then. "There has been some splitting of the seams of the industrial structure in the United States. We are losing our competitiveness in basic industries such as steel, chemicals, electronics and machine tools. This also has a negative effect on the industries that depend on steel, chemicals, electronics and machine tools – and that means just about everything." Japan was thought to have an advantage in its manufacturing system.

On a broader basis, the Robert Wang Center for International Business would team up with other entities for more general seminars, such as one of many it conducted in 1992 to help emerging exporters. This particular half-day workshop, for instance, was developed by the center in partnership with the Tennessee Small Business Development Center, the International Trade Center, the Memphis Area Chamber of Commerce, the Department of Commerce, the Tennessee Export Office of Economic and Community Development. Topics included assessing a firm's export potential, focusing on markets, and selecting a freight forwarder and international broker.

A key conference for 1992 covered the entire NAFTA scenario under the title "Business without Borders." Attendees learned how the economic borders between the U.S., Canada and Mexico were parting and a panel of business and government experts discussed implications of the proposed NAFTA treaty. The still relatively young center had sponsored more than 30 seminars, conferences and workshops to help business people open new markets in other nations by that stage.

Just as the formal programs and offerings matured, the seminars became more and more focused over time. One presentation in the fall of 1993 covered the topic of managing diversity for strategic advantage. It featured four speakers who addressed a range of topics about managing a diversified workforce and using diversity as a competitive edge. Dr. Marilyn Gowing, assistant director of research for the U.S. Office of Personnel Management, discussed initiatives for managing workforce diversity. She had served as a national officer for the Society for Industrial and Organizational Psychology and was a past president of the Personnel Testing Council in Washington, D.C. Robert Hayles, president of cultural diversity for Pillsbury Center's Metropolitan Food Sector, gave the seminar a corporate perspective. He had directed research and human resources at the Office of Naval Research and was the first behavioral scientist to manage the Department of Navy Technology with an annual budget of more than $1 billion. Speaker Lewis Griggs was known for his marketing and sales skills and new enterprise management. The author discussed workforce diversity in international competition. Thomas T. Smith, principal consultant with Rafael Gonzalez

Enterprises, talked about diversity in the marketplace and ways to deal with an increasingly pluralistic consumer.

The emerging North American Free Trade Agreement was an increasingly talked about eventuality as the year 1993 closed. Many business people were interested in learning about NAFTA, so the Wang Center staged a conference titled "Doing Business with Mexico and Canada: After the Vote." Stephen Gill, then a partner with a Nashville law firm, discussed the overall implications of NAFTA during his keynote address. Gill had completed a one-year White House Fellowship, during which he served as director of intergovernmental affairs for the U.S. Trade Representative's office. In that position, he acted as a liaison between the government officials at various levels. Other speakers on the panel hailed from Morris and Associates, the Eden Group, IDA, Drexel Chemical, Dover Elevator Systems, VVP America, Flavorite Laboratories, Gentec, AZO Inc., and National Bank of Canada. Again joining as cosponsors were the Memphis Area Chamber of Commerce, the Tennessee SBDC, the MidSouth Exporters Roundtable, the Memphis World Trade Club and the Department of Commerce International Trade Administration - Memphis office.

In 1994, the conferences and seminars which the center created grew in their weight and magnitude. Dr. Konstanin Remchukov, professor of economics at People's Friendship University in Moscow, came to discuss social, political and economic reform in Russia. Other programs concerned the General Agreements on Tariff and Trade (GATT) proceedings.

The concept and practice of "total quality management" was much in vogue in the summer of 1994. Thus, 56 people participated in a conference at the University of Memphis that dealt with this management philosophy, which had its genesis in Japanese manufacturing after the war and grew steadily in popularity in America since the 1980s. The total quality philosophy stresses, among other things, a focus on customers, teamwork, continuous improvement and fact-based management practices. In this instance, the American Production and Inventory Control Society participated with the Wang Center in bringing about the conference. IBM started in 1992 to award grants to universities that encourage the growth of total quality and higher education. That boost helped many educators start seeing this emphasis as an investment in the educational realm.

In 1995, the center hosted timely back-to-back business workshops: one on Doing Business in Mexico and the other on Doing Business in Germany. Consider, for example, the timeliness of the German seminar when the effects of unification and the emergence of the European Union had created a new and different business environment in that nation.

At several key invitations, Kedia would travel the world to address audiences in various venues. *The Financial Express* newspaper in New Delhi, India, in 1995 quoted him as saying that the large emerging nations of India, China, Indonesia and Mexico would provide the engine for world economic growth in the 21st century and that present-day developed countries would forge business and economic alliances to take advantage of labor and resources in these countries. He talked in India about global economic transformation and managerial challenges at a conference organized by the Indian Institute of Finance. Kedia stressed that in order to make alliances stronger, today's managers needed to have a multicultural perspective and create a worldwide web of relationships with stakeholders in the alliance. They must leverage and integrate through their bargaining power and manage the interdependent entities through the flow of knowledge. These guiding principles help eliminate the fear of foreign investment and move from a guarding of the status quo mindset to that of an architect of change.

A Global Logistics Conference in 1996, which was a resounding success, had as its premise that competition is taking place in a new climate where products, resources, capital and services must flow unimpeded, and that those in the industry have much to learn about how it can become a major strategic variable for gaining competitive advantages. Joining in this event were the Council of Logistics Management, the American Production and Inventory Control Society, FedEx Logistics Services, Memphis Uniport Association, the Chamber and the Wang Center. "Logistics has become critically important due to creation of international, long-distance value chains and international transactions," Kedia said. "In the past, domestically, logistics was primarily considered a support function for marketing, but it's increasingly being examined, especially in an international context, as a strategic weapon. This may be a factor on which companies compete by providing on-time delivery, better service and more integrated operations." Global economic and business trends, as well as the impact on gaining an edge through cycle time reduction, intermodal transportation and other topics were covered by seven seminar speakers at this major logistics conference. In addition, the event planners conducted focus group meetings to find out what people perceived as educational needs in the field. The prior year, the city was host of Air Cargo Shippers Conference – the first time it had been held in Memphis in years.

Brazil was rightfully the focal point of a workshop in 1997 that emphasized trade and investment opportunities there. At that time, American firms were focusing a fresh attention toward Brazil as a market for trade and investment. With the largest economy in Latin America and an estimated $760 billion gross domestic product with a population of 160 million people, the stakes were enormous. At the time, Brazil's policies for currency stabilization, economic restructuring and pro-market reforms were expanding economic opportunities through privatization, deregulation and the removal of impediments to competition.

India's Information
Technology: A 21st Century
Resource for U.S. Companies
May 10-12, 2000

By 2000, information technology was as much in vogue in conversation as ever before. Therefore, it was appropriate to launch a conference called, "India's Information Technology: A 21st Century Resource for U.S. Companies." This conference, presented in conjunction with FedEx, the Government of India, Memphis in May International Festival and the Memphis Chamber, included the Honorable Naresh Chandra, Indian ambassador to the United States. Firms were able to meet and hear from some of the faster-growing information technology firms in India and learn new applications and resources for doing business in the region. Executives from America and India discussed opportunities for business development, collaboration and matchmaking, including offshore services and information technology.

Earlier that year, the Wang Center also held a forum on the e-commerce explosion. Electronic commerce has been touted as the business strategy of the new millennium, involving a dramatic shift from an industrial-based to an information-based economy with all of its implications.

On an even more major participatory and regional scale, Fogelman Executive Center was the setting for the ninth annual East-West International Business Conference, highlighted by special guest Sen. Howard Baker; FedEx CEO Fred Smith; Johnny Adams, director of AutoZone, and also leaders from Tyson Foods International, Storage USA, and Drexel Chemical, among other companies.

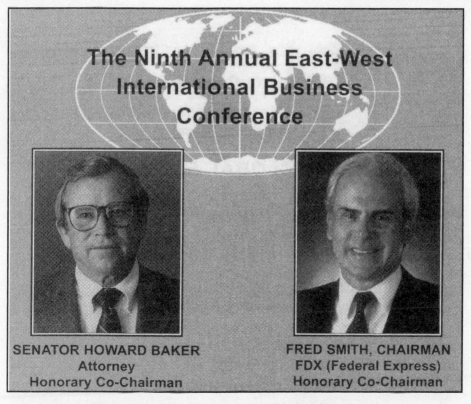

New Opportunities in the Global Economy
April 9-10, 2001

International breakfast forums were going full speed ahead by 2003, featuring such topics as practical strategies for negotiating cross culturally and leveraging China. They continued into the next year with more information about NAFTA, the stock exchange and work performance.

Topics for 2005 seminars and forums included successfully exploring and exporting to Asian markets, an analysis of the Seven Revolutions (population, resources, technology, information, integration, conflict, and governance), and engaging in African business developments. In 2006, an ambitious February conference covered the waterfront with an analysis of the future of every major geopolitical region in the world. This innovative, futuristic seminar featured Erik Peterson, senior vice president and director of the Global Strategy Institute's Center for Strategic and International Studies.

As time went on, seminar topics were tweaked and changed to stay relevant. For instance, a 2009 workshop took on the topic of how to meet renewable energy's technology challenges, along with various innovative solutions from Japan. That year also had workshops that addressed economic and financial crisis lessons and actions in addition to a cyber security exposition. The year 2010 covered export investment opportunities with India and also with Tunisia in separate, freestanding sessions. That year the multimodal conference covered everything from cargo security to intermodal collaboration. A November 2010 seminar treated the topic of doing business with Spain. Because cyber security is such a hot, ongoing topic and the first conference had been so successful, a larger scale follow-up seminar was presented in October 2011, in collaboration with Dr. Dipankar Dasgupta, a professor of computer science and internationally known expert in cyber security,

Fast forward to the present day and near future. To develop international business acumen in the local business community, the Wang Center and the Memphis Regional Chamber's International Business Council will continue to develop programs offering international education and networking opportunities. The Wang Center will continue to partner with the Japan Outreach Initiative (JOI), the Japan-America Society of Tennessee (JAST) and the Memphis Department of Foreign Languages and Literatures to offer regular Japanese language and culture workshops and seminars to the region's business community. JOI, housed on the U of M campus, is sponsored by the Japan Foundation and the

Center for Global Partnership (CGP), and administered by the Laurasian Institution and CGP. Recent programs include seminars, cultural demonstrations at the Japanese Festival at Memphis Botanic Garden, and Noh Drama performances at the university. Planned activities include a bilingual website highlighting local resources, programs and events; a Japanese language telephone hotline; and access to business programs featuring experts from leading Japanese financial and economic institutions.

The Confucius Institute operates as a non-profit, public institute with the goal of promoting Chinese language and culture and supporting local Chinese teaching internationally through affiliated Confucius Institutes around the globe. These goals were established by the China National Office for Teaching Chinese as a Foreign Language, headquartered in Beijing. The University of Memphis is home to the only Confucius Institute in the state of Tennessee and the first in the Mid-South. In conjunction with its partner institution, Hubei University in China, the Confucius Institute at the University of Memphis promotes understanding of the Chinese language and culture among the people of the United States, develops friendly relations between the U. S. and China, accelerates the expansion of multiculturalism, and provides opportunities for students studying the Chinese language.

The Confucius Institute is closely affiliated with the university's new Asian Studies and International Trade program, whose aim is to provide students with the critical combination of skills that an increasing number of companies seek: international business knowledge, foreign language proficiency, cultural sensitivity and experience abroad. The program was created by an anonymous donation to the university. The university has long participated in educational exchanges with a number of universities in China, including Hubei University, its partner in the Confucius Institute. See Appendix E for a list of Organizational Relationships.

Finally, to increase the relevancy of internationally focused business education and MBA programs at U of M, the Memphis CIBER and Fogelman College of Business will host a guest speaker series drawing on the experience of chief executives from internationally-focused businesses. Leveraging U of M's IMBA and CD MBA, the guest speaker program supports select presenters to speak at luncheons. The core audience will be U of M MBA students and alumni.

High-Level Exchange Delegations

In line with these themes, the importance of a special two-week training session for Shanghai executives in Memphis in the early 1990s cannot be overstated, because it had far-reaching implications. Shanghai, in the past as is the case now, is an economic power center for China and also for much of Asia. It has undeniably grown into one of the great financial centers of the world – just like New York, London, and Frankfurt.

Former Chinese Premier Deng Xiaoping traveled to Shanghai in 1992 to make a speech from the podium at the Wisteria Guest House, in which he told of his plans to rebuild the city and financial center into the major player it has become today. Up until that moment, the economy had been very much centrally run and planned. After this order, the Shanghai government searched for ways it could transform from a planned economy to a market economy. Premier Xiaoping encouraged a significant decentralization and local municipalities and provinces were allowed to invest in industries that they considered most profitable, which encouraged investment. Thus, his reforms shifted China's development strategy into a fresh emphasis on light industry and export-led growth.

Soon, Shanghai was rebuilding its financial center all across the east end. Its leaders invited several business heavyweights to speak; among those invitees was Robert Wang. In fact, he was invited to the same prestigious podium at the Wisteria Guest House where Deng Xiaoping addressed leaders only one year before. Most of the

High Level Shanghai Executive Delegation
1994

other speakers before this group of government decision-makers and business leaders were from places such as Hong Kong and Singapore. "They told me, 'You know distribution and retailing and you could have something important to tell the various heads of government operations as they make the needed transitions'," said Wang. Also among the members of the audience were the chairmen of two of the largest department stores in China and leaders of the grocery and garment industries.

Robert Wang soon conceived of the idea of a specialized training session in Memphis, and shared that idea with Kedia. The Wang Center subsequently designed a specialized two-week course to offer an intensive learning environment at Fogelman Executive Center, where the high-level attendees lived during the workshops. All were key representatives of the commercial government industry sectors – people who later became chairmen and executives of business enterprises once the large operations were converted to new management models.

The special invitee program's basic framework was that in the mornings, the guests toured local large firms, and in the afternoons,

The high-level visiting executive delegation from Shanghai
presented an appreciation plaque of
"FRIENDSHIP FOREVER"
to the University of Memphis

they were involved in sessions to learn the "how's and why's" of American business practices. "Here in Memphis, these leaders were learning key information that helped them in becoming the leaders of future change in China and the start of what has been called the Shanghai Miracle," Wang stated. They toured the Port of Memphis, the Central Business District downtown, the Defense Depot, the Southern Pacific Container Yard, Fleming Corp., FedEx, Wang's International, Kroger Distribution Center, retail shops and Williams-Sonoma's warehouse. Lectures included topics on transportation, distribution, logistics, wholesaling channels, customer service, inventory approaches, marketing segmentation and competition. Before departing, this high-level delegation presented the Wang Center with an appreciative "Friendship Forever" plaque with their signatures.

As an offshoot of the sessions, one of the visiting business leaders asked Wang if he could recommend to them an excellent, large department store chain to enter into potential conversations for licensing in China. Since Wang was one of the largest suppliers at that time to Wal-Mart, he talked with the president of the company. After a number of conversations and agreements, Wang accompanied Wal-Mart chairman Rob Walton and its international president, Bobby Martin, to China for a week in 1994, along with the company's vice president of international operations. China then opened the door for Wal-Mart to have nearly 300 stores in that vast nation, and it has as a result become a giant retailer there. All of these events stemmed from Robert Wang's speech at the government house. In subsequent visits to Shanghai, Wang was invited as a special guest to the opening of the Pearl Tower, an impressive television tower there. In addition, he has spoken twice at Beijing University.

Quite interestingly, Robert Wang led in 1992 a whole series of economic business programs on the large Chinese television station, CCTV. For the show titled "American Corporate Profile," which introduced and described how international companies operate, Robert and his company – much in the style of *60 Minutes* – filmed and interviewed executives with household-name American companies, including Disney, Johnson & Johnson, Wal-Mart, Anheuser-Busch, General Motors, and Goodyear. He talked about the details of how they operated. Premier Deng Xiaoping often watched these shows. At the launch of this series, in fact, the vice premier and three ministers of China attended the press conference in a great hall. "Robert planted the seeds of so many things and has enjoyed unique opportunities when he shared the lessons of how market economies work," Susie Wang said of her husband's endeavors.

Visits by High-Level Dignitaries Built on Success after Success

An important delegation representing the China Machinery and Automobile Industrial industry visited Memphis in the mid-1990s, which nicely coincided with a conference at the university about forming joint-venture alliances among companies, both domestic and international. "The joint venture workshops were highly informative and had practical relevance for companies contemplating or currently engaged in a business alliance with the partner outside the continental U.S.," said Judy Scales, then assistant director of the Wang Center. Workshop participants learned how a firm could benefit from a business alliance using various types of financing, ways to identify partners, and the means to negotiate and structure a deal legally and contractually.

The Wang Center and the Department of Commerce in 1995 played host to His Excellency Nitya Pibulsonggram, ambassador to the United States at the Royal Thai Embassy. Immediately prior to his appointment, the ambassador had served for eight years as permanent representative of Thailand to the United Nations in New York City. He was the son of one of Thailand's first constitutional prime ministers and had a distinguished career in the Ministry of Foreign Affairs.

The very same year, the center hosted a delegation from the Quingdao Textile Corp., which was established in 1951 and had 72 enterprises and a textile university and research institute. Another delegation, one from the Peoples Government in Tianjin, China, visited in 1998. That select group of five included a standing district vice president, a foreign economic relations commissioner, and members of trade groups there.

True to its promise and form, Asia and China were a focus of an important consortium Memphis hosted on "Doing Business with that Giant Nation of China" as the decade and the millennium closed. In March of 1999, China's market opportunities for

American firms was the centerpiece of such a seminar attended by Li Yong, the director of the Center for Marketing Trade Development in China, and Dr. Shi Yonghai, head of the Chinese Academy for International Trade and Economic Cooperation, a major economic think tank and advisor to the Chinese government. The two important Chinese delegates spoke at the conference at the University of Memphis before taking a tour of the FedEx hub operations and also the inner workings of the Defense Supply Depot, Nike, Williams-Sonoma and other large-scale local companies. They in turn presented an overview of the Chinese economy and opportunities and pitfalls of penetrating that market.

Doing Business in China Conference
March 25, 1999

Dr. Shi Yonghai (left) of Beijing talks with Ting Ho (Chief Economist, FedEx), Ben Kedia, and Ted Weise (COO, FedEx).

An interesting executive forum called "Planes, Trains and Trucks... Learning About NAFTA" was held in January of 2004 to celebrate the first 10 years of NAFTA and to also discuss opportunities and security challenges for the coming decade. Phil Newsom, international sales manager for FedEx, spoke on the topic "From Toronto to Toluca: The Air Transportation Side of NAFTA," which focused on security concerns for clearing goods.

"Education, Health, and Information Technology" convened in March of 2004, which brought in specialists from the university's sociology department as well. That conference featured a presentation by F. W. de Klerk, former president of South Africa, on how information technology can facilitate development, conflict resolution and nonviolent political change in the world.

Over time, seminars became even more specialized. In the fall of 2004, the Wang Center cosponsored a half-day business conference on international trade compliance issues featuring officers with the U.S. Department of Commerce and with the Office of Export Assistance.

Furthermore, the Wang Center in the fall of 2005 hosted a conference with FedEx on the topic of security issues and related concerns on the Memphis logistics industry. That program addressed how security screening of trade merchandise could be facilitated at the point of origin as well as the point of entry. The Memphis World Trade Club, the Council of Logistics Management and the Memphis Traffic Club all participated in that seminar.

The Memphis in May International Festival brings in business experts from the host country to open the economic lines of communication. In 2005, for instance, the Memphis Regional Chamber's International Council, the Memphis Export Assistance Center, the Memphis World Trade Club, Northwest Airlines and the Wang Center for International Business held a conference on doing business in Ireland. Dale Tasharski, the senior commercial officer at the U.S. Embassy in Dublin, Ireland, was one of the presenters.

A unique program provided by the CIBER is the Global Executive Network, which links Mississippi Delta executives with potential clients or partners in other countries. Delegations from various Chinese regions, Africa, Ireland and Germany have participated in related events. Furthermore, the CIBER organizes a series of ad-hoc business conferences on subjects of current interest of importance to the international business community of Memphis and the region, often in collaboration with the U.S. Commercial Service of the U.S. Department of Commerce and the Memphis Area Chamber of Commerce.

An innovation to the range of program offerings is the International Business Breakfast Forums, where leading business consultants, government officials, and academics are brought to campus and offer their views on current events to a large audience of regional business people. Jointly sponsored by various business associations and local corporations, the Breakfast Forum format allows a large impact at relatively low cost. Speakers included the chief economist of the New York Stock Exchange, a well-known consultant and author who is an expert on cross-cultural negotiations, and leaders from the Pearl River Delta region of China.

These activities have proven to be well-grounded in the needs of the region and therefore fill an obvious need among local businesses. The large numbers of participants, along with the fact that most of the programs are co-sponsored by local business associations, government agencies or local businesses, are indicative of the support these programs enjoy and the value that they represent to the community. It is without a doubt that these programs create a tremendous amount of goodwill for the CIBER and the university, as well as develop a strong network of businesses that can help the Center with its other programs, such as providing internships for IMBA students and potential supporters for the academic outreach activities.

More than 6,500 participants from the business community have attended various international business sessions since 1991. These included participation in the global executive network, the international business breakfast forum and numerous international business conferences and seminars offered for executives. See Appendix L for a list of business conferences and visiting business delegations.

Global Education (Global Ed) Seminars for FedEx Customers and Executives

Managers have come to realize that while thinking and operating globally, they must act locally. This means that they should know the language, customers, institutions, government relations, social values and corporate culture of the various countries in which they are doing business. That is why executive development became a major function of the center, which had the intention to develop an understanding of global competition, marketing and financial issues in overseas operations and strategies for joint ventures and strategic alliances. The GlobalEd seminars have been a springboard in themselves for reaching various clients and executives of FedEx. These clients have included such companies as Abbott, Canon, Cargill, Cessna, Citrix, Anheuser-Busch, Colgate-Palmolive, Dow Corning, Medtronic, Rolls Royce, Texas Instruments, the Department of Commerce, and other notable customers.

Kedia addressed this ongoing global need in an article in the *Journal of World Business* back in 1999. "There is increasing evidence that large-scale globalization is rendering traditional ways of doing business largely irrelevant. There is a constant need for managers to become global managers with a global perspective that is supported by appropriate skills and knowledge." He said this takes into account not only regional and country pressures, but a holistic strategy which moves an organization and its people and processes from autonomous business units to a more integrated, effective approach. Achieving this goal often involves realignment of strategies to a more complex reality. "This will allow a manager from one part of the world to be comfortable in another on account of knowledge and skills that are based on understanding and awareness."

"This is a major effort that has had tremendous impact on the business community and that responds effectively to the mandate of the Title VI legislation," said Dr. José de la Torre, dean of the Graduate School of Business at Florida International University CIBER, in his peer review of 2005. "Originally conceived to serve FedEx's own customers and run in Memphis, these programs have broadened to include third-party businesses and have been offered throughout the United States in places such as San Francisco, Seattle, New York and Miami. With an average participation of 30 business representatives, the programs have focused on the cultural, political, economic and practical issues of doing business in specific areas of the world."

European Culture and Business Practices Seminar
January 2001

(Front, left) Mike L. Ducker, Chief Operating Officer and President of International, FedEx Express, meets with FedEx customers and FedEx executive participants.

For several years, Memphis CIBER Director Kedia had served as a guest instructor at the FedEx Leadership Institute. This relationship evolved into a national executive training program about the understanding of countries, cultures, and business practices in Asia, Europe, Latin America, and the Middle East. By using native cultural trainers and regional experts to lead the seminars, the program has earned rave reviews from senior FedEx directors for providing a clear picture of various cultures and business practices of different countries. The program, however, was suspended due to the downturn in the economic situation.

A GlobalEd course conducted on Asian cultures is illustrative. The first day of the program dealt with doing business in a global village, while the next three days focused on one nation each day, with the last day covering "becoming a global leader." Everything from bureaucratic rules to core values to culturally adaptive leadership was covered. One on Latin America added elements on flexibility and adaptability, traditions within church and family, institutions and other nuances. Meanwhile, the European component provided its own slant on behavioral patterns, cultural insights, and business practices. The GlobalEd educational seminar on the Middle East inserted such specificities as the monarchy in Saudi Arabia, Israeli values, and the basic foundation of Islam among session components.

Longtime Wang Center staffer Jeanne Tutor vividly recalls these seminars and their formats. "For all of the culture seminars, Monday was the day to learn more about our own U.S. culture," she said. "There was always an amazing 'A-ha' moment after playing the BARNGA card game on Monday. There were four to five tables and the participants did not know that each table received slightly different rules for playing the game. Also, participants weren't allowed to talk or write notes during the card game. After 15 minutes, the winner at each table was asked to move to another table. He/she went to a new table and tried to play the card game with the rules learned initially," Tutor added.

"When the new player (with his set of rules) joined another table (with a different set of rules), the players at each table got frustrated and confused but were asked to silently continue to play the game without any communication among the players.

Following the card game, the participants discussed how they felt when everyone didn't play by the same rules," Tutor explained. The exercise was a good simulation for real-life adaptations of cultural nuances and particulars.

The center organized two Middle Eastern cultural seminars in 2003 largely for the perceived need to have an increased awareness of the Arabic mindset. The expansive agenda included one day on the American cultural perspective, and one day each on the various perspectives of the Arab world, Israel, and Egypt/Saudi Arabia. The last day summarized how the mindsets differed and how such differences can sometimes precipitate conflicts. The program contributed to a greater understanding of Islamic cultures by the various participants.

Testimonials from FedEx executives and their customers have been overwhelmingly positive regarding the overall specialized series. "This is an excellent program and one that I would sincerely recommend for any of our customer executives or sales account managers who traveled to Asia," said D. B. Newill, senior executive, marketing and strategy for Rolls-Royce Corporation's Helicopter Engine Business. "I have been through cultural and pre-travel conditioning courses as part of my GM background, but this one was clearly better in teaching the participants how to interact with Japanese, Chinese and Indian business people. I was particularly impressed with the fact that the session later brought in subject and country experts for each nation. They brought out details and customer relationship building in ways that books and notes alone cannot. Their practice exercises clearly embed the knowledge you need to remember when traveling."

"It was the best learning experience I've had in a long time," said Melissa Jones of the human resources department at Pacific Northern Inc. "On my first day back at work, I was able to implement things I've learned."

"I was on the edge of my seat for three and a half days," said James Martin, a vice president with Saturn Electronics and Engineering Inc. "By far, it was the best training on Asian culture I've attended. The class was so well done, I was unable to come up with much for improvement input. It is clearly a big motivator and learning experience for the FedEx and client attendees."

"We had some Japanese businessmen come to our company to check out our products," said Gary Smith, distribution manager at Eaglevision. "My president said he used some of the information learned from the Asian Cultural Seminar that I had reported in the management meeting in dealing with our Japanese visitors. He said that was life-saving information on properly dealing with the Japanese."

"This seminar was by far the best and most useful that I've ever attended in my professional life," noted Jim Newton, senior director of Global Operations at Intermec Technologies. "My big take-away was that I didn't know how much I didn't know about Asian culture. The class exercises helped me break through my previous paradigms of how other cultures view Americans and how I viewed other cultures. At times, I felt as if I was submerged into another culture."

"I had the pleasure of attending the Global Ed seminar in Miami and I cannot express enough how valuable I found it to be," noted Renee Beech of FedEx. "As a native of Cuba and having lived since age 4 in the South Florida area, I thought I was in tune to the nuances of the different Latin American cultures. I was

Latin American Cultures and Business Practices
Seminar for FedEx Customers and Executives
March 2004 - Miami, Florida

mistaken. The seminar provided me with very valuable insights to other cultures and I can see value to front-line managers in culturally diverse markets."

Her colleague, Eileen Paternostro of FedEx, was equally impressed, according to her own seminar observation form: "I have conducted business along the Texas/Mexico border for years, both as a ramp manager and as a sales professional; however, after learning more about the Latin culture through this program, I quickly realized why I was successful at times and unsuccessful at other times with regard to local personnel."

And Muzaffar Qurashi, then global sales manager with FedEx added: "In my 17-plus years in global sales and operations with our company, I can unequivocally say that this is the most influential training that I've attended. It combines academic with real-life applications. I walked away completely prepared and motivated to deal with my counterparts in the respective locations around the world." Such were commentaries derived from feedback forms.

"My exposure to CIBER is connected with the Global Education Culture Seminars," said Lee Alcott, managing director of International Sales with FedEx. "From these, we've also invited Dr. Kedia to participate and present to various marketing events. The GlobalEd seminars were fantastic. They gave us a unique opportunity to have FedEx employees learning right along with our customers. This allowed us to target the right level contacts because they had no concern that it would turn into a FedEx commercial. That said, it did help us learn more (and candidly) about the concerns and issues our customers were facing as they expanded out of the US."

For the FedEx people, GlobalEd really gave deeper understanding of regional differences, Alcott said. "So often, people look at LAC or APAC or even Europe as one country (each) and don't understand that there are some very significant differences. Having lived outside of the U.S. myself, I was particularly impressed with the portion on the U.S. values and what drives us. All too often, we just take these for granted and, while I didn't expect much from this portion, it really helped remind me that everything is relative when dealing with multiple countries. It's wonderful that Memphis has been able to attract this center and the interest of people from diverse cultures. I hope my company will find many more ways to work with it in the future."

"A program that I have been particularly impressed with and involved with is the GlobalEd leadership series," said Mike Ducker, chief operating officer and president International of FedEx Express. "It was one of those types of stories where you met someone for breakfast and asked them about a program to educate future business leaders for the global marketplace. That was now 10 years ago for our discussion. At that time, many of our leaders were underexposed in terms of doing business on a global scale. Ben Kedia and his team designed and delivered an outstanding globalized business initiative. A combination of FedEx leaders and our customers together would attend and get a much deeper understanding of the culturally different parts of the world. This included cultural norms, value systems and business practices. The course is a weeklong immersion program. You can target individual sessions, for instance, if your business is heavily expanding into Latin America at the time.

"I've had people who were ex-patriots tell me after the fact that they would've given anything to have had this program years earlier," the FedEx senior executive added. "The efficiency of doing something like that on the front end of a process has everything to do with success, quality and damage control."

Russ Musgrove, managing director with Global Vehicles at FedEx, also gained experience with the center via the GlobalEd Culture Seminars. Such seminars typically were focused upon one of four geographic regions: Asia, Europe, Latin America and the Middle East, at a given time. "These GlobalEd Culture Seminars were an important part of my shift to a global manager. I attribute a great deal of my personal success in shifting to a global perspective to these classes. The vast majority of my team is outside the United States, and the training I received via those seminars had a material impact on my ability to be effective managing these teams. While hard knocks and years of experience might have eventually filled the knowledge gap, this program fast-tracked my transition. The format, structure and resources made the difference in these classes. I still use the material given in the class today! This specific group of classes under-committed and over-delivered.

"Managing on the global stage can be very complex for an unprepared American, but with the support of the Robert Wang Center, I was prepared for the most difficult part of understanding and adapting to cultures."

Chapter Seven

❧

Faculty Members Moving Out
to Meet the World

Traditionally speaking, faculty members have had a lack of exposure to international business training and overseas experiences – the types of experiential skill sets which would greatly help in conveying global concepts and intercultural truths to their students.

The Wang Center acted as a catalyst to promote faculty development in several ways. Initially, it sent U of M business, language and area studies faculty members to the University of Antwerp in Belgium to study European business methods, while on the home front, the center offered international faculty development workshops at the University of Memphis. In a mere five-year span, more than 80 faculty members from across the U.S. participated in the Antwerp Study Abroad in Belgium while more than 120 faculty members attended the programs offered on the campus in Memphis. The center also promoted the teaching of foreign language from a business perspective both at the University of Memphis and at other colleges and universities. In 1993, the center hosted its first annual business language workshop (which would continue for 20 years), designed to teach college instructors how to teach language from a business perspective.

Still focused on filling the gap regarding international curriculum, the Memphis CIBER has encouraged U of M faculty members to attend a domestic program offered by the University of South Carolina CIBER, where functional courses are taught with an international perspective. This is an international capacity-building effort within the business school to facilitate business faculty in adding international curricula to their existing courses or to establish new international courses. Also along these lines, Fogelman faculty members have been supported to participate in special programs in international human resource management and international entrepreneurship offered by the CIBER at the University of Colorado at Denver.

In addition to the domestic international faculty development program and the study abroad program, there is a third component encouraging faculty members to free their time to do research on an international topic of their choosing. Also, the Wang Center supported faculty members to attend conferences and present papers on topics of international significance. "This gives a multi-pronged approach to get U of M business faculty members involved in the Wang Center, thus facilitating capacity-building for international teaching and research overall while the participating faculty members acquire more knowledge and experience in their own specific business disciplines," Kedia explained.

The center has supported research streams (which have been presented at many national and international conferences and published in major journals) during the various program cycles, long-term streams that have yielded significant past results and which still offer opportunities for new development and updated areas of emphasis. They are designed to complement continuing research streams. As a whole, these areas contribute to our understanding of: (1) managerial action in the context of U.S.-based international firms; (2) U.S.-based firms in the context of their global environment; and (3) strategic alignment between both.

David Allen, professor of Management at Fogelman College, said he also has benefited personally and professionally from these activities of the Wang Center. "Ben has supported my efforts to internationalize my teaching and research in several ways. For example, the center has supported me to participate in a Faculty Development in International Human Resource Management Program at the University of Colorado at Denver, to participate in a Faculty Study Abroad Program in Latin America, and to present some of my research at an international business conference in Spain. These opportunities have had a profound impact on my own career."

Faculty Study Abroad

Faculty Study Abroad (FSA) programs coordinated by the center are robust and have been growing through refinements since the first one was conducted in Lille, France, in 1991. Subsequently, FSA's have been organized in Antwerp, Belgium; Strasbourg, France; and Brussels, Belgium. These intensive programs include informative and focused lectures combined with tours in the host country for visiting faculty during the summertime. Political, economic and cultural dimensions are among categories examined.

The Memphis CIBER organizes and conducts these FSA programs primarily in Europe while also cosponsoring a wide array of additional Faculty Study Abroad opportunities organized and coordinated by other CIBERs. Various CIBERs that have actively coordinated FSA programs since 1998 include: Florida International University, University of South Carolina, University of Colorado-Denver, University of Connecticut, University of Pittsburgh, Brigham Young University, University of Wisconsin, and University of Hawaii. See Figure 8 for an overview of CIBER FSA programs offered in 2009-2010.

Antwerp is a highly desirable location for faculty development in business, foreign language, and political science. This program includes lectures by government and business leaders and site visits to international firms, financial organizations and key government offices. Focused topics have included pan-European marketing, distribution structures, and an analysis of banking. The objective of the program is to raise faculty awareness of the social, political, economic and business environments and practices in Western Europe through hands-on experiences. See Appendix M

Faculty Study Abroad in Antwerp (May 1995)

(Front row, left) Dr. Liliane Van Hoof (FSA Coordinator, University of Antwerpen), Dr. Rose Rubin, Dr. Sherry Sullivan, Dr. Sidney McPhee, Dr. Ashvin Vibhakar, Dr. Denise Stanley, Dr. Christopher Forth; (Back row, left) Dr. C. Jayachandran, Dr. Clarence Mann, Dr. William Smith, Dr. Stephen McDaniel, Dr. Dinah Payne, Dr. Ben Kedia, Dr. Thomas Davies, Dr. Delano Black, Dr. Milton Pressley.

2009-2010 CIBER Overseas Programs for Faculty

FACULTY DEVELOPMENT IN INTERNATIONAL BUSINESS (FDIB)

FDIB-INDIA
Mumbai & Chennai
December 16-23, 2009
Florida International University CIBER
ciber.fiu.edu

FDIB-EUROPEAN UNION
France & Germany
May 9-19, 2010
University of Memphis CIBER
memphis.edu/wangctr

FDIB-EASTERN EUROPE
Croatia, Czech Republic & Turkey
May 20-31, 2010
University of Pittsburgh CIBER
www. business.pitt.edu/ibc

FDIB-INDIA
New Delhi & Agra
January 4-15, 2010
University of Connecticut CIBER
www.business.uconn.edu/ciber

FDIB-TURKEY
Istanbul & Ankara
May 23-June 3, 2010
University of Kansas CIBER
www.ciber.business.ku.edu

FDIB-EcoBiz (GREEN)
CENTRAL AMERICA
Costa Rica
May 14-25, 2010
Texas A&M University CIBER
cibs.tamu.edu/CostaRica

FDIB-CHINA
China & Hong Kong
January 3-15, 2010
University of Colorado Denver CIBER
www.ucdenver.edu/CIBER

FDIB-MERCOSUR
Argentina, Brazil & Chile
May 8-19, 2010
Florida International University CIBER
ciber.fiu.edu

FDIB-AFRICA
Kenya, South Africa & Tanzania
May 10-26, 2010
University of South Carolina CIBER
mooreschool.sc.edu/moore/ciber

FDIB-VIETNAM
Ho Chi Minh City & Hanoi
January 2-14, 2010
University of Wisconsin CIBER &
University of Hawaii CIBER
www.bus.wisc.edu/ciber/vietnamfdib

CIBER Covers the World

Figure 8. CIBERs offer Faculty Study Abroad
programs across the breadth of the world.

for information on the European study abroad program. In 2011, the following FSA programs were offered by various CIBERs: the EU regulation and integration (Brussels), Mercosur (Argentina, Brazil and Chile), European economics in transition (Hungary, Bulgaria and Turkey), Africa (Kenya and Tanzania), and Russia (Moscow, St. Petersburg and Yekaterinburg).

"I have been supported by the Wang Center on two important occasions: a Faculty Development in International Business (FDIB) seminar at the University of South Carolina on international marketing teaching and research in the early 1990s, and more recently, a Faculty Study Abroad program on European Community (EU) held in Brussels, Belgium coordinated by the University of Pittsburgh and the University of Memphis CIBERs," said Emin Babakus, Palmer Professor of Marketing in the Fogelman College of Business and Economics. The Memphis CIBER provided funding for him to attend in 2011. "I have benefitted immensely from both experiences in terms of teaching and research. As a result of the EU experience I now have connections with researchers from European universities. There is no question in my mind that these programs helped me and my students in significant ways, which would not be possible if Wang Center support was not available. I remain grateful to Ben and the Center, and of course, Mr. Wang who made all this possible."

David Smith, a faculty member participant in the 2000 FSA in Antwerp, wrote a paper about his experience. "We attended over 20 in-class lectures delivered by experts in their fields and visited several prestigious European institutions. Lecture topics covered the spectrum, touched on issues from the balanced scorecard to cross-cultural management and to e-commerce within Europe."

The faculty study abroad program in South America (Argentina, Brazil, and Chile) involves collaboration among four CIBERs, including the Wang Center. Business and scholarly presentations and site visits focus on the political, economic, and trade/investment environment in each country. Mercosur underscores the significance of the Southern Cone in Latin America. The program is composed of lectures, discussions sessions, visits to companies, and opportunities to interact with management faculty and students. Speakers are drawn from business, government, mass media and academia.

Support from the University of Memphis CIBER was granted for trips to South America, China, and India. Lloyd D. Brooks, chair and professor of Management Information Systems, recalled through his own experience in regard to the Faculty Study Abroad initiative. "Taken together, these trips provided a contrast and overall global understanding about differing cultures and financial aspects. These provided many examples that can be used in the classroom to acquaint students with first-hand experiences. This adds more credibility because the instructor has lived what he is teaching. I developed a slide presentation for each of the trips and often use the presentation during lectures relating to culture to provide students with a better understanding about the global environment. While visiting universities in each country, opportunities were provided to better understand the higher education system in the country and the ability to provide a contrast with ones in the USA.

"On a personal note, the CIBER experience made me more knowledgeable and grew my understanding about global societies," Brooks said. "I serve as an advisor for the MSBA degree program in which over half of the students are from India. The trip to India provided insights into the country and culture and made me a better advisor for these students. In my comment about visiting India, I include some pictures of my travels on a personal part of my professional website, so students see them and know that I understand their society and culture."

"I was able to visit Eastern Europe and India in different years through the Faculty Development in International Business program. In Eastern Europe, we traveled to Croatia, Bulgaria and the Czech Republic," said Dr. Robin S. Poston, associate professor of Management Information Systems and associate director of the Systems Testing Excellence Program at the Fogelman College. "What those types of trips do is to place attendees in a type of quick-immersion program led by knowledgeable lecturers who are usually social science faculty and who have studied the country and have deep knowledge of its economic, political, and social structures. After morning lectures, where we are briefed, we would take company tours in the afternoons. Nights and weekends are for more tourist-related interests. Every part of the program is a learning experience.

"I will never forget a business person I met briefly in Eastern Europe. He had opened a chain of gas stations. We asked him, 'What is your greatest cost?' and he told us it was the bribes he had to pay for protection of his business. That was an eye-opener. It was part of the cost of doing business there. It was fascinating to see nations in transition experience the dawn of capitalism and the opening of markets. Still, they were learning about what it meant to have true individual initiative in business there. Faculty participants bring those kinds of stories back to inform their research and share with their students," Poston said.

These trips are designed for learning and knowledge growth in a particular locale. There also is value in meeting other faculty members from different universities, such as a professor from the University of Florida with whom she compared notes about various professorial efforts and experiences. About 12-15 U.S. faculty members attend each trip.

"A few years after the Eastern Europe trip, my brother and I went back to Croatia and rented a sailboat," she said. "A spinoff gained from the trip, therefore, is that you realize the beauty of an area and can navigate through a certain country easier when you return in the future.

"India was quite distinct," Poston noted. There was the same basic scheduling structure, but it was more rustic than many other nations, at least in certain areas, she said. There were rolling power outages at the time, and also is a much higher population density. "I particularly recall the Honda motorcycle factory, where they still were doing much of the assembly in a hands-on manual fashion. There were hundreds of workers there with specialty tools. With the cost of labor, they could make the motorcycles less expensively than with full automation. What made that trip interesting, too, was that I was able to get some pre-approvals from FedEx to take a side trip, interviewing some of their existing vendors about how FedEx could work with them better and I reported on those findings. I was able to publish three research papers so far from the data I gleaned." The professor participated in yet another such activity in 2012 to Brazil-Argentina-Chile as part of this Faculty Development in International Business program.

The center also has provided partial funding for international conferences where Poston has presented papers at various times over the last nine years. "The Wang Center brings us international opportunities and applicable speakers and forums," she said. "The world is global, and they keep that dialog in the forefront of peoples' thinking here at the University of Memphis. The staff brings opportunities for us to participate in learning more about international business concepts and practices. What they deliver is not just a-nice-to-have, but a must-have to survive in today's business environment."

Dr. Robert R. Taylor, professor of management and former chair of Management at the University of Memphis, taught in the IMBA program and has been involved in Faculty Study Abroad programs. He now teaches in continental Europe yearly. "I most admire Ben Kedia for providing a mechanism for international involvement for our faculty," Taylor said. "In regard to my own connection, he supported me to go to conferences – one in Antwerp, Belgium, and another in South Carolina on how to teach from international perspectives."

Kedia would also send students to Germany and other locations to complete internships. One of these happened to be in Ingolstadt, Germany, at the university. A professor there had been assisting the Wang Center, primarily in helping facilitate internship placements in Germany. They in turn asked the center in Memphis at one stage what it could do for them. The result was that the University of Memphis sent some professors to the university in Germany to teach in English. "I went and taught an organizational behavior class in English," Taylor explained. "I have now done that for 10 years. I bring an experiential approach with role-playing and teambuilding exercises. It has really helped me learn the culture there. I do a condensed class for two weeks. Ben Kedia has the charisma and confidence with an understanding of international topics," Taylor said. "He relates well to business people and academics."

The Wang Center partners with the University of Pittsburgh CIBER, Pitt's European Center of Excellence and other CIBER co-sponsors to offer an FDIB in Brussels, Belgium – the headquarters of the European Commission. The 12-day program, held each May, includes briefings by EU experts and visits to EU institutions for the purpose of educating U.S. business and language faculty on European Union (EU) regulation policy and integration issues. This new program format will continue the Memphis CIBER's highly successful EU-focused programs.

The Memphis CIBER is a co-sponsor of FSA programs hosted by other CIBERs. The following programs recently have been part of the seasonal lineups:

- India (Mumbai and Chennai; coordinated by Florida International U.)
- New Delhi and Agra (coordinated by the U. of Connecticut)
- China and Hong Kong (coordinated by the U. of Colorado)
- Southeast Asia (Singapore and Malaysia; coordinated by U. of Wisconsin and the U. of Hawaii)
- "Green" Central America (Costa Rica; coord. by Texas A&M U.)
- Mercosur (Argentina, Brazil and Chile; coord. by Florida International U.)
- European Union (Brussels; coordinated by U. of Pittsburgh)
- Africa (Kenya, South Africa and Tanzania; coord. by U. of So. Carolina
- Eastern Europe (Croatia, Czech Republic, Turkey; coordinated by U. of Pittsburgh)
- Turkey (Istanbul and Ankara; coordinated by U. of Kansas)
- Vietnam (Ho Chi Minh City and Hanoi; coordinated by U. of Wisconsin and U. of Hawaii)
- Latin America "Sustainability" (Brazil; coord. by Indiana University)
- European Economies in Transition (Hungary, Bulgaria, Turkey; coordinated by U. of Pittsburgh)
- Russia (Moscow, St. Petersburg and Yekaterinburg; coordinated by the U. of Connecticut)

Chapter Eight

∾

Bringing the World Into U.S. University Classrooms

In order for faculty to be in positions to truly impart international knowledge and vision, they first must possess it themselves. In general, for a long time faculty members needed to move beyond a world viewed through glasses polarized by only home country experiences. The need to internationalize faculty members at schools of business factored into Kedia's mind as a most urgent goal. As part of this process, many faculty members report a professional rejuvenation and cite examples of how international issues have positively benefited their own research and teaching.

Building strategies for internationalizing various schools of business (including the Fogelman College of Business and Economics at the University of Memphis) was part of the CIBER agenda in its early stages. Kedia addressed this need formally in a 1991 white paper in which he said sharing such expertise with other institutions of higher learning was all part of a larger intention to develop an understanding of global competition, issues in overseas operations and organizational strategies for effective joint ventures and strategic alliances. Beneficiaries would ultimately be not only faculty, but also students.

Train-the-Trainer: A Capacity-Building Formula

As part of its outreach endeavors, the Memphis CIBER is committed to building capacity in the U of M, the region and in the country. A key mission is to conduct train-the-trainer programs that ultimately carry focused, transferable and experiential knowledge to various classroom settings. The programs developed in this chapter are orchestrated through a three-pronged approach: Globalization Seminars, Business Foreign Language Workshops, and Faculty Study Abroad programs. The knowledge, experience and expertise accumulated through all three programs are synergistic and transferable to students.

The Globalization Seminars comprising six concurrent courses represent a four-day, intensive program which is offered annually in June. Also referred to as FDIB (Faculty Development in International Business), the seminars are intended to teach faculty members how best to incorporate international content into their own courses. In essence, they then are able to artfully adopt and blend whatever they have learned from these informative sessions as content and dimensions of their own pedagogy. Over the years, 1,020 persons from 318 schools in 48 states have participated in these annual seminars, according to Jeanne Tutor of the Wang Center.

A second annual program is the Business Foreign Language Workshop that involves intensely practical applications in contrast to traditional literature and linguistic-based approaches to teaching foreign language. Specifically, this intensification involves an approach to business language that is conducive to commerce. Professors at University of Memphis became the first tier for enriched training in how to teach business language.

Then, the center in partnership with the Department of Foreign Languages and Literature at the U of M started a similar array of offerings to faculty around the country on how to teach foreign language specifically to conduct global business. In turn, their students can receive more practical language training relevant to doing business in another country using business-oriented foreign language skills.

Thirdly, as part of this key triad, the center offers an annual Faculty Study Abroad program mentioned in detail in Chapter Seven. These opportunities for exposure and interaction are not confined solely to CIBER faculty attendees. This is conducted for University of Memphis faculty and also is available to faculty across the U.S. with a heavy emphasis on the European Union. The first was offered at the University of Lille in France and the second at the University of Antwerp. After these programs were conducted for many years, another one was also developed at the University of Strasbourg. An advantage of operating out of Antwerp was that it was close to the business center and European Commission locale of Brussels, Belgium. Meanwhile, Strasbourg is the seat of the European Union Parliament. Last year, a program was conducted in Brussels in cooperation with the University of Pittsburgh. Overall, 313 faculty members from 140 schools in 45 states have participated in these programs.

Faculty Development in International Business (FDIB) Globalization Seminars

A primary vehicle for promoting international curriculum in the business school is found in the "Globalization Seminars" taught by some of the most renowned international business professors in the world. A group of CIBERs have formed a consortium led by the University of Memphis each June. The Globalization Seminars provide six concurrent two-day intensive seminars at the U of M Fogelman Executive Center currently titled: Introduction to International Business, International Finance, International Accounting, Global Supply Chain Management, International Marketing and International Management. These are intended for U.S. business faculty members who wish to deepen their understanding of the international aspects of their functional field. The seminars are taught by faculty drawn from the sponsoring universities. The end objective is to help business faculty bring international content into the classroom and expand teaching and research skills.

"Participating faculty evaluations of the programs were uniformly high," noted Josse de la Torre, dean of the Graduate School of Business at Florida International University. "All instructors but one earned an 'effectiveness' score above 4.25 on a 5-point scale.

"Participants' comments were also unanimously enthusiastic in terms of their learning and, most importantly, their ability to take that learning back into their respective classrooms," the FIU dean continued. "This is a remarkable achievement and one that has leveraged the U.S. DOE grant funding dramatically across a broad cross-section of academia."

Such seminars for faculty development in international business were strongly underway in the summer of 1994. These are designed to assist faculty to teach in a global context by infusing international material into existing courses and for developing specialized international courses. The clinics also help business schools fulfill their missions to internationalize their curriculum within the American Assembly of Collegiate Schools of Business Accreditation (AACSB) framework. Another way to view this is that the programs are designed for faculty who want to add international content to their courses through the development of new knowledge and teaching skills.

Today, each globalization seminar is built around a comprehensive course pack designed to support and demonstrate this multifaceted impact on business. These course materials are available to participants for future use and application at their respective institutions. Each participant receives course outlines, presentation slides, experiential exercises, case studies, and reference materials. Additionally, half-day workshops focusing on teaching, research and grant opportunities are provided as well.

To gain a better idea of the depth of each column of study, here are examples of several representative topics covered within each seminar:

- Introduction to International Business: evolution of global business, foreign direct investment, the multinational enterprise, trade policies, economic integration, managing acquisitions internationally and corporate governance;

- International Accounting: development of worldwide accounting standards, rules-based versus principles-based accounting, the future of convergence, and the role of auditor in performing global audits;

- International Finance: currency and Eurocurrency markets, parity conditions and real exchange rates, managing transaction exposures, asset pricing, cost of capital, and multinational capital budgeting;

- Global Supply Chain Management: knowledge of logistics intricacies, distribution and transportation methods, global sourcing and supply;

- International Management: institutional and cultural environments, structuring and managing strategic alliances, organizational structures, global strategy and leadership;

- International Marketing: resources for teaching international marketing, implications for marketing managers, entry decision-making, conducting research, international pricing, product policy and branding.

"In addition to its intellectual contributions, the Wang Center is literally a physical center for thriving international business activities," noted Mike W. Peng, Jindal Chair of Global Strategy in the Jindal School of Management at the University of Texas at Dallas. He is also author of *Global Business* and *Global Strategy*. "I say this because every June, between 60 and 90 business faculty members travel to Memphis to participate in the FDIB Globalization Seminars. As a faculty seminar leader, I have been going there every year since 1999."

What has brought Peng back year in and year out? He describes the magnet pull as the unparalleled dedication to IB education and research. "The Memphis CIBER/Wang Center has brought me back every year to be in the company of like-minded colleagues eager to contribute to IB education and research."

Peng said the Wang Center's ability to draw like-minded colleagues together is quite remarkable. "Ben Kedia and colleagues at the Wang Center have definitely made a huge impact on IB education and research. I deeply appreciate their vote of confidence in me. Fourteen years ago when I was an assistant professor, they brought me in to teach faculty, some of whom were full professors." Peng leads the Introduction to

Participants of the FDIB Globalization Seminars
June 7-10, 2012

International Business seminar at the Globalization Seminars. He takes a pragmatic dialogue-style approach with his sessions and liberally sprinkles the latest business headlines and statistics with participants in a 'did-you-know' kind of interactive approach.

"The Wang Center has raised the competencies of faculty members with valuable train-the-trainer exposure. In sum, I am very proud to be a comrade-in-arms in these wonderful endeavors."

Lee Radebaugh, professor of Accountancy and CIBER Director at Brigham Young University, leads the International Accounting seminar within the Globalization Seminars. He said the Wang Center has leveraged its strengths and advantages in its region well with its extensive outreach record to other higher learning institutions. "Ben has been very focused in finding these strengths. He works very hard to establish networks and put the things in place to enable them to work effectively."

Tomas Hult, CIBER director and professor of Global Supply Chain Management at Michigan State University, leads the Global Supply Chain Management section of the Globalization Seminars. He mentioned that Ben Kedia started an array of strong programs before other educators latched onto the same underlying international need. "He started very early on with all of these curriculum elements and has maintained the IMBA so well over all of these years, which is quite a legacy."

Hult has participated with the Globalization Seminars for more than a decade. "There is quite a track record there too, for chiefly helping underserved markets. Ben steadily has been forming and molding programs for what needs to be done in the region. He had the foresight to get to know others, and through networking, made this a converging point for a lot of international things in the Mid-South. He has built an alliance model and is very good at managing those alliances."

"I have been directly taking part in the annual globalization seminars that Memphis CIBER has organized and hosted for the past two decades," said Dr. Tamer Cavusgil, CIBER director at Georgia State University. "Each June, we typically gather about 60 faculty across the United States who come for a four-day professional program. We have been teaching them about instructional resources and strategies for teaching international management, finance, supply chain management, marketing and so forth. Dr. Attila Yaprak and I led the seminar on international marketing. I am able to observe Memphis CIBER's activities, meet their team and experience their successful ways in which they cater to the constituents."

Dr. Michael Pustay, professor of International Business at Texas A&M University, has been a co-leader in the Introduction to International Business (IIB) component of the FDIB program for over a decade, working with Mike Peng of the University of Texas at Dallas for most of that period. "During that span, we've had the pleasure of teaching, interacting with, and learning from some 250 or so participants in the Intro to IB seminars, who in turn have passed on the benefits of their experiences to untold thousands of students back at their home colleges and universities.

"None of this could have happened without the vision, talents, and perseverance of Ben Kedia, Jeanne Tutor, and the dedicated staff at the Wang Center," Pustay continued. "Their graciousness and concern permeate the program. They carefully and thoughtfully designed the program, starting from participants' arrival on Thursday afternoons until their departures on Sunday afternoons, all to ensure that the formal and informal dimensions of the program promoted learning and, perhaps, more importantly, the sharing of ideas and experiences."

Placing people from different backgrounds together in such a teaching atmosphere often leads to unexpected learning and insights. For example, during a class discussion regarding the quality of GDP data among countries, one student (a former intelligence service analyst) recounted that they often resorted to measuring the length of trains entering and leaving factories to assess the productivity of Soviet heavy industry. See Appendix N for information on co-sponsors, seminar leaders, and participants of the Globalization Seminars.

Business Foreign Language Workshops

Language provides communication between cultures, but how does language itself provide insights into the cultures that are being studied? There is an ongoing need to discover how languages of business help zero in on cultural norms of business. Clearly, languages play a key ingredient in cross-cultural understanding, so each business school should emphasize fluency in other languages to deliver a full-orbed education in this manner.

The Wang Center provides Business Foreign Language Workshop opportunities to foreign language faculty members and has done so for the past 20 years. This program has drawn language faculty from across the United States, as well as a rapidly growing number of area high school teachers. The center also provides financial support for U of M foreign language faculty to attend business language conferences offered by partner CIBER institutions.

One of the original Memphis CIBER projects, the long-standing Business Language Workshop, has been held annually in February. Current business language workshops include German, Spanish, French, and Japanese. Business Language Workshop leaders provide a well-rounded offering that includes discussions on how to develop and teach a business language curriculum. This program recently expanded to include high school teachers to better prepare students for college-level classes. Over the years, there have been 711 participants in these workshops, coming from 360 schools in 48 states.

"In addition to the international business curriculum, Professor Kedia made good use of his CIBER funding by organizing the annual business language workshops," said Ralph Albanese, professor and chair of Foreign Languages and Literatures at the University of Memphis. "For many years, faculty from institutions of higher learning around the county (including a few local high school teachers) came for a weekend to attend intensive, language-specific workshops to learn how to organize a course in business language. The University of Memphis became a major training site for foreign-language faculty throughout the U.S. Each workshop was organized by a well-known business language specialist in collaboration with our university language faculty. Each workshop began with a stimulating lecture by Ben Kedia, which was followed by engaging questions and answers. We often received laudatory comments from these foreign language faculty members in attendance, who appreciated the breadth and depth of information they received during the workshops."

Yuki Matsuda, associate professor of Japanese at the University of Memphis' Department of Foreign Languages and Literatures, initiated the Japanese business language workshop – a new addition to the annual business language workshop organized by the Memphis CIBER.

"I have been working with Dr. Robert Russell from Brigham Young University since 2001 to co-teach the Japanese group during the language specific portions of the annual business language workshop. We always kept up with the rapid changes in this global society and new trends in the business language education," said Matsuda. "As a language educator and linguist, I was able to contribute to the development of the field of foreign languages for specific purposes (FLSP) and was able to exchange ideas with participants of the workshop every year. Many of those who came to the business language workshop also developed their skills and consequently became the leaders in the field. I think the contribution to the field of business language education made by the Wang Center over the years is tremendous."

"The program is unique in that the participants spend two half-days on issues related to how to structure a business language class, trends in teaching business languages, and on student-centered learning techniques," said Dean José de la Torre of FIU. "They then split off into two other half-days, during which the participants meet in language-specific workshops where they can discuss the use of specific materials, examinations, available resources, etc. Faculty members for the workshops are again drawn from the most successful programs at the sponsoring universities, which resulted in extraordinarily high marks in the program evaluations.

Participants of the Business Foreign Language Workshop
February 17-19, 2011

"Once again, this is an excellent example of CIBER collaboration under the leadership of the Memphis CIBER providing valuable opportunities for faculty in other institutions to incorporate state-of-the-art materials and techniques into their programs and their teaching," José de la Torre added.

Anecdotal comments from faculty, such as one by Dr. John Bednar of the language program at Clemson in 2003, are noteworthy, too: "The need for Americans to speak foreign languages and operate with ease in foreign cultures is growing with the market." Over time, such workshops bore focused titles such as this one: "The Impact of Globalization: New Directions in Teaching Foreign Language and Culture."

The workshops held on the campus at Fogelman Executive Center encourage language departments at universities to better educate students to compete in international business. Traditionally, foreign languages had been taught from the humanities perspective, but with globalization on the march, there was an increasing interface across departmental lines.

"For the past 20 years, the Memphis business foreign language workshop was a fixed point on my February calendar," said Dr. Bettina F. Cothran, professor of German at Georgia Institute of Technology, a professional who led the German workshop since its inception. "It was the conference and workshop I most looked forward to. It was the best-organized event of its kind and a wonderful mix of meeting longstanding friends and new colleagues. It was amazing how many answered the call year after year. With an attendance of about 50 to 70 foreign language educators representing universities, colleges and high schools, the message of the value of applied and content-based language programs was spread far beyond the region. To this day, strangers come up to me at professional gatherings telling me they attended one (or more) of the Memphis workshops and how much they learned. So: Mission accomplished!"

The team of presenters and organizers coalesced over the years into a finely-tuned organism. The language groups composed of one faculty member each from University of Memphis and another institution having a CIBER center provided the know-how for the individual language groups. Spanish, French and German (Japanese was later added) were studied to provide a fully covered field of languages. The German workshops accomplished important goals in familiarizing instructors on all levels, and from all over the United States, with current and emerging trends of curriculum design, teaching concepts and specific examples.

"We introduced participants to German Business Examinations, developed by institutions such as the Goethe Institute and used worldwide; we shared the pros and cons of the latest teaching materials and presented successful models of applied language curricula, including immersion programs, study abroad and internship experiences," Cothran recalled.

One unique aspect of the Memphis CIBER conference was its integration of the business viewpoint and language teaching. The undisputed highlight seemed to be Kedia's opening presentation on the "Global Mindset." He aptly provided a framework for discussion from the business angle using facts and figures of international business. Cothran said a logical conclusion reached was that those in the U.S. must be much more open-minded and adept when it comes to global engagement. The role of the foreign-language classroom is defined as not only providing the requisite communication skills, but more importantly, the cultural concepts necessary as a basis for successful interaction on the global stage.

"Of course, these conferences were not all work, play also was part of the program," she recalled. "For years, my image of Memphis was synonymous with Beale Street at night: the 'Blues' in various 'speluncas' (as we would say in German for somewhat questionable, dark, cave-like localities), sometimes reaching highest artistic levels, as in the Center for Southern Folklore. This is where my friend and colleague Monika Nenon would take me after we both had worked hard to introduce the German instructors to the more sober topics related to business language and culture. Typically, the German group's evening program would start with a visit of the ducks at the Peabody Hotel, followed by dinner at Automatic Slim's where we enjoyed jerk chicken and other Caribbean spiced foods. The evening would end with a walk through Beale Street. Over the years, our associations have grown into lifelong friendships."

The focus has adapted over the years, but this once revolutionary orientation for the academic setting has proven to be the right way in the context of the globalization of America's higher education. The Memphis Business Language Workshop combined theoretical presentations as well as extensive and intensive workshops for practical application. It was the only one of its kind focusing exclusively on business language teaching and its integration in the general curriculum, Cothran said. "Ben Kedia's foresight, his initiatives and hard work with the University of Memphis CIBER Center have been a cornerstone for global education in the United States."

The Department of Foreign Languages and Literature led by Dr. Ralph Albanese at the U of M has enjoyed a long history in the teaching of business language. Albanese's early commitment to business-language training was essential to the success of the workshops. Various faculty members gave valuable expertise in this particular field during the seminar. Today's foreign-language educators recognize the need to understand the importance of international business as well as business language and culture in order to adapt their curriculum to reflect these new trends in the field of business-oriented foreign language instruction. Participants gain numerous insights into the relationships between foreign language, culture and international business and are able to discuss how to develop and teach a business-language curriculum.

"It has been a great honor and privilege for me to participate as a co-director for many years of the Business Spanish component of the Business Language Workshops hosted by the Wang CIBER," said Dr. Michael Scott Doyle, professor of Spanish, Translation Studies, Business Language Studies, and Latin American Studies at UNC-Charlotte.

"In that time, running from 1996-2010, I worked with two outstanding colleagues, friends, and national leaders in Business Spanish and Business Language Studies (BLS): the inimitable and always engaging Dr. Felipe LaPuente (emeritus) of the University of Memphis, and the pioneering and hard-driving Dr. T. Bruce Fryer (emeritus) of the University of South Carolina at Columbia. In Spanish, we worked alongside other distinguished colleagues in

Business French (Dr. Stephen J. Sacco, San Diego State University, and Dr. Will Thompson, University of Memphis), Business German (Dr. Bettina Cothran, Georgia Institute of Technology, and Dr. Monika Nenon, University of Memphis), and Business Japanese (Dr. Robert Russell, Brigham Young University, and Dr. Yuki Matsuda, University of Memphis).

"I believe that the Business Language Workshops served as unique and powerful catalysts for the ongoing development of BLS in American higher education in the areas of teaching, creation of pedagogical materials, and research," Doyle said. "The development of the center over time has included the increased incorporation of cultural studies, grant writing, internships, and technology. Each year, I witnessed firsthand the increasing depth and breadth of subject matter treatment in the Business Language Workshops. All of this, of course, was facilitated by a wonderful staff (Jeanne Tutor and Amelia Cole) and by the vision, energy, and personality of Dr. Ben Kedia, the Robert Wang Chair of Excellence and Director of the Wang CIBER."

As stated on its web page, the Wang CIBER serves as a catalyst and a forum for ongoing analysis, training and discourse on the global economy and the challenges of global competition for American business and higher education. Doyle firmly believes that the Wang CIBER, via its Business Language Workshops, has provided the impetus for many American colleges, universities, and several high schools to design and implement successful courses and programs in BLS. This goal was often achieved with external funding assistance that they first learned about in the workshops and then later secured. He said that it has also supported the directors of the Business Language Workshops in developing new teaching approaches and materials. "In terms of BLS, the Wang CIBER has provided remarkable, undeniable, and sustained leadership."

Continuing, the language educator noted that "the Wang Center Business Language Workshops have played a key role in developing the faculty who teach business-language courses to the students who then graduate and apply their skills and knowledge in the real-world arena of international business, in which the ability to communicate effectively in other languages and across cultures is often the difference between success and failure, or between real success and partial success. For every individual faculty member trained in BLS, there are in turn many students (perhaps an average of 12-15 per business-language class, which must then be multiplied over the years) who have engaged more fully and productively in the global economy." See Appendix O for more information on the co-sponsors, workshop leaders, and participants of the Business Language Workshops.

Chapter Nine

❧

Bringing the World to Minority Institutions

Beginning in 2002, the Wang Center joined hands with several other CIBERs, along with the Institute for International Public Policy (a special project of the United Negro College Fund), for an outreach to assist business and language faculty at Historically Black Colleges and Universities (HBCUs). This initiative, titled Globalizing Business Schools (GBS) Program for HBCUs, focused on internationalizing business schools at HBCU institutions. The purpose of this initiative was to raise awareness of the importance of international and interdisciplinary business education, equip faculty with new knowledge and tools, and incorporate international content into existing business courses. Moreover, it provided for one-on-one assistance with the acquisition of federal grant funds to facilitate implementation of the program.

Susanna Easton, the senior program specialist with the U.S. DOE, was particularly helpful in connecting Kedia with Mark Chichester, then director of the Institute for International Public Policy (IIPP), without whose help the program could not have taken off. Subsequent IIPP directors Blair Alexander and Nicholas Bassey also continued to support the GBS program and personally visited Memphis to participate in this initiative.

The GBS program was developed as a four-year, lockstep program designed to internationalize business education on the campuses of historically black colleges and universities. Twelve HBCU institutions participated in the first four-year program held during 2002-2006. Annual CIBER partner contributions, funds from IIPP, and in-kind or modest contributions covered program costs. Since HBCU institutions typically did not have extra resources, it was considered important that the program minimize financial burdens upon them. Fourteen HBCU institutions were involved in the 2006-2010 phase and 20 HBCU institutions are currently participating in the 2010-2014 phase.

The Globalizing Business Schools program incorporated the existing triad of faculty development programs mentioned in previous chapters that are part of the core of the Memphis CIBER, namely the capacity-building, train-the-trainer type exposure that carry focused, transferable and experiential knowledge ultimately to the classroom settings. Again, these are: Globalization Seminars, Business Foreign Language Workshops, and Study Abroad programs. These are integrated, mutually reinforcing, knowledge- and experience-based programs designed to ultimately benefit students in the classroom through their professors.

"We customized our existing programs as part of the capacity building for minority institutions," Kedia said. "In addition to arranging for curriculum linkages with our various array of existing programs, we added something new, namely mentoring the HBCU faculty for writing grant proposals for the Business and International Education (BIE) grant program to secure finds from the U.S. Department of Education to expand and sustain their internationalization efforts." In most cases, minority institutions were not fully aware of the availability and varied potential uses of this particular grant. "More minority institutions have been supported by the BIE program during the last 10 years than at any time during the previous 20 years," said Tanyelle Richardson, BIE program director, U.S. Department of Education.

Lockstep Phases of the Globalizing Business Schools (GBS) Program

The first phase began with an orientation workshop to introduce sources of grant funds and grant-writing techniques and continued throughout the program with one-on-one consultations between each HBCU and its respective CIBER partner. The intent of these consultations was to develop an internationalization plan designed uniquely to fit each HBCU's strengths and resources. Utilizing their international plan, the HBCU institutions worked on a Business and International Education (BIE) grant proposal in consultation with their CIBER partners to submit to the U.S. Department of Education for funding consideration.

The second phase of the program consisted of inviting HBCU faculty to participate in three faculty development programs. The initial platform of these was an annual business-language workshop to enhance foreign language faculties' ability to bring business foreign language and culture into their foreign language curriculum. The supplemental stage involved attendance and participation by three business faculty members each year in the Globalization Seminars. These are discipline-specific seminars designed to help business school faculty incorporate international content across the business courses.

The final phase of the project included a faculty study abroad for two faculty members from each participating HBCU institution. This two-week study tour included visits with educational, business and government officials in the destination countries, providing faculty firsthand experiences with the socio-cultural and political structures under which business operates abroad. In essence, this initiative also laid the foundation for future institutional linkages, overseas teaching, student internships and study abroad opportunities.

**GLOBALIZING BUSINESS SCHOOL (GBS) PROGRAM
FOR HBCU INSTITUTIONS**

HBCU Successes in the GBS Program (2002-2006)

Faculty Development in International Business Seminars .... 92 HBCU Faculty

Business Foreign Language Workshops .... 31 HBCU Faculty

Area Studies on Africa Programs... 35 HBCU Faculty

Faculty Study Abroad to South Africa & Botswana .... 22 HBCU Faculty

Faculty Study Program to South Africa and Botswana
for HBCU Faculty
June 2005

GBS Success Stories

A key result has been that more HBCU institutions have received Business and International Education (BIE) grants during the existence of Globalizing HBCU Business Schools program than during the two decades preceding this initiative. They can utilize the funds to revise and/or create new international courses and curricula, defray expenses for study abroad for their faculty and students, and pay for conferences and workshops on international topics. Such BIE grants typically range in federal funding from $70,000 to $95,000 per year for two years.

In many instances, the HBCU business faculty have established linkages with foreign universities as a result of their participation in the Faculty Study Abroad opportunities. These links lead to study abroad opportunities for HBCU students. An extended part of the mentoring process also covers how to establish existing relationships with foreign universities so that the deans and faculty of these universities will support such programs. In order to orient faculty with this process, two to four faculty members from each participating HBCU are invited to attend the CIBER-sponsored "Short-Term Study Abroad" program – a primer for how to organize study abroad programs, along with particulars on topics such as insurance, safety, program planning and other things that need to be considered for planning study abroad programs. After attending this program, the faculty members become the lead persons at their institutions for establishing student study abroad programs.

Specific Experiences in Globalizing Business Schools for HBCUs

The University of Memphis' initial partnering with several CIBERs and the United Negro College Fund's Institute for International Public Policy established the Globalizing Business Schools (GBS) initiative for HBCU institutions. For the 2006-2010 time period, these HBCU-CIBER partnerships had grown to be 14, and now for the 2010-2014 grant cycle, they stand at 20. Designed in five phases, this program provides the continuous involvement of the CIBER partners with their respective HBCU institutions.

HBCUs have traditionally faced challenges such as financial resources, coordination between program areas, competition for institutional priority, and incentives for participation in the internationalization process as was learned during the first GBS Planning Workshop in 2002. The purpose was to understand the barriers and challenges of internationalization among these institutions. Some of the long-term goals were to develop new international courses, increase student participation in study abroad programs and develop partnerships with their own regional business communities.

These outcomes, in effect, equip faculty at HBCU schools with the knowledge, pedagogical tools and materials, and international experiences to transform their current courses or develop new ones to fit the global business environment, notes José de la Torre. "It makes use of the full range of existing programs that the partner schools have already in place, such as the Globalization Seminars, Business Language Workshops and Faculty Study Abroad programs. This, of course, allows the U of M and its CIBER partners to accelerate the impact of the transfer of knowledge to the HBCU schools and to minimize the fixed costs associated with the program. It provides, furthermore, an economical delivery mechanism by combining the skills and market power of a diverse set of CIBER schools with different orientations and strengths. There also is a compounding effect whereby participants in one program can come back the following year to complete another program."

To provide a catalyst for HBCU and CIBER collaboration during the 2010-2014 grant cycle, the University of Memphis CIBER staged a HBCU Globalizing Business Schools Orientation Conference. Seventeen HBCU deans and one business faculty member from each of the invited HBCUs participated as guests of the conference sponsors, along with directors or associate directors of 20 CIBER institutions. The result of the conferences was to establish a consortium of 40 institutions. See the HBCU four-year summary reports and participants in Appendix P.

Ralph Hines, director of the international office for the U.S. Department of Education at the launch of the program in 2002, commented: "It is among the most sweeping efforts to help predominantly African-American schools sharpen their competitive edge in an increasingly global economy."

HBCU Successes in the GBS Program (2006-2010)	
GBS Orientation .... 29 HBCU Faculty	New Undergraduate IB Courses 44
Business Language Wrksp ... 49 HBCU Faculty	New Graduate IB Courses 8
BIE-HBCU Workshop .... 30 HBCU Faculty	Int'l Content Added to Bus. Courses.......44
FDIB-Globalization Seminars .. 110 HBCU Faculty	Students Attended Study Abroad..........152
BIE Proposals Submitted .... 14 HBCUs	Faculty Attended Study Abroad..............54
BIE Grant Awards (7 HBCUs).................. $1.2 M	Int'l Research (Pres. & Publ.) 141
Alabama St. U. (twice), Bowie St. U.,	New IB Minors...4
Hampton U., North Carolina Central U.,	Int'l Business Collaborations 7
South Carolina St. U., Winston Salem St. U.	Int'l Academic Collaborations.................33

Witnesses to the Efficacy of the Dedicated HBCU Program

"During my tenure at the Wang Center, we launched the major, collaborative initiative to reach out to Historically Black Colleges and Universities," said Deborah Hernandez, who worked as an associate director of the Wang Center beginning in 2001. The focus of the effort was 1) to involve faculty from HBCUs in existing faculty development programs designed to support globalizational/internationalization of teaching and research; and 2) to pair established CIBERs with HBCUs to coach and consult in order to produce institutional change that would sustain the effort, she noted. In the academic year 2010-2011, 32 HBCU deans and faculty attended the Globalizing Business Schools Conference, 27 language faculty attended business foreign language workshops, and some 53 HBCU business faculty attended one or more of six Globalization Seminars that year.

The Florida Memorial University (FMU) School of Business participated in the Globalizing Business Schools program as part of the HBCU initiative. FMU's annual progress report to the Wang Center served to inform its experience with the program. "The Wang Center helped our faculty to develop and introduce global perspectives in the classrooms and courses, engage in scholarly research related to global business, network with colleagues by attending global seminars, and meet global business leaders," said Abbass Entessari, Ph.D., dean of the FMU Business School. His school also has been able to effectively add courses in International Accounting, International Business, International Marketing, and International Finance to its curriculum as a result.

University business and language faculty see how much progress they have made in the internationalization of the curriculum. Faculty from business disciplines other than management now want to participate in the internationalization efforts.

"They have made steady growth and have reached out to different universities, especially from the HBCU standpoint," said Dr. Kanaata Jackson chair of the Department of Management at Hampton University. "Earlier, the Department of Management had not been internationalizing the curriculum. After we had partnership with the Memphis CIBER, then we started really seeing a big difference. I am really appreciative for their helping us get that started. We at first had few members participating in international issues and there was even some resistance. However, with the BIE grant and faculty development opportunities, we have been able to send more than 15 different faculty members for training in business and languages. There is cooperation and cross application among various departments."

As an outgrowth, Hampton University started an emphasis on student study abroad programs. The university also now has established an international office. Thus far, about a dozen students have been able to go abroad to study for summer sessions.

"The quality of the faculty training that the Wang Center conducts is exemplary," Jackson said. "They perform a top-notch job and that is from the perspective of someone who attends training programs elsewhere. They are accommodating and helpful. The information is practical and you can use it immediately. It is a model on how to bring universities along in the international piece, because as a country, we need it. We cannot be isolationists; rather, we must prepare our students to compete in the world market. I teach organizational behavior and one of my many class requirements of students is that they get a passport."

At Alabama A&M University's School of Business, 2008-2009 was a productive year for international programs. Three students received a B.S. degree with a major in business administration and a concentration in international business. All programs in the School of Business offer and require at least one international course for graduation.

Twelve business faculty and three language faculty attended the GBS programs. As a result, Alabama State University's business faculty are quite enthused about the importance of international business education, and the College of Business Administration is now offering a new IB Minor, including six new IB courses.

The Bethune-Cookman University School of Business hosted two international guests from Florence, Italy; the President of Florence University of Arts (FUA) and the Vice-President of Marketing, to discuss international business programs, hospitality and culinary programs and the prospects for alliances/partnerships for Study Abroad/Internships for BCU students.

Bowie State University has formed overseas linkages with Ethiopia, Senegal, Gambia, and Cameroon. One faculty member attended a conference and lectured at a university in Senegal. Another met with faculty and scholars in Cameroon.

Fayetteville State University signed a Memorandum of Understanding with ESC Bretagne Brest (a French university) for the exchange of students and faculty. Attending the Short-Term Study Abroad Conference marked a turning point for Florida Memorial University as it is working through approaches to study abroad, both short- and long-term. One of the presenters distributed an "Embedded Education Abroad Faculty Toolkit," which was found to be helpful in considering each step of the development of such programs.

The College of Business at Grambling State University continues to require all faculty to indicate explicitly in their syllabi how globalization will be covered in the courses and to indicate how many lecture hours are dedicated to covering the topic of globalization.

Business faculty members at Mississippi Valley State University participated in the FDIB-European Economies in Transition program, boosting the knowledge of international business through interaction with Polish and Turkish industry leaders, firsthand cultural experiences, and discussions with U.S. and European faculty.

An international research project underway at North Carolina Central University includes a survey of outsourcing companies in the North Carolina area, and also a research proposal to study immigrant entrepreneurs.

South Carolina State University launched a minor in International Business with 20 students declaring an IB minor. It also was able to get a *Spanish for Business* course approved.

Texas Southern University hosted a nine-day African Executive Development Symposium featuring nine senior executives from firms in various industries located in Ghana, Tanzania, and Malawi. The FDIB Africa program provided an awareness and knowledge of the economic, political and cultural environment that exists in sub-Saharan Africa. This education should leverage that firsthand knowledge into a higher level of expertise in the classroom said a business faculty member at the University of Maryland-Eastern Shore.

The School of Business & Economics at Winston-Salem State University established two new overseas linkages with BEM Management School, Talence; Cedex, France; and Lycee Bremontier University, Bordeaux, France.

All of these initiatives prospered through effective alliances attained through a collaborative project of HBCUs, the Institute for International Public Policy-United Negro College Fund Special Programs (IIPP-UNCFSP), Centers for International Business Education and Research (CIBERs) and the United States Department of Education (USDOE).

HBCU Successes in the GBS Program 2010-2014 (Year 1)*

GBS Conference (May 2010) ... 32 HBCU Faculty	New Undergraduate IB Courses................ 7
Business Language Wrksp ... 27 HBCU Faculty	New Graduate IB Courses 2
FDIB-Globalization Seminars ... 53 HBCU Faculty	Int'l Content Added to Bus. Courses...... 32
BIE Proposals Submitted 5	Students Attended Study Abroad 49
(Note: BIE Grant Cancelled in 2011)	Faculty Attended Study Abroad 20
	Int'l Research (Pres. & Publ.).................. 64

*** Year 1 (2010-2011) of 4-year program.**

Chapter Ten

※

Bringing the World to University Researchers

When the U.S. government started in the 1980s to actively pursue and fund linkages between educational institutions and U.S. businesses by establishing the Centers for International Business Education program, grant proposals from various universities sprang forth. Each one of the 33 current CIBERs across the country is involved in some facet of research, in addition to the provision of advanced educational programs and focused workshops and seminars. In essence, the CIBERs from the very beginning were meant to serve as national resources and repositories for teaching, outreach, and research in relevant aspects of international business and management including language, culture, commerce, markets, and today, even security considerations. They are vested with the responsibility of not only monitoring change but facilitating it, often through research.

The ongoing core areas of research at the Memphis CIBER have been these: knowledge acquisition and management; global mindset, leadership and culture; emerging markets; and institutional environments. Global sourcing; cyber security; and innovation and collaboration are newer areas of research focus. For a graphic portrayal of these research areas and their interconnectedness, see Figure 9, "Helping U.S. Firms Meet the Challenges of Globalization."

All such research activity ultimately contributes to the body of knowledge on competitiveness across global markets. Research has been conducted, for instance, on emerging markets that comprise more than half of the world's population and account for an increasing share of world output, also experiencing high growth rates which can translate to market potential for American companies. U.S. firms can benefit as these markets need larger

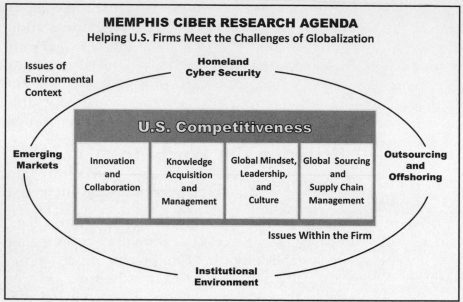

Figure 9. Memphis CIBER Research Agenda

amounts of capital goods, machinery, power transmission equipment, transportation equipment and high technology and consumer products.

Then, there has been continuing research on technology and knowledge management. The pace of technical change embodied in the adoption of information and communication technology has no doubt accelerated. The ongoing digital revolution has made knowledge management key requisite for global success. New knowledge is generated through local innovation as products and processes are adapted to suit different locations.

Fine-Tuning Research to a Changing Global Economic Landscape

More specifically, the growth in emerging markets is often attributed to economic liberalization, privatization, and/or restructuring of state-owned enterprises. The increasing prominence of emerging markets leads us to ask questions, such as, how do institutional constraints within emerging markets affect the ability of U.S. firms to profit in those locations? And, how will the rise of emerging market multinationals affect U.S. firms' ability to compete in a globalized economy? Thus, research in this stream includes exploration of: 1) ways in which supra-national and national level policies impact competitive environments; 2) factors affecting the surging rates of emerging market integration into the international economy; 3) challenges the U.S. faces for creating economic, social, and environmentally sound partnerships with emerging economies; and 4) the rise of emerging market multinationals as global competitors. A number of papers in this line of inquiry already have been presented at prestigious national and international conferences and published in top journals.

Research on global mindsets, leadership and culture are areas of emphasis. Growth in the global economy has increased the significance of the cognitive orientations of managers in global business success. This orientation has given rise to a number of new concepts, such as the "global mindset," associated with management across cultures. Furthermore, scholars are exhorted to integrate informal institutions such as culture into studies of economic and/or firm performance. As U.S. firms expand operations and/or enter new markets, how can they ensure that their managers have optimal cognitive orientations when interacting with culturally diverse stakeholders? Also, how can firms be certain management can formulate an optimal strategy when it is highly questionable if a simple extension of domestic strategy will be effective? The theories and practices of global leadership are being examined relative to global mindsets and cross-cultural management. Again, a number of papers in this domain have been presented and published in top journals.

Research on global sourcing and supply chain management also is a key area of inquiry. Global sourcing is fast becoming one of most significant industrial shifts in modern history. U.S. competitiveness increasingly depends on the ability of firms to organize globally and connect with specialized service providers and science and engineering clusters around the world. The partnership between FedEx Corp. and the U of M's FedEx Center for Supply Chain Management allows nationally recognized researchers to examine supply chain issues via case studies, field experiments, and computer-based modeling in a region containing one of the most strategically located transportation hubs in the world. Other aspects of this research address the use of technology in global supply chain management and its relationship to homeland security, listed by the Department of Homeland Security (DHS) as a top concern.

One of the most challenging issues facing U.S. businesses are the increasing needs to integrate DHS requirements while maintaining international competitiveness. The Memphis CIBER collaborates with faculty in the Department of Computer Science to develop a wide research stream relative to cyber security. Collaborative research in this area will include associated issues such as risk assessment, modeling, planning, cooperative response, critical information flow, computer and data security, simulation, public safety and the political/socio-economic consequences of mitigation choices at both the regional and national levels. This research explores how applied intelligent agents, genetic algorithms, neural networks, Fuzzy Logic and immune system techniques may increase national computer security.

Faculty Support to Present Papers and Attend Conferences

The global financial crisis and issues related to sustainable development have highlighted the impact of a nation-state's institutional environment on firms. Today, we not only ask how American firms can better compete within a broad array of institutional matrices, but also how firms can balance traditional goals such as profitability, job creation, and global competitiveness with global imperatives related to sustainability and transparency. Thus, research in the area of multinational enterprises and the institutional environment focuses on integrating this relationship through an exploration of issues, such as, lessons the financial crisis holds for U.S. firms, the impact of institutions on the relationship between U.S. firms and profit opportunities and institutional moderators of U.S. firm performance amid an interrelated network.

In a similar vein, the global financial crisis and the accounting scandals associated with firms such as Enron, WorldCom and Global Crossing have highlighted the importance of global corporate governance. This is an area the Wang Center is well-positioned to address due to its relationship with acclaimed faculty members such as the Thompson-Hill Chair of Excellence and Professor of Accountancy, Zabi Rezaee. He is one of three academics appointed to the Standing Advisory Group (SAG) created by Sarbanes-Oxley, and was invited as a speaker at over 120 conferences and workshops worldwide. He and other professors of the business faculty will contribute to the inventory of knowledge regarding corporate governance reforms and their impact on research, education, and business practices across a multicultural world stage.

Knowledge acquisition and management research examines the results of cultural dimensions and network dynamics on knowledge creation and acquisition among international subsidiaries and affiliates. The Memphis center focuses on the continued impact of the digital revolution, information technology, knowledge management, and the logistics revolution in the global economy. Again, a number of papers in this area have been presented and published in top journals.

Success in today's global economy often is defined by the ability to develop and engage in innovations. However, innovation is rarely carried out by a single company; rather, multiple organizations forming collaborative networks are needed to create new technologies and institute complementary business practices. Research on innovation in collaborative environments examines how the structure, leadership, and management of such collaborations drive the types of innovations that are developed, and the resulting impact of those innovations.

The Memphis CIBER co-sponsors annual conferences that promote innovative research and teaching in international business. The center in Memphis is a founding member and supporter of the American Society of Competitiveness (ASC). Kedia is the editor of the Society's journal, *Competitiveness Review*. The Wang Center co-sponsors the *Journal of International Business Studies'* paper development workshops, as well as Duke University's Offshore Research Network initiative.

Recently, two research conferences were coordinated by the University of Connecticut and Memphis CIBERs. These invitation-only programs were titled "Enhancing Global Competitiveness through Sustainable Environmental Stewardship" and "Restoring America's Global Competitiveness through Innovations." One book edited by Subhash Jain and Kedia (titled the same as the conference) was published by Edward Elgar Publishing in 2011 and examined the impact that climate change and other environmental factors have on global business. A second book, edited by Kedia and Jain (titled the same as the second conference), will be published in 2013 and will focus on how different context and content of innovations will improve America's economic competitiveness.

Traditionally, the study of foreign languages for business purposes has lacked a more serviceable and academically communal name by which to identify itself as a theory-based field of scholarship. Therefore, the Wang CIBER supported Michael Doyle (University of North Carolina-Charlotte) to conduct an important investigation focused on the articulation of a broader, more systematic, and theory-based business language studies research agenda to break new ground and provide additional insights into the decisive roles of language and culture in a highly competitive global economy. He published a landmark article entitled, "Business Language Studies in the United States: On Nomenclature, Context, Theory, and Method" in *The Modern Language Journal* in 2012.

Ph.D. Candidates Are Mentored To Foster Original and Advanced Research

The future of tomorrow's managers as well as international business education is in the hands of today's doctoral students as they go on to become tomorrow's professors. It is the level of education in international business that reproduces itself in future faculty. In light of rapid and profound changes sweeping the world, doctoral education must explore phenomena such as global markets, relationships and environments. As mentioned, greater economic interdependence among nations is a motivating reality behind the drive to internationalize doctoral programs. Such programs also act to correct deficiencies in the ability of business school faculty to conceptualize problems globally and teach classes from a global perspective. Good arguments exist for teaching international contents in specific functional areas, so that faculty are provided a higher level than just simple awareness of international issues. As doctoral students in the Wang Center graduate and go on to become faculty members at other business schools, they will impact all levels of students in international business as the future cadre of faculty.

In addition to supporting thematic research in the areas of emerging markets, knowledge management, and global mindset, the center continues to support other activities that encourage research in the international domain, including faculty summer research grants, travel support to present research papers, and acquisition of materials and databases necessary for completing internationally related research (over 220 faculty/students supported in over 520 activities to date). The center also provides support to two to three international business-oriented doctoral graduate assistants per year.

The presence of the Memphis CIBER will continue to attract internationally focused scholars to the Fogelman College of Business and Economics. In turn, these scholars recruit and train the next generation of internationally focused Ph.D. students. In the past decade alone, with assistance from the center, these scholars have helped Ph.D. students develop at least 20 internationally focused dissertations and 60 IB-themed papers, many of which were presented at international conferences and then developed and published in top journals. See Appendices Q and R for U of M faculty and Ph.D. students who presented international research at major conferences.

Chapter Eleven

❧

Testimonials to the Wang Center

Reviews Provide a Mirror for Performance Evaluation and Benchmarking

Testimonials abound regarding the efficacy of the Wang Center and its various programs over the years. Rajiv Grover, Dean of the Fogelman College of Business & Economics and Chair of Excellence, Sales and Marketing, offers a significant vote of affirmation from his own vantage point: "We are absolutely delighted that Dr. Kedia could renew the grant six times. His steady leadership at the CIBER and all the related programs over the years has been a boon to the Fogelman College of Business and Economics. The achievements that Ben has attained are listed throughout this book and it was the steadfast and stable nature of his leadership over the years that allowed him to accomplish for us all what he did. Thank you, Ben, for all you did for the Fogelman College."

Tamer Cavusgil, currently CIBER director at Georgia State University and formerly faculty member of global marketing at Michigan State University's Eli Broad Graduate School of Management, took an in-depth tour of the center some 10 years after it was established. In 2001, he was able to conduct a comprehensive review of the center's scope and activities and its plans for the future. During that visit, he had the opportunity to meet with a large number of faculty, staff, students, administrators, business executives and members of the Advisory Council of the Memphis CIBER. Thus, he was able to make an objective assessment. Then in its fourth round of the grant cycle, the center had already built a strong reputation for innovative programs such as the International MBA, strong faculty development programs, business outreach and an exceptionally talented staff, in the words of Cavusgil. "Indeed, the Memphis CIBER is a mature organization and is well integrated into the university, the business community and the region," Cavusgil summarized.

Cavusgil remarked that "the Memphis CIBER has accomplished an enviable work agenda." He cited its establishment of the International MBA in its first funding cycle, the introduction of the faculty development in international business seminars in its second cycle, along with the faculty study abroad programs and business workshops for foreign language faculty. The professor and then CIBER director from Michigan State was also quite impressed with the Wang Center's implementation of on-site foreign-language instruction for business firms and the local community.

"Within the Fogelman College of Business, this center has worked hard to enhance global curricula at all levels," Cavusgil said. "As a result, courses at all levels now contain significant global content. Efforts also have begun to enhance the international component in the undergraduate program and to expand the study abroad and internship opportunities for undergraduate students."

The professor was also quite interested in the faculty development in international business strides. The objective of such programs is to provide professional development opportunities for business and language faculty and to equip them with the most recent comprehensive knowledge that they can use in their various classes. Participation nationwide in FDIB programs has grown tremendously since the CIBER's inception.

"The evaluations that I've seen of these programs are truly outstanding," Cavusgil remarked. "These evaluations have been very consistent over the years and speak to the excellent organizational capabilities of the Memphis CIBER team and the faculty leaders assembled to teach these programs."

Not only that, the professor from Michigan State found that the Memphis CIBER has done an excellent job in forging alliances with other colleges on campus. For instance, several arts and sciences faculty members indicated that the CIBER staff had been proactive in launching projects that involved their areas of study and teaching.

In another important realm, the Wang Center had been aggressive in providing faculty and doctoral students with opportunities to promote research related to global competitiveness of U.S. enterprises. Research funds were provided for language faculty to pursue curriculum development and participation in professional development activities. Examples of research up to that point included international market entry modes, regionalism, firm globalization and a competitive framework, and cultural influences in the management of knowledge and other topics.

Cavusgil went so far as to say that part of his on-site visit led him to the conclusion that Memphis CIBER has one of the most talented staffs in the entire CIBER network. He labeled it as "dedicated, experienced and very impressive." Furthermore, he said that Kedia, its director, has the credentials of a nationally renowned international business educator. "He impresses me as an excellent leader who has been able to build and motivate an exceptional team."

Also noteworthy was the prominence of the center across campus. The president and the provost of the University of Memphis spoke very knowledgeably about the campus-wide mission of the center and showed enthusiasm in charting out new directions.

Other testimonials herald from civic leaders in Memphis. For instance, Mayor Bill Morris served on the university's Board of Visitors for 25 years because of his role in the mayor's office and his interest in getting Memphis recognized as a source of growth for international companies. That scenario started with Holiday Inn Corporation, even before the growing FedEx enterprise came onto the horizon. "I said to myself, 'Here is where we are, but we have a long way to go to meet an emerging international marketplace.' It starts with the study of languages and cultures for people to become interested with the global economy," Morris noted.

"Robert and Susie Wang became friends of mine and I went to Taiwan when his family hosted us there at the Grand Hotel," Morris said. "We were together and able to have top leadership meetings in Asia and in Memphis. In the process of talking with the University of Memphis, we collectively knew that we needed an international business center here. I approached Robert about making a donation, and we would match it to create a center or school of international business. Both Robert and Susie are dynamic leaders and fine examples of being persistent and growing a business that reaches across borders.

"Academics must be transformational and entrepreneurial. You must have the ability to get results from knowledge attained, and both the Wangs and Ben Kedia understand this well. Since its establishment, I am proud that the Wang Center has hosted groups from Mexico, England, Australia, Africa, and Russia, whereby we have been able to dialogue about mutual business interests."

Even in 1995, the center was cited for its dramatic influence in the region. Edwin Miller, of the University of Michigan business school in Ann Arbor, spoke of how the Wang Center provided instrumental forces energizing and guiding the internationalization of the faculty, curriculum, research and outreach efforts of the university. During his visit, Miller obtained a quote from Dr. Rawlins, to the effect that the center was "a catalyst for internationalization, leveraging its funds to develop outreach programs to the communities in the Delta region and having a significant impact on academic programs at the University of Memphis."

"The CIBER has contributed to the ascendancy of the university as a magnet for those interested in international business and infused into their academic programs of study," Miller of the University of Michigan said. "Without that, it is highly questionable if the university could have made all the progress that it had in the last five years. It has offered high-quality, innovative programs to members of the academic and business communities, it has staffed these programs with high quality instructors, and it has done this effectively and with amazing speed." That is saying quite a lot, keeping in mind that the comment was made in 1995, only a few years after the center opened its doors. He clearly saw that the center was viewed by others as entrepreneurial in its mission, reflected in terms of program innovation, involvement by faculty members representing diverse academic units and its outreach to the various communities it intended to serve.

Dr. William R. Folks, director of the CIBER at the University of South Carolina, noted in 1993 that the region is enhancing its economic competitiveness. He said the University of Memphis thus had perhaps one of the most important missions of all CIBERs, namely the provision of CIBER services to the entire Mid-South Mississippi Valley. He envisioned then that the institutional commitment of the University of Memphis to the center formed a critical part of a carefully crafted strategy of internationalization, which in turn would lead the university to a position of leadership in education for international business.

Interestingly, the structure of the International MBA differed from the program at the prestigious University of South Carolina in a number of interesting ways, director Folks summarized. First, the business courses are integrated rather than differentiated; that is, a particular subject, such as finance, is taught with international material integrated into the total finance curriculum, as opposed to presenting the fundamental finance concepts in one course and then subsequently providing an international finance course built upon the foundational concepts. The relative effectiveness of the two approaches is heavily debated. The first method is preferred as students are only taking one finance course; however, differentials in effectiveness of approaches may be pronounced in the results achieved. These decisions also are determined by availability of faculty for staffing the courses.

"Given the national scarcity of trained international business faculty, internationalization by course integration is the preferred strategy for almost all schools of business," he said. In this area, the approach of the University of Memphis was particularly effective. He knew that the adoption of such a strategy required a significant effort in terms of the development of functional-discipline faculty who understood the international dimension. The CIBER at the University of Memphis thus provided incentives to faculty for internationalization of both their research and their teaching. Significantly by 1993, a number of University of Memphis faculty had entered some form of international business enrichment programs, so that the university had in place a body of faculty capable of staffing integrated courses to bolster the International MBA program.

When the U.S. Department of Education presented a formal report entitled "Taking Business into the 21st Century," it recognized the center at the University of Memphis as a key example of 10 year accomplishments among CIBERs nationwide: "The Robert Wang Center for International Business provides a full array of international education and research services to meet the needs of local businesses. It organizes and sponsors activities for companies of all sizes in a wide variety of industries by using programs centered on custom language classes, placement of International MBA student interns, specialty conferences and briefings, facilitation of meetings with visiting foreign executives, and custom global leadership training programs. These activities have not only benefited the participating companies through tangible research, employee training and networking, but also the university and its students. Programs designed for such powerhouse companies as Federal Express have helped deepen the university's relationship with these firms."

The Sparks Bureau of Business and Economic Research in its spring 2003 magazine, *Business Perspectives*, highlighted the work of the Wang Center in an expansive article. It told how the U of M center helps guide professionals and students toward opportunities to become culturally conscious and globally competent amid a diverse, global society. "By developing results-oriented programs that foster international competencies among students, faculty and professionals, the Wang Center advances the body of knowledge in international business teaching. The center continually responds to the emerging needs and growth opportunities while maintaining its focus on each constituency's unique needs," the report reads.

The article also expounded on how the IMBA program helped students develop business skills, country and regional understanding, cultural competencies and the global mindset to do business just about anywhere in the world. This is because experiential learning is at the heart of that program which features a mandatory overseas summer study session and a full-time fall semester internship at a foreign host company. Moreover, the magazine article touted the undergraduate international business degree, study abroad for the executive MBA program, faculty development and international business seminars, business workshops for foreign language faculty, faculty study abroad program, and international business research carried out by the Wang Center.

In this instance, its role in research was particularly interesting. Issues examined included international economic trends, exploring emerging organizational forms and practices, and discovering linkages between management practices and competitive advantage. Additionally, research activities included the development of international business-related teaching modules, courses and pedagogies, and research on the competitiveness of American business. Furthermore, such programs as one-day specialty conferences, half-day workshops, luncheon briefings, breakfast forums, customized training programs, and overall global networking were also illustrated through the article.

Anecdotal comments from participants far and wide verify further credence of the efficacy of programs through the center. Here are some of the testimonials:

"It was by far one of the best learning experiences I have had in my professional career... the course content and presentations, not to mention the interaction, sharing of knowledge and information was beneficial far beyond any of my expectations. What I learned during the week at the five-day GlobalEd cultural seminar, I can use every day." Rick Rounds, Emergency One, Inc. (2003).

"The 2001 globalization seminar provided both exceptional content and extraordinary inspiration. I left Memphis with an armful of directly related materials and a head full of ideas to strengthen my institution's commitment to global education." Dorothy Luffing-Wright, Suffolk County College, Selden, New York (2001).

The recollections of a key inside player especially sum up the story well. "I remember well the issues, especially in establishing the IMBA," said veteran university president Rawlins. "I don't believe I understood at the time what a bold and challenging endeavor that was. One trip, to visit students in Germany, stands out as one of my most enjoyable adventures. Also, walking London and talking with Ben about the British Empire gave me insights that I cherish. Often, I miss those days. Great memories."

"It was clear to me that the Memphis CIBER is a well-respected and appreciated center by the university administration, the faculty, students and the business community," said José de la Torre of Florida International University. "Its wide range of activities and the dedication of its director and staff are exemplary. Just the evidence provided by the allocation of prime space for the center's offices and for the IMBA classroom is indicative of this position. I congratulate the Memphis CIBER for its broad range of high-quality interventions and programs. Whether judged in terms of its impact on students, faculty, knowledge creation or international business practice, the cumulative results of all of these activities is impressive and commendable."

Chapter Twelve

❧

Epilogue and Outlook

As one major newspaper cast its headline, we are witnessing "Wrenching Times Across the Globe." We started this book with a macroeconomic overview of the world, then progressively focused the view to the national, regional and local levels. The current world economic focus in 2012 fixes upon the European Union and the Euro currency. Nonetheless, the truth is that the world's ability to regain economic health will no doubt be tough overall. Complicating this and more so than ever before, we find that the inner workings of a given nation's own fiscal health have the capability to spill over with global ramifications to countries far afield.

Wherever one looks, we see several powerful market trends significantly altering the economics of the financial industry. To remain competitive, many companies are reassessing their business models, operations, and technology structures. Given the magnitude of the forces involved – margin pressure, regulatory changes, globalization complexity, and fast-moving technology innovation – the formula is complex and changing.

Even the pillars of the global economic leadership – Europe, America, China and the Arab world – are hurting and will find painful ways out of the malaise, there is little to no doubt. Compounding this idea is an unsteady political climate alongside a contentious citizenry and business public in America, Greece, Italy, Spain, and Portugal to varying degrees. Germany, meanwhile, given the advantage of its stronger economy alongside the weaker economies, presents a lopsided stance when averaged together as a whole. Indeed, the president of the European Central Bank, Mario Draghi, warned in June that the structure of the Euro currency union had reached the *verge* of unsustainability. Eurozone citizens and politicians alike are tiring after three years of a bailout here or a stop-gap measure there to only calm things for a while. Half-measures and delays have only made the situation worse, with even various measures enraging national populaces who took to the streets in stormy waves of protestations.

Meanwhile, we also have witnessed the Arab Spring more recently with a shift toward democratization and often at a cost. The settling out of this maelstrom is not yet evident and is sharply different from country to country. Syria still boils and roils in the streets, and Iran plays a chessboard game with its intentions and arms buildup. Today, the Arab picture is a fractured one as it tries to find its new identity, nation by nation.

China is slowing production, relatively speaking, as it looks at both internal and external consumer demand. It has been quick to streamline its economic superstructure to coalesce with world commerce, but slower in terms of becoming more flexible with its institutional rigor and bureaucracy. Ultimately, political reform will have to follow economic reforms.

America finds itself politically polarized as ramifications continue to address problems of a diminishing Social Security and Medicare picture for the future. The costs of the two wars have taken economic tolls, as has the subprime mortgage crisis aftermath. Stimulus packages which have cost billions of dollars are now making the public consider that they were stimulators only in name. The more real jobless numbers are true revealers to the national portrait. Whatever medicine is in store for the world – even the best the world has to offer up – will be a bitter pill to swallow for some time to come.

However, the other part of the big picture today is one in which emerging market nations are yard by yard reaching a new prominence on the global scene, the furtherance of a trend cited early in this book. Consider as an illustration the petrochemical industry as one indicative substructure of change, a trend line noted by Booz & Co. Not long ago, the center of the global chemical industry seemed destined to be moving to the Middle East from North America and Europe, propelled by the ready availability in the Arab world of relatively inexpensive oil. A wave of drilling activity has unearthed giant supplies of natural gas in shale rock around the world, but mostly in the United States, creating a surfeit of raw material for making ethylene-based plastics inexpensively, even as the cost of oil skyrockets. This discovery has altered chemical industry dynamics in significant ways. Demand for most petrochemicals is climbing as their prices fall in line with natural gas. This demand is particularly true in fast-growing markets in emerging nations.

As a result, many large companies are adding to their natural gas reserves in North America with a goal of manufacturing ethylene polymers locally and shipping them to factories worldwide, where the chemical can be used for everything from sandwich bags and cling wrap to car covers, squeeze bottles, water pipes, and cable insulation. This trend could force an ethylene price war and profit margin pressure for the chemical companies with the most invested. Couple that with an impending price war that is further punctuated by activities in China, where natural gas resources are substantial and ethylene factory capacity is increasing at a rate equal to that of the rest of the world combined.

Finally, several overriding and underlying influences are embedding themselves in the marketplace today, some on a less obvious, quieter level. These include such welcome trends as reverse innovation, sustainability, and corporate social responsibility – independent in their own rights. Reverse innovation is likely to be used first in the developing world before spreading to the industrialized world. It refers broadly to the process where goods developed as inexpensive models to meet needs of developing nations, such as battery-operated medical instruments in countries with limited infrastructure, are repackaged as low-cost innovative goods for Western buyers. The process of reverse innovation begins by focusing on needs and requirements for low-cost products in countries like India and China. Once products are developed for these markets, they are then sold elsewhere at low prices, which creates new markets and uses. This leads to products that are created locally in developing countries, tested in local markets, and, if successful, upgraded for sale and delivery in the developed world.

Corporate social responsibility, also called corporate conscience, corporate citizenship, social performance, or sustainable-responsible business, is in vogue now. It involves a form of corporate self-regulation integrated into a business model.

This functions as a self-regulating mechanism where a business monitors its compliance with the spirit of the law, ethical standards, and international norms – often going beyond the mere lawful considerations. The goal is to achieve a positive impact through its activities on the environment, consumers, employees, and communities.

Truly, the business and economic map of the world is being recharted by the week, and even the day. The trends change and the facts change and the players at the top also move around. This trend is all the more reason why there always will be an inherent need for dedicated and capable advanced global business education. As evidenced across the span of this book, the Wang Center has responded to the macroeconomic changes of the last 25 years and will need to consistently chart a new pathway to meet the new challenges and changes unfolding across the global economy.

A Timeline of Progress

1973 – Robert Wang arrives in Memphis and enrolls in Memphis State's graduate school, concentrating in sociology and business management.

1975 – Wang receives his MA from Memphis State University and undertakes the risky business venture of becoming a road salesman of home craft items.

1976 – Dr. Kedia, holder of the Wang Center Chair of Excellence in International Business, receives his Ph.D. from Case Western Reserve University with a research focus on international comparative management, strategic management and business policy, and international organizational structure.

March 1976 – Wang's business becomes incorporated and subsequently rises from a *mom-and-pop* business into a successful international enterprise selling home craft items.

1981 – Wang receives the Small Business Executive of the Year Award.

1984 – The Tennessee State Assembly creates new Chairs of Excellence with a $44 million appropriation to be matched by private funds to attract eminent scholars and a new research initiative to the state's various public institutions.

1985 – An exchange agreement between Memphis State University and Huazhong Normal University in China is signed.

1986 – The Fogelman Executive Center, a state-of-the art conference center, opens.

1988 – Memphis State University becomes member of the International Student Exchange Program which arranges one-to-one exchanges among 200 foreign universities and 35 nations; Gov. Lamar Alexander helps create the Chairs and Centers of Excellence for universities in Tennessee.

1988 – The Robert Wang Center is established and the U.S. Congress passes the Omnibus Trade and Competitiveness Act.

1989 – The U.S. Department of Education awards a Business and International Education (BIE) grant to the Wang Center.

1989 – The Wang Center stages a seminar on challenges of doing business in the Soviet market via a two-hour nationally broadcast video conference.

1989 – J. Taylor Sims, Dean of the Fogelman College of Business and Economics, goes on a 10-day trip to Japan to build ties between the Fogelman college among several Japanese universities.

July 12, 1989 – Robert Wang Center is officially dedicated and located in the Fogelman Executive Center.

November 1989 – Dean Sims, professor of marketing and Dean of the Fogelman College of Business and Economics, postulates that the greater Memphis area is highly poised for international business development.

1990 – Dr. Henry Kissinger, former U.S. Secretary of State, featured at first Arthur Andersen international business symposium, titled "Memphis: Seizing the Global Opportunity."

1990 – The Commissioner of Economic and Community Development speaks at the Wang Center about exporting to East Asia and the Pacific Rim and expanding international business.

1990 – Memphis State University, in conjunction with Southern Illinois University, is awarded $1 million to establish a Center for International Business Education and Research (CIBER) through a grant from the U.S. Department of Education.

1990 – Memphis State applies for a federal grant of $200,000 to establish an interdisciplinary program of language and culture in the departments of international studies and foreign language in both bachelor's and master's programs.

April 1990 – The U.S. Department of Education and Tennessee Department of Economic and Community Development approve a grant for a series of seminars for Mid-South business representatives.

Summer 1990 – Memphis State uses an $80,000 federal state grant to expand its interdisciplinary programs that allows students to attend classes in Spain and England and professors to teach at universities in Hong Kong and Czechoslovakia.

1991 – V. Lane Rawlins named 10th president of Memphis State University.

Early 1991 – Dr. Rawlins expresses his goal for the university to become a major urban research center, with research applied to problems facing modern society.

Early 1991 – Otis W. Baskin becomes the new Dean of the Fogelman College of Business and Economics and seeks to cultivate useful ties among business schools, local companies and promoters of economic development.

Spring 1991 – William Cavitt, director of the Canadian office of the U.S. Department of Commerce and the minister for Congressional Relations from Mexico, visits the university in an effort to sell the idea of free trade agreement academics across the nation.

Spring 1991 – Robert Wang and Shelby County Mayor Morris express the need for the Memphis business community to expand from a regional to a strong international hub by branding itself as a center of international learning.

July 1991 – *Commercial Appeal* writer Lisa Jennings posits how former Memphis State University's Fogelman College plays a pivotal role in international business and in the city's economic development as a whole.

December 1991 – Directors of the CIBER at Memphis State University and Southern Illinois University stage a seminar to teach other college-level educators how to establish international business curricula.

January 1992 – Wang Center invites Professor Oleg Gurbin of the Department of Political Sociology at Moscow State University to visit Memphis State University and speak about Russia's attempt to march toward a market economy.

1992 – Communist countries move toward open-market economies and a unified European community begin doing business en masse, placing greater emphasis on America's need to learn foreign languages and understand global cultures.

May 1992 – *International Business Chronicle* discusses how business schools in the Southeast are getting serious about international business education; this article singles out Memphis State University as one of the few to offer such an undergraduate degree in the Southeast region.

1993 – An international business data library is established to provide information on markets, culture, laws affecting businesses and local customs in foreign nations.

Fall 1993 – Directors from the Fogelman College, the Robert Wang Center and the College of Arts and Sciences offer a new graduate program in international business, the International MBA, which provides a new full-time lockstep program to be completed within two years.

1994 – Memphis State University officially becomes The University of Memphis.

1994 – Interim Dean Ferrell notes that university is in a good position to take advantage of increased opportunities in international business.

Spring 1994 – The Academy of International Business names Robert Wang the "International Business Executive of the Year" in the Southwest Region.

Summer 1994 – Dr. David Kemme, who is recognized as an authority on Eastern Europe and on the developing business concerns of former Soviet Union bloc nations, is named to fill the Shelby County Chair of Excellence in International Economics.

1994 – University of Memphis President Rawlins and Dr. Kedia sign formal agreements with the University of Dortmund in West

Germany, the University of Antwerp in Belgium and the University of Birmingham in England.

1994 – Fifteen University of Memphis International MBA students intern in companies in France, Germany and Mexico.

1994 – Assistant Director Erwin Williamson brings the growing, positive narrative about the Wang Center to a large readership in an article for the *World Business Review*.

Fall 1994 – A delegation of 19 high-level business and government officials from Shanghai, China, arrive in Memphis to participate in the inaugural Chinese executive training program at the University of Memphis.

1995 – The China Machinery and Automobile Industrial Delegation visit Memphis, coinciding with a conference at the university about forming joint-venture alliances among companies.

1996 – The center hosts its third annual business-language workshop designed to teach college instructors how to teach language from a business perspective.

Summer 1996 – More than 100 educators from around the world gathered at the University of Memphis to discuss ways to internationalize the curriculums at their business schools.

Late 1996 – The University of Memphis president Rawlins and Dr. Kedia embark on a 17-day visit to China, Hong Kong and Japan to sign faculty and student exchange agreements with six Asian universities.

1996 – Dr. Kedia looks further into developing dual degree programs – one where students can earn a law degree and an International MBA, and another where students can earn an engineering degree and an International MBA.

1996 – U.S. Department of Education renews the CIBER grant for the third time.

1997 – International MBA program expands to add a Chinese component to the curriculum.

December 1997 – Mayor William Morris, mayor of Shelby County, Tennessee, delivers a commencement address to The University of Memphis graduates in terms of a true interest and concern for the global arena.

1998 – Dr. Kedia plans to add Japanese and Brazilian-dialect Portuguese as components of the International MBA program.

February 1998 – The University of Memphis establishes its 24th Chair of Excellence and seeks a top-ranked scholar in international business to fill the new professorship.

October 1998 – The Asian economic crisis causes some temporary problems in the transportation industry as the demand for Asian goods creates an influx of imports and severely devalues the American currency.

March 1999 – China's market opportunities for American firms is the centerpiece of a Memphis-hosted consortium attended by the director of the Center for Marketing Trade Development in China.

September 1999 – Wang Center celebrates its 10-year anniversary by inviting key faculty from overseas universities, U of M administrators, Fogelman faculty, and business executives to participate in a one-day seminar.

October 1999 – Governor Ned McWherter takes 15 businessmen and officials on a foreign trade mission to Japan; strengthens ties between industries in Tennessee and Japan.

December 1999 – Wang Center expands its emphasis to offering conversational and business foreign language classes for area employees through the Tennessee Foreign Language Institute satellite office in Memphis.

2000 – Lane Rawlins leaves the university to become president of Washington State University; Dr. Ralph Faudree, dean of the College of Arts and Sciences, is named interim president.

2001 – Dr. Shirley C. Raines is named the 11th president of the University of Memphis.

2001 – The subject of homeland security brings increased relevance to international competitiveness and the ability to work globally unfettered.

2002 – The Wang Center joins hands with seven other CIBERs along with the Institute for International Public Policy to conduct outreach, mentoring and development programming for faculty at Historically Black Colleges and Universities.

August/September 2003 – Wang Center presents two Middle Eastern culture and business practices seminars.

October 2003 – Memphis Regional Chamber's international commerce day, co-sponsored by the Wang Center, features a presentation by the senior advisor to Tom Ridge.

January 2004 – "Planes, trains and trucks....learning about NAFTA" is an executive forum held to celebrate first 10 years of NAFTA and to discuss opportunities and security challenges.

June 2004 – The Tennessee Homeland Security Consortium, a partnership to provide leadership, visionary solutions, training and technology for homeland security challenges facing the nation, is formed by the University of Memphis and includes Tennessee's other top research institutions.

Fall 2004 – Wang Center co-sponsors a business conference on international trade compliance issues featuring officers with the U.S. Department of Commerce and with the Office of Export Assistance.

2005 – GlobalEd seminars broaden cultural and leadership understanding among executives in order to prepare them for conducting business in the global marketplace.

2005 – The Memphis Regional Chamber's International Council, the Memphis Export Assistance Center, the Memphis World Trade Club, Northwest Airlines and the Wang Center for International Business hold a conference on Doing Business in Ireland.

Fall 2005 – Wang Center hosts a conference with FedEx on the topic of security issues and related impacts on the Memphis logistics industry.

May 2007 – A total of 245 faculty members participate in the Faculty Study Abroad program focusing on the European Union from 1991 forward.

June 2007 – Beginning in 1994 to present, 620 business faculty members participate in the annual FDIB-Globalization Seminars, which offer six concurrent international courses.

2007 – A landmark is reached from 1993 through this year, with a cumulative 467 language faculty members from 249 institutions participating in the annual business-language workshops for Spanish, French, German and Japanese foreign language faculty members

2009 – Fogelman College of Business and Economics begins an online master's in business administration, requiring two on-campus residency sessions.

2010 – Study Abroad program, supported with student fees, provides scholarships for programs offered by 200 institutions in 45 countries.

2011 – The University of Memphis' Centennial Celebration begins in September 2011 and runs through December 2012.

2012 – *Moving Out to Meet the World* is published, marking a quarter-century of bringing the ever-changing business world to faculty, students, business executives and the local community.

Appendices

Dr. Ben L. Kedia, Director (1988-Present)

Ms. Tonna Bruce, Associate Director (1991-1994; 2004-2006)
Mr. Erwin Williamson, Assistant Director (1994-1995)
Ms. Judy Scales, Assistant Director (1995-2000)
Ms. Deborah Hernandez, Assistant Director (2001-2003)
Mr. Jeff Morris, Assistant Director (2003-2004)
Ms. Barbara Stevenson, Associate Director (2007-Present)

Dr. Otis Baskin, Director, IMBA Internships (1992-1994)
Mr. Gene Odom, Assistant Director, IMBA (1995-1997)
Mr. Rob Marcynski, Assistant Director, IMBA (1998-1999)
Dr. Joseph Keith, Assistant Director, Academic Programs (2000-2001)
Dr. David Dickson, Assistant Director, Academic Programs (2001-2002)
Mr. Dwayne Stevens, Assistant Director, IMBA (2002-2004)

Ms. Pat Taylor, Coordinator, International MBA (1997-2011)
Ms. Dottie Shelton, Sr. Administrative Secretary, IMBA (1997-2006)
Ms. Kay Molpus Hefty, Secretary, International MBA (1995-1996)

Mr. Richard Marcus, Manager, Memphis Foreign Language Inst. (1998-2001)
Mr. Charles Fitzgerald, Manager, Corporate & Inst. Relations (2000-2001)
Mr. Harold Gulley, Manager, Undergrad Int'l Business (2002-2003)

Ms. Ann Brock, Administrative Assistant (1991-1994)
Ms. Jeanne Tutor, Program Coordinator (1994-2007; 2008-Present)
Ms. Amelia Cole, Program Coordinator (2007-2012)

Ms. Sherry Henson, Assistant Program Specialist (1998-1999)
Ms. Vera Martin Perry, Assistant Program Specialist (2001-2011)

Ms. Susan Kelly Hance, Secretary (1988-1998)
Ms. Frankie M. Perry, Office Supervisor`(1999)
Ms. Franchiska Dorse, Sr. Admin. Secretary (1999-2001)
Ms. Jeanne Monger, Sr. Admin. Secretary (2001-2002)

Ms. Maha Baragat, Data Management Specialist (2002-2004)
Ms. Joanna Beames, Data Management Specialist (2004-2007)
Mr. Chris Videll, Data Management Specialist (2008-2010)

University Administrative Representatives

Dr. Ralph Faudree, Provost
Dr. Ivan Legg, Provost
Dr. Linda Brinkley, Vice Provost for Research and Graduate School
Dr. Dianne Horgan, Vice Provost for Research
Dr. Andrew Meyers, Vice Provost for Research
Dr. John Haddock, Vice Provost, Academic Affairs
Dr. Chrisann Schiro-Geist, Vice-Provost for Academic Affairs
Dr. Van Oliphant, Vice Provost for Extended Programs
Dr. Tom Nenon, Asst. Vice Provost,Undergrad Prog./Dir., Int'l Programs
Dr. H. O'Neal Smitherman, Executive Assistant to President
Dr. Cal Allen, Executive Director, International Programs & Services
Dr. Blaine Brownell, Executive Director, Center for Int'l Programs and Services
Mr. Kevin Roper, Vice President for Marketing & Advancement
Dr. Will Thompson, Assistant Dean, College of Arts and Sciences
Dr. W. Theodore Mealor, Vice President for Planning

Professional Schools Representatives

Dr. Marty Alberg, Assistant Dean, K-12 Programs, College of Education
Dr. Lillian Bargagliotti, Dean, School of Nursing
Dr. Nathan Essex, Dean, College of Education
Dr. Francis Gabor, Professor of International Law, Humphreys School of Law
Dr. Mary Lee Hall, Assistant Dean, College of Education
Dr. Marjorie Luttrell, Dean, Lowenberg School of Nursing
Dr. Robert M O'Halloran, Director, Wilson Sch. of Hospitality & Resort Mgmt.
Dr. Donald Polden, Dean, Humphrey's School of Law
Dr. Richard R. Ranta, Dean, Communications and Fine Arts
Dr. John Ray, Dean, College of Engineering
Dr. William Terry Umbreit, Director, Wilson Sch. of Hospitality & Resort Mgmt.
Dr. Ralph Wilcox, Chair, Human Movement Sciences and Education
Dr. Richard A. Zurburg, Director, Wilson School of Hospitality & Resort Mgmt.

College of Arts & Sciences Representatives

Dr. Ralph Albanese, Chair, Department of Foreign Languages and Literature
Dr. Cal Allen, Assistant Director, Center for International Programs and Services
Dr. Linda Bennett, Anthropology
Dr. Robert Blanton, Political Science/ Dir., Interdisciplinary Studies Center
Dr. Jack Carpenter, Dean, College of Arts and Sciences
Dr. Dipankar Dasgupta, Computer Science
Dr. Cliff Dixon, Geography/Planning
Dr. Randy Dupont, Chair, Criminology and Criminal Justice
Dr. Rex Enoch, Chair, Sociology
Dr. Ruth Finerman, Anthropology
Dr. Jane Henrici, Anthropology
Dr. Ken Holland, Political Science

Dr. Henry Kurtz, Dean, College of Arts & Sciences
Dr. David Mason, Political Science
Dr. Charles Williams, Anthropology

Fogelman College of Business Representatives

Dr. Rajiv Grover, Dean
Dr. John Pepin, Dean
Dr. Donna Randall, Dean
Dr. O. C. Ferrell, Dean
Dr. Coy Jones, Associate Dean for Academic Programs
Dr. Dan Sherrell, Associate Dean for Faculty & Research
Dr. Emin Babakus, Marketing & Supply Chain Management
Dr. Otis Baskin, Management
Dr. Lloyd Brooks, Management Information Systems
Dr. Carolyn Callahan, Director, School of Accountancy
Dr. Bettina Cornwell, Marketing
Dr. Jasbir Dhaliwal, Management Information Systems
Dr. Mark Gillenson, MIS/Director, MBA Programs
Dr. Kanji Haitani, Economic
Dr. Julie Heath, Economics
Dr. P. K. Jain, Finance
Dr. Brian Janz, Director, Institute for Managing Emerging Technologies
Dr. Ben Kedia, Director, Wang Center for International Business
Dr. Philip Kolbe, Director, EMBA
Dr. Jeffrey Krug, Management
Dr. Ken Lambert, Director, School of Accountancy
Dr. James Lukawitz, Accounting / Director of Undergraduate Programs,
Dr. John Malloy, School of Accountancy
Dr. Earnest L. Nichols, Director, FedEx Center for Supply Chain Management
Dr. Albert Okunade, Economics
Dr. Mars Pertl, Chair, Finance, Insurance & Real Estate
Dr. C. S. Pyun, Marketing
Dr. Zabihollah "Zabi" Rezaee, Thomson-Hill Chair in Accounting
Dr. Judy Simon, Chair, Management Information Systems
Dr. William Smith, Chair, Economics Dept.
Dr. Ronald W. Spahr, Chair, FIR
Dr. Marla Stafford, Chair, Marketing & Supply Chain Management
Dr. Tom Stafford, Asst. Prof., MIS
Dr. Robert Taylor, Chair, Management
Dr. Shelley White-Means, Prof. Economics

Representatives of the State of Tennessee

Mr. Frank Barnett, Tennessee Governor's Representative
Mr. Allen Neel, Assoc. Comm., Int'l Mktg., Dept of Economic & Comm. Dev.
Mr. Robert Parsons, Asst. Comm. Int'l Marketing, Dept. of Econ. & Comm. Dev.
Mr. Andy Pelych, Director, Tennessee Export Office

Representatives of Local and Regional Business

Mr. Lyman D. Aldrich, Partner, Financial Solutions Worldwide, LLC
Mr. Alex Alvarez, Manager, Cummins Engine Co.
Mr. Robert Bell, Director, Cummins Engine Co.
Mr. Bob Bennett, VP, Human Resources, FedEx Express
Mr. Ray Bryant, Executive Director, Lower Mississippi Delta Center
Mr. Kathy Buckman David, Chairman of the Board, Bulah Holdings, Inc.
Mr. M. L. 'Maury' Bush, VP Public Relations, Sharp Mfg. Co. of America
Mr. Jerry Cardwell, VP, Corporate Dev. & International Sales, Orgill, Inc.
Mr. Brad Champlin, Exec VP (ret.), Entrepren./Public Serv., Regions Financial
Mr. Wei Chen, Chief Exec. Officer, Sunshine Enterprise, Inc.
Ms. Patricia Covingtin, Director of Operations & Transp., Cummins Engine
Mr. Samuel Cox, Director, Information Systems, Brother Industries (USA) Inc.
Mr. Steve Cox, Managing Director, Global Program Mgmt., FedEx Express
Mr. Mike Demster, VP Int'l & Tech Bus. Dev., Greater Memphis Chamber
Mr. James W. Drake, Sr. VP, International, Varco-Pruden Buildings, Inc.
Ms. Misty Duke, Mexico Merchandising, AutoZone, Inc.
Mr. James Gannaway, Partner, Athur Anderson & Co.
Mr. Mike Harless, VP Human Resources, ThyssenKrupp Elevator
Mr. Wilbur Hawkins, Department of Commerce, Washington DC
Mr. Dennis Kenny, Vice President, Human Resources, FedEx Corp.
Mr. Patrick Kern, Vice President International Operations, VP Buildings, Inc.
Mr. Malcolm Koch, Vice President, International, First TN Bank
Mr. Paul M. Langenus, Director, Global Bus. Dev., International Paper
Mr. B. Lee Mallory III, President, Mallory Distribution Centers/Exec VP
Mr. Larry McMahan, VP, Human Resouces, FedEx Leadership Institute
Mr. Bill Morris, Former Mayor of Shelby County
Mr. Max Painter, Mktg. Dir., US Biologic Trauma Div., Medtronic Spinal & Biologics
Mr. Edson Peredo, President, International, Buckman Labs
Mr. Frank J. Poper, Controller, International Paper
Ms. Carole Presley, Sr. VP Marketing, Comm. & Customer Service, FedEx Corp.
Mr. Dennis Roche, Vice President Global Compensation & Benefits, FedEx
Mr. Ruben Rosales, VP International, Smith & Nephew Richards
Ms. Ree Russell, The Commercial Servcie, U.S. Depart. Of Commerce
Mr. Matthew Rutherford, Global Business Manager, International Paper
Mr. Don Scott, Vice President Marketing, Memphis Group, Inc.
Mr. David Spann, Director, U.S. Export Assistance, U.S. Dept. of Commerce
Mr. Steve Stapleton, Mgng. Dir., Executive Servs. Worldwide Operations, FedEx
Mr. Darrick Starling, Director, Engine Marketing, Cummins Engine Co.
Ms. Leigh Shockey, International Sales Manager, Drexel Chemicals
Ms. Betty Steele, Baker, Donelson & Caldwell/TN Council Global Compet.
Mr. Mark Sutton, Vice President Corp. Strategic Planning, International Paper
Mr. Bruce Thompson, Sr. Vice President , International, Smith & Nephew
Mr. Robert Wang, CEO, Wang's International/President, Creative Co-op
Ms. Susie Wang, Chief Operating Officer, Wang's International/Creative Co-op

University of Antwerp, Belgium

The University of Antwerp is characterised by its high standards in education, internationally competitive research and entrepreneurial approach. It was founded in 2003 after the merger of three university institutions previously known as RUCA, UFSIA and UIA. Their roots go back to 1852. The University of Antwerp has about 13.000 students, which makes it the third largest university in Flanders.

Antwerp Management School is the autonomous business school of the University of Antwerp. It was founded in 1959 and is the most prestigious school for management education. The university had a major impact on the development of Antwerp, Flanders, Belgium and beyond by delivering top managers in large companies and organizations.

The school has evolved to a business school that has carved out an important place for itself on the international stage, preparing future managers and leaders for key roles in the global business community and passionately promotes global citizenship, leadership and professionalism.

University of Birmingham, Birmingham, U.K.

The Birmingham MBA staff are delighted to announce that we have been ranked 9th in the UK by the 2011 Economist Rankings, moving up three places from 12th. We have now achieved one of our targets to be in the top 10 of UK Business Schools. With ever increasing and fierce international competition, we are also pleased to report that we have mostly maintained our global position in the rankings – a slight movement from 68th to 70th. The impact of such competition does make our other target more challenging – to be ranked in the world top 50. Nevertheless we strive towards this achievement and seek to consolidate our UK top ten standing.

Birmingham Business School is renowned for its research. With over 80 lecturing and research staff, many internationally recognized authorities in their fields, our research contributes to academic debates worldwide. We undertake projects funded by the Research Councils, major trusts, professional institutions, government departments and the EU.

University of Ulster, Londonderry, Northern Ireland, U.K.

Ulster is a university with a national and international reputation for excellence, innovation and regional engagement. We make a major contribution to the economic, social and cultural development of Northern Ireland and play a key role in attracting inward investment. Our core business activities are teaching and learning, widening access to education, research and innovation and technology and knowledge transfer.

Magee Campus of the University of Ulster: Located in Derry (Londonderry), the Magee campus is named after the College founded by Martha Magee in

1845. It is located only a short walk along the River Foyle away from the city walls and comprises a mixture of historical and new buildings and modern and traditional facilities. Teaching strengths include business, computing, nursing, Irish language and literature, social sciences, law, psychology, peace and conflict studies and the performing arts.

University College, Dublin, Ireland

UCD is one of Europe's leading research-intensive universities where undergraduate education, postgraduate masters and Ph.D. training, research, innovation and community engagement form a dynamic continuum of activity. The university was established in 1854 by John Henry Newman whose classic work, *The Idea of a University,* is one of the most enduring texts on the value of higher education and a source of inspiration for UCD's current educational philosophy.

UCD School of Business is Ireland's leading business school and research center. In 2009 we officially celebrated 100 years of business education. One of the keystones of our reputation as one of the world's leading business schools is the quality and expertise of our Faculty. We are the only business school in Ireland to hold the triple crown of accreditation from AACSB (US), EQUIS (Europe) and AMBA (UK). We are also the only Irish member of CEMS, a global alliance of leading business schools and multinational companies.

UCD made history back in 1964 when it became one of the first schools in Europe to offer the MBA. Our MBA programmes are designed for professionals with at least 3 years experience. Programmes can be taken full-time (12 months) or part-time (24 months). Our MBA programmes are consistently ranked in the world's top 100 and Europe's top 50 by the Financial Times and the Economist Intelligence Unit.

Lille Catholic University, Lille, France

Founded in 1875, is France's largest private university with 22.500 full-time students and 5.000 staff members. Lille Catholic University is well known for its academic quality and its international dimension.

As a comprehensive university, it is home to 30 different faculties and schools: traditional faculties, graduate engineering and business schools, and vocational training colleges.

It offers 140 distinct degrees in four major fields of study:

- Law, Economics and Management
- Sciences and Engineering
- Humanities
- Health Sciences and Social Work

EDHEC Business School of Lille Catholic University, France

EDHEC Business School's goal is to train current and future executives via teaching and research programs geared to the needs of the economy and businesses. This objective is enshrined in our "EDHEC for Business" strategy. Internationalism is one of the pillars of EDHEC Business School's strategy. We have continued to expand internationally in 2010, particularly by strengthening our presence in Europe and Asia via the opening of two Executive Campuses in London and Singapore. Further initiatives include the recruitment of professors from prestigious foreign universities, the creation of international education tracks and programs, and the dissemination of our research work in the world's leading economic publications. All in all, no less than 75 nationalities are currently represented on EDHEC Campuses while 85% of our corporate funding comes from international corporations. During 2009-2010, we organized executive education and research seminars in 28 international economic capitals. Lastly, EDHEC is one of the few among the world's select business schools to have been awarded the three international accreditations, attesting to the quality of our education and training, our teaching faculty and the methods we employ.

Montpellier Business School, France

The Montpellier Business School is the only Group Grande Ecole of Management of the Languedoc-Roussillon region, Member of the Conférence des Grandes Ecoles. The mission of the Group Sup de Co Montpellier is to train students who desire to become socially responsible managers, endowed with a strong entrepreneurial spirit and able to adapt quickly to their professional context, whether it is local, national or international. Through its various programs, the Group Sup de Co Montpellier educates each year more than 2400 students, sends annually 600 students abroad on academic exchange programs, and welcomes 250 students coming from 137 partner universities representing 34 states. It graduates 560 students per year, of which 80% are recruited before obtaining the diploma.

EM Strasbourg Business School, Strasbourg, France

EM Strasbourg Business School is the only French Business School to be part of a multidisciplinary academic centre of excellence: the University of Strasbourg. This model, inspired by international references, enables the combination of academic benefits and university support while relying on solid partners from the public sector, local authorities, E.M. Strasbourg-Partners (involving 170 partner companies), and the network of its 13,000 alumni. Enjoying extensive autonomy with regard to its development policy, located within a first-rate academic environment and benefiting from an EPAS accreditation for its Program Grande Ecole, EM Strasbourg Business School will facilitate your development in a globalised world and teaches new forms of managerial behavior.

University of Dortmund, Germany

The University of Dortmund was founded in 1968, during the decline of the coal and steel industry in the Ruhr region. Its establishment was seen as an important move in the economic change (Strukturwandel) from heavy industry to technology. The university's main areas of research are the natural sciences, engineering, pedagogy/teacher training in a wide spectrum of subjects, special education, and journalism. The University of Dortmund was originally designed to be a technical university, but in 1980, it merged with the adjacent Pädagogische Hochschule Ruhr that housed mostly humanities.

The Faculty of Business, Economics and Social Sciences was established in 1973 and, since then, has educated students in the fields of business administration, economics and sociology. Longstanding experience in both integrated courses of study, and cross-faculty cooperation, particularly with the Industrial Engineering and Business Mathematics programs, make the faculty an important component of the TU Dortmund. Located in the heart of North Rhine-Westphalia, young people from all over the world are attracted to the Ruhr region. Due to its strategic location, close to the Dortmund Technology Park, the area offers outstanding partners for conducting research and gaining practical experience. This is a major advantage for our students. Within the framework of collaborative events, internships and trainee activities, students have the opportunity to establish contact early on with potential employers.

Catholic University of Eichstaett-Ingolstadt, Germany

The WFI – Ingolstadt School of Management was founded in 1989 and is part of the Catholic University Eichstaett-Ingolstadt, which can look back on more than 400 years of superior education in various disciplines. Constantly ranked as on of the top business schools in Germany, the WFI´s goal is to encourage and enable its students to fulfill executive and managerial functions in a national and international environment in a responsible and competent way. Focusing on the individual, practical, methodical and internationally orientated training of our students – facilitated by our professors, lecturers, teachers, economic luminaries and guest lecturers from abroad – has proved exceptionally fruitful. Furthermore, progressive integration of the department into the university, as well as regional and supraregional economic structures, have led to great successes in scholarship, research and business practice.

Monterrey Institute of Technology, Mexico

Monterrey Institute of Technology (Tecnológico de Monterrey) is a higher education institution that educates students to become responsible citizens who trigger the development of their communities. We promote in our students humanistic values, an international perspective, and an entrepreneurial culture. We are present throughout México with our 31 campuses and in several other countries through our sites and liaison offices.

It's Master's programs of EGADE Business School lead in Latin America. The new ranking Best Masters of Eduniversal ranks the OneMBA program of the EGADE Business School of the Tecnológico de Monterrey as number one in Latin America. Another of its programs, the Master's in Business Administration (MBA), holds the same ranking in the category of General Management; and the Master's programs in Finance, Manufacturing Management, Marketing and International Business were also highly ranked.

ESAN, Lima, Peru

ESAN is a Peruvian institution, private, international in scope and not-for-profit, academic and managerial autonomy. ESAN is the first academic institution to offer a graduate degree in Administration created in Spanish-speaking world. It was established on 25 July 1963 under an agreement between the governments of Peru and the United States of America and its organization and implementation was entrusted to the Graduate School of Business Stanford University, California.

Transformed into a university from July 12, 2003 (Act No. 28021), ESAN now offers master's degrees in Business Administration, master specialized (in Organization and Personnel Management, Supply Chain Management, Marketing, Management of Health Services, Management and Real Estate Development Management Information Technology, Finance and Corporate Law, Finance), eight runs in the level of undergraduate and executive programs in various formats, corporate programs and other academic and professional services.

Indian Institute of Management, Bangalore, India

A 100-acre oasis in south Bangalore, the Indian Institute of Management Bangalore (IIMB), with its all-stone architecture, lush verdant woods and landscaped gardens provides an idyllic environment to engage in management studies, academics and learning. IIMB has world-class infrastructure that facilitates excellence in teaching, research, consulting and other professional activities.

Located in India's high technology capital, IIMB is in close proximity to some of the leading corporate houses in the country, ranging from information technology to consumer product companies, giving it the added advantage of integrating classroom knowledge with practical experience.

Established in 1973, the Institute has since then built on its base of highly accomplished faculty, world class infrastructure and motivated student body to emerge as one of the premier institutes for management education and research promoting managerial excellence in the country. IIMB strives to achieve excellence through partnerships with industry, and leading academic institutions, the world over. IIMB's mission is to "build leaders through holistic, transformative and innovative education."

Alliance University, Bangalore, India

To be a world-class university that nurtures talent and catalytically transforms the lives of millions through excellence in teaching, research, service, and community development. To uphold a commitment to shaping lives through scholarly teaching and learning, and that which contributes to an equitable and holistic transformation of society at large.

The Master of Business Administration (MBA) course offered by Alliance University School of Business is the flagship course of the School and is accredited by the International Assembly for Collegiate Business Education (IACBE), USA — a premier international accreditation body for business management programs. Crafted with utmost care and with the cooperation of academics and practitioners worldwide, the curriculum offered is rigorous, contemporary and forward-looking. The course is designed to equip graduates with the skills, abilities and knowledge that will enable them to take up positions of higher responsibility in the corporate world anywhere, or to become entrepreneurs.

Nankai University, Tianjin, China

A key multidisciplinary and research-oriented university directly under the jurisdiction of the Ministry of Education, Nankai University, located in Tianjin on the border of the Sea of Bohai, is also the alma mater of our beloved Late Premier Shou Enlai.

Nankai University was founded in 1919 by the Famous Patriotic Educators, Mr. Zhang Boling and Mr. Yan Xiu. During the war (1934-1945), Nankai Univeristy, Peking University (Beijing University) and Tsinghua University (Qinghua University) united in Kunming to form the renowned Southwest Associated University. It was compared to be "The North Star of Higher Learning." In accordance with its motto of "Dedication to the Public Interests, Acquisition of All-Round Capability and Aspiration for Daily Progress," the University has produced batches of prominent talents such as Late Premier Zhou Enlai, Dr. Shiing-Shen Chern, Dr. Ta-You Wu and Playwright Cao Yu.

In 2004, Business School was awarded as: "The Advanced Collective Organization for the Tenth Five-Year Plan." The MBA Program of Nankai University is one of the top three MBA Programs in the First Accreditation held by the Ministry of Education in 2002. The organic committee of the world managers listed among the most influential MBA of China Ranks, and the MBA Program of Nankai University was ranked fifth in the Survey of 1,000 Professional Managers in 2003.

Nanjing University, Nanjing, China

NJU consists of three beautiful campuses, Gulou, Pukou, and Xianlin. As a top university in China, it boasts advanced teaching and research facilities. The master programs at the NUBS cover 11 majors and 14 research directions (excluding MBA, EMBA, and MPAcc), including political economics, western economics, world economy, human resource and environment economics, national economy, finance, industrial economics, international economics and trade, econometrics, accounting, and enterprise management (with the directions of human resource management, marketing, and electronic business). Among them, political economics and enterprise management are national key disciplines, and accounting is the key discipline in Jiangsu Province. Currently, the NUBS has 775 master students at school. It has a strong faculty team and 82 of its faculty members are supervisors for master students.

The master student training at the NUBS is characterized as "high caliber, solid foundation, and strong ability." Great importance has been attached to both professional education and comprehensive quality of students. The graduates are of high theoretical level and teamwork spirit, and very competitive in scientific research and management.

Sophia University, Tokyo, Japan

The origin of Sophia University can be traced back to more than 450 years ago when the Jesuit missionary Francis Xavier came to Japan in 1549 to spread Christianity in Japan. The actual foundation of the university began in 1908, when three Jesuit priests arrived in Japan in response to a request from the Roman Pontiff at that time, Pope Pius X. Five years later, in 1913, they opened the first Catholic university in Japan on this Kioi site where Sophia still stands. The university will celebrate its centennial in 2013.

Graduate School of Economics: Important economic and environmental issues such as Japan-U.S. Trade Imbalance and Economic Issues, Fluctuating Exchange Rate, Japanese Economy and Employment are covered. The programs are designed for students to acquire the skills to study modern important economic issues with a positive and normative approach.
- Master's (Doctoral) Program in Economics
- Master's (Doctoral) Program in Management

Osaka University, Japan

The Graduate School of Economics at Osaka University is arguably one of the best graduate schools in the field of economics and management and business in Japan today. Currently, the school has nearly 50 faculty members, who are leading economists and business scholars in the world.

Economics and Business at Osaka University: The Business Course in the Major of Management and Business has the main objective of fostering professionals equipped with a high degree of knowledge required in the business field. Thus, it is fundamentally important that students complete the course in the Master's Program. The Business Course in the Major of Management and Business, different from specialist graduate schools at other universities, has a Doctoral Program. Students who have enrolled in the Business Course to become highly skilled professionals can change careers by becoming researchers or advance to the Doctoral Program if an outstanding master thesis is provided. Thus, the Business Course, in the same way as the Major of Policy Studies, allows you to choose your future between finding a job after the Master's Program and advancing to the Doctoral Program as a researcher.

In 2008, we started a new area of research in the Major of Management and Business, the Global Management Course, which aims to raise capable individuals who have a thorough grounding in global perspectives and strong management skills to manage urban and regional developments as well as technological advancement. Students who have completed this area of research will enjoy the same diverse career options as the ones offered in the Business Course. The Global Management Course primarily focuses on management education and technological development needed particularly for emerging markets in Asia, learning about its languages, regions, cultures, and economy.

1991	
Dr. Andrew Lomax	Buckinghamshire College, U.K.
Dr. Carl Reyns	University of Antwerp UFSIA, Belgium
Dr. W. V. Grembergen	University of Antwerp UFSIA, Belgium
Dr. Alicja Kozdroj	Polish Academy of Science, Poland
Dr. Noel Kavannah	University of Birmingham, England
Dr. J. R. Slater	University of Birmingham, England
Dr. Niels Noorderhaven	Tilburg University, The Netherlands
Dr. Martin Welge	University of Dortmund, Germany
Dr. Yoshio Yoshida	Ashai University, Japan
Dr. Liliane Van Hoof	University of Antwerp UFSIA, Belgium
Dr. Oleg Gubin	Moscow State University, Russia
Dr. T. K. Tanahashi	Tokyo Kenzai University, Japan
Dr. S. Prakash Sethi	New York
Dr. Oleg Gubin	Moscow State University, Russia
1992	
Dr. Mohammed Ariff	National University of Singapore
Dr. Harold Wiese	Koblanz School of Management, Germany
Dr. Owen Nankivell	Westminster College, Oxford Unive., U.K.
Dr. Stefan Kesenne	University of Antwerp UFSIA, Belgium
Prof. Dr. Martin Glaum	Justus-Liebig University, Germany
Dr. Hamzah Ismail	University of Utara, Malaysia
Dr. Richard W. Pollay	University of British Columbia
Dr. Abu Baker	University of Malaya, Malaysia
Dr. T. K. Tanahashi	Tokyo Kenzai University, Japan
1993	
Dr. Claude-Isabelle Bossi	ISCID, France
Dr. Leland Yeager	Auburn University
Dr. Liliane Van Hoof	University of Antwerp UFSIA, Belgium
Dr. J. R. Slater	University of Birmingham, England
Dr. Lisa Dumas	University of Hull, England
Dr. Alena Ockova	Czechoslovak Management Center
1994	
Dr. Onitsuka	Momoyama University, Japan
Dr. Hirokazu Imamitsu	Aichi Gakuin University, Japan
Dr. J. D. Agarwal	Indiana Institute of Finance, Delhi, India
Ms. Judy Lambert	La Rochelle Grad. Sch of Business, France

Dr. Yoshio Saito	Chuo Gakuin University, Japan
Dr. Konstantin Remchukov	Moscow People's Friendship University
Dr. Jim Slater	University of Birmingham, England
Dr. Norbert Kolhase	University of Geneva
Dr. Ravi Kanungo	McGill Univ., Montreal, Quebec
Dr. Miriam Erez	McGill Univ., Montreal, Quebec
1995	
Dr. Anne Smith	McGill University, Montreal, Quebec
Mr. Robert F. Moore	AZO Inc., Memphis, TN
Dr. Shu-Hai Cong	Shanghai Security & Futures Institute, China
Dr. Lester Johnson	Australia
Dr. Patricia Neuhaus	Catholic University of Eichstatt, Germany
Dr. Ingemar Skog	Luftfartsverket Swedish Civil Aviation Adm.
Mr.Jim Hibberd	British Embassy, Washington
Dr. Martin Welge	University of Dortmund, Germany
Dr. Yoshio Yoshida	Asahi University, Japan
Dr. Yan Islam	Griffith University, Brisbane, Australia
Dr. J. D. Agarwal	Indiana Institute of Finance, Delhi, India
Mr. Michael A. Weininger	City University of Hong Kong, Hong Kong
Mr. Wang Haisheng	Embassy of the P.R. China in the U.S.
Mr. Liao Zhihong	Embassy of the P.R. China in the U.S.
Dr. Yvonne Desportes	Sup de Co Montpellier, France
Dr. Pierre Siklos	Wilfred Laurier University, Ontario, Canada
Dr. Chen Jiyong	Wuhan University, China
Dr. Tibor Palankai	Budapest University of Economic Sciences
Dr. Norio Aoyama	Chuogakuin University, Japan
Dr. Ichiro Uchida	Asia Foundation, Washington, D.C.
1996	
His Excellency Nitya Pibulsonggram	Ambassador to the U.S., Royal Thai Embassy
Dr. Arie Lewin	Duke University, Durham, NC
Dr. Mauricio Gonzalez	Monterrey Institute of Technology, Mexico
Dr. Gerardo Luyan	Monterrey Institute of Technology, Mexico
Dr. G-bor Hamza	Budapest, Hungary
1997	
Prof. Paola Bielli	Bocconi University, Milan, Italy
Dr. Jorge Pedroza	Monterrey Institute of Technology, Mexico

Lic. Mauricio Gonzalez	Monterrey Institute of Technology, Mexico
Prof. Dr. Bernd Stauss	Catholic University of Eichstatt, Germany
Dr. Curtis E. Harvey	University of Kentucky
Dr. John Kraft	Florida
Prof. Yasuo Sakakibara	Doshisha University, Japan
Dr. Kazuyuki Tokuoka	Doshisha University, Japan
Prof. Kazusei Kato	Kansai Gaidai College, Japan
Dr. R. D. Nair	University of Wisconsin-Madison
Dr. P. Moeller	Aachen, Germany
Prof. Dr. Hans Tummers	Univ. Robert Schuman, Strasbourg, France
Dr. Carl Reyns	President, University of Antwerp, Belgium
Dr. Yvon Desportes	University of Montepellier, France
Dr. Ian H. Stewart	Acadia University, Nova Scotia, Canada
Dr. T. J. Pempel	University of Washington
Dr. Gregosz Kolodko	First Deputy Prime Minister and Minister of Finance, Poland
Dr. June Dreyer	University of Miami
1998	
Dr. Ludwig Kreitz	Univ. Robert Schuman, Strasbourg, France
Prof. Dr. Bernd Stauss	Catholic University of Eichstatt, Germany
Dr. Axel Markert	Eberhard-Karls-Univ. Tubingen, Germany
Prof. Guihua Li	Nankai University, Tianjin, China
Prof. Dr. Dieter Cassell	Gerhard-Mercator Univ., Duisburg, Germany
D. Camille Becker	Citizen of Luxembourg, Belgium
Dr. Jaime Alonso Gomez	Monterrey Institute of Technology, Mexico
Prof. Dr. Joachim	Catholic University of Eichstatt, Germany
Prof. Dr. Martin Groos	Catholic University of Eichstatt, Germany
Prof. Dr. U.Hoffman-Lange	University of Bamberg, Germany
Dr. Michael Doyle	University of North Carolina, Charlotte
Dr. Mauricio Gonzalez	Monterrey Institute of Technology, Mexico
Dr. Shirley Daniel	University of Hawaii
Dr. Meera Kosambi	S.N.D.T. Women's Univ., Bombay, India
Dr. Dolores O'Reilly	University of Ulster, Northern Ireland
Dr. Mariano Tommasi	Univ. of San Andres, Victoria, Buenos Aires
1999	
Prof. E.Pausenberger	University of Giessen
Prof. Gwinder Singh	Amity Business School, Delhi, India

Prof. Bernd Stauss	Catholic University of Eichstatt, Germany
Prof. Martin Welge	University of Dortmund, Germany
Prof. Nicholas Hendrichs	Monterrey Tech, Mexico
Prof. Hans Tummers	Robert Schuman Univ. Strasbourg, France
Dr. J. D. Agarwal	Indiana Institute of Finance, Delhi, India
Prof. Liliane Van Hoof	University of Antwerp UFSIA, Belgium
Prof. Johannes Schneider	Catholic University of Eichstatt, Germany
Mr. Li Yong	Center for Market and Trade Develop., China
Prof. Paul Crowther	Catholic University of Lille, France
Prof. Christopher Cripps	Groupe ESC Grenoble, France
Prof. Yvon Desportes	Sup de Co Montpellier, France
Prof. Aquayo	Monterrey Tech, Mexico
Dr. Shi Yonghai	Chinese Acad. for Int'l Trade & Econ. Coop.
Mr. Li Yong	Center for Market and Trade Develop., China
2000	
Prof. Sundararajan	Indian Inst. of Management Bangalore, India
Prof. M. R. Rao	Indian Inst. of Management Bangalore, India
Prof. Bernhard Schipp	University of Dresden, Germany
Prof. Hans Tummers	Robert Schuman Univ. Strasbourg, France
Prof. Shuming Zhao	Nanjing University, China
Prof. Dirk Holtbruegge	University of Dortmund, Germany
Prof. Masa Ota	Massachusetts Institute of Technology
Stewart Cox	Thomas & Betts, Memphis, TN
Len Parker	Loctite Corp, Japan
John Gurney	First TN Bank, Memphis, TN
Pat Kern	VP Buildings, Memphis, TN
Pritpal Bansal	Orgill Corp., Memphis, TN
Sergio Anguiano	VP Buildings, Mexico
2001	
Dr. Louis Balthazar	Laval University, Quebec
Prof. Ludwig	Univ. Robert Schuman, Strasbourg, France
Prof.Rachel Kreitz	Univ. Robert Schuman, Strasbourg, France
Prof. Dr. Deiter Cassell	Duisburg University, Germany
Prof. Dr. Alex Kohlstedt	Duisburg University, Germany
Herbert W. Schulz	Singapore Embassy
Jonathan M. Bensky	Singapore Embassy
Robert Gelbard	Indonesia Embassy

Alice Davenport	Indonesia Embassy
Michael R. Frisby	Vietnam Embassy
V. Lane Pascoe	Malaysia Embassy
Michael Hand	Malaysia Embassy
Richard Hecklinger	Thailand Embassy
Aren Ware	Thailand Embassy
George F. Ruffner	Philippines Embassy
Ken Richeson	U.S.-ASEAN Business Council
Prof. Michel Guerive	Groupe EGC, Nantes-St.Nazaire, France
Prof. Laurence Briand	Groupe EGC, Nantes-St.Nazaire, France
Oleg A. Tolochek	Russian Delegation for Global Logistics
Mikhail Gurevich	Russian Delegation for Global Logistics
Valentina N. Vlasova	Russian Delegation for Global Logistics
Vladimir Y. Kukushkin	Russian Delegation for Global Logistics
Vyacheslav P. Sfronov	Russian Delegation for Global Logistics
Lenar T. Hakimullin	Russian Delegation for Global Logistics
Sergei Karalov	Russian Delegation for Global Logistics
Ross McAllister	FedEx Corp.
Adti Madhok	Infosys, India
2002	
Michael Anyiam Osigew	African Inst. Leadership Res. Dev., Nigeria
Coetzee Bester	African Insti. Leadership Res. Dev., SoAfrica
Johannes Britz	African Inst. Leadership Res. Dev., SoAfrica
Bhisma K. Agnihotri	Ambassador-at-Large, India
Exec. MBA Class(14 stud)	Catholic University of Eichstatt, Germany
Dr. Iemoto	Osaka University, Japan
Alice LeMaistre	Diplomat-in-Residence
Hilary Sadler	U.S. Dept. of Commerce, Washington D.C.
Dr. Michael Hitt	University of Arizona
Prof. Le Wean	Nankai University, China
Prof. Li Guihua	Nankai University, China
Prof. Tan Liyang	Nankai University, China
2003	
Prof. Larry McCurry	University ofUlster, Ireland
Paul Dacher	Office of E U, U.S. Dept. of Com., Wash. DC
2004	
Prof. Michael Doyle	University of North Carolina, Charlotte

Luisa Elder	State of Illinois, NAFTA Opportunity Center
Phil Newsom	FedEx Corp.
Prof. Dr. Hartmut Kiehling	Catholic University of Eichstatt, Germany
Prof. Javier No Sanchez	University of Salamanka, Spain
Prof. Kjell Lundmark	Umea University, Sweden
Prof. Dr. Helmut Assafalg	University of Applied Sciences, Germany
Prof. Dr. Gunter Buerke	University of Applied Sciences, Germany
2005	
Prof. S. Raghunath	Indian Inst. of Management Bangalore, India
Prof. John Makumbe	University of Zimbabwe, South Africa
Prof. Elisabeth Asiedu	University of Kansas
Prof. Barbara McDade	University of Florida
Prof. Glenwood Ross	Morehouse College
Prof. David Smith	Southeast Missouri State University
Prof. Ernie Betts	Michigan State University
Prof. John Metzler	Michigan State University
Prof. Anthony Ross	Michigan State University
Ann Bacher	East Asia Pacific, U.S. Commercial Service
Mark Patterson	VP, FedEx Corp.
2006	
Shanghai Brilliance Group	18 Executives from Shanghai, China
Prof. Ciaran Lynch	Tipperary Institute, Ireland
Prof. Gary Posser	Tipperary Institute, Ireland
Prof. Michael Ryan	Tipperary Institute, Ireland
Dr. Talib Issa Al-Salmi	Culturale Attache, Sultanate of Oman
Eric Peterson	CSIS, Washington, D.C.
Derrick Starling	Cummins Corp, Memphis, TN
Luis Zertuchi	Vitro Corp, Mexico
2007	
Prof. Xiaohong Chen	Sun-yat Sen Univ., Guangzho, China
Prof. Y. K. Bhushan	ICFAI Business School, India
Prof. Zang	Director, Hubei University, China
Prof. Lee	Director, Hubei University, China
Dr. Wu, Chuanxi	President, Hubei University, China
Prof. Iemoto	Osaka University, Japan
2008	
Dr. Francis Schillio	Ecole Du Management, Strasbourg, France

Dr. Iris Varner	Illinois State University
Dr. Len Trevino	Washington State University
Prof. Iemoto	Osaka University of Economics, Japan
Prof. Dean Ottmar Schneck	European Sch. of Bus., Reutlingen U., Germany
Prof. Dr. Hans Tummers	European Sch. of Bus., Reutlingen U., Germany
Prof. Dr. Titmar Hilpert	European Sch. of Bus., Reutlingen U., Germany
2009	
Masaaki Shirakawa	Governor, Bank of Japan
Prof. S Rajagopalan	S.P. Jain Center of Management, Singapore
Mr. Adaunio Senna Ganen	Consul General of Brazil
2010	
Denise Wood	VP, CIO, FedEx Corp.
Prof. Li Guihua	Nankai University, China
Wei Chen	Sunshine Enterprises, Inc.
Bill Fisher	Contract Warehouse Associations, Inc.
Don Harkleroad	Global Network Found., SIBF, Atlanta, GA
Lane Carrick	CEO, Sovereign Wealth Mgmt (Spkr, IMBA)
Emily Greer	Chief of Staff, ALSAC/St. Jude (Spkr, IMBA)
Jay Myers	CEO, Interactive Solutions (Spkr, IMBA Class)
Tom Kadien	SVP, International Paper (Spkr, IMBA Class)
Rob Fredericks	VP, Medtronic (Spkr, IMBA Class)
Gary Shorb	CEO, Methodist LeBonheur Health (Spkr, IMBA)
Tom Grimes	SVP, Mid-America Apartments (Spkr, IMBA)
Carolyn Hardy	CEO, Hardy Bottling (Spkr, IMBA Class)
J. R. (Pitt) Hyde	President, Pittco Mgmt. (Spkr, IMBA Class)
Doreen Edelman	Attorney, Baker Donelson (Spkr, IMBA Class)
Mark Luttrell	Sheriff, Shelby County, TN (Spkr, IMBA Class)
Brent Alvord	President, Lenny's Subs (Spkr, IMBA Class)
Jan Bouten	Partner, Innova (Spkr, IMBA Class)
Gary Henley	President, Wright Medical Tech. (Spkr, IMBA)
Mike Glenn	EVP Marketing, FedEx (Spkr, IMBA Class)
Mark Colombo	SVP, Marketing, FedEx (Spkr, IMBA Class)
2011	
Randy Walker	Oak Ridge National Laboratory
Jeff Shipley	CISCO
Tom Pigg	JSCC
Owen McCuster	Sonalyst, Inc.

Andrew Nell	FedEx
Tim Bailey	National Security Agency
Gary O'Neal & Joe Stewart	Dell
Bill Hagerty	Economic & Community Development, TN
Mark Colombo	SVP, Solutions & Digital Access (Spkr, IMBA)
Mike Sherman	Partner, MB Venture Partners (Spkr, IMBA Class)
Robert Carter	Exec. VP & CIO, FedEx Corp. (Spkr, IMBA)
2012	
Bettina S. Roberts	U.S. VP & General Manager - Great Southern Region, McDonald's USA (Spkr, IMBA Class)
Mary Day	Principal, Tradewind Group LLC (Spkr, IMBA)
Raymond Berglund	Sr. Dir. of Finance, Smith & Nephew (Spkr, IMBA)
Fred Towler	International Paper (Spkr, IMBA Class)
Ruchin Kansal	Sr. Manager, Deloitte Consulting (Spkr, IMBA)
Pitt Hyde	Pittco Management (Spkr, IMBA Class)

International Business Council of the Greater Memphis Chamber of Commerce

The International Business Council of the Greater Memphis Chamber of Commerce brings together businesses interested in facilitating the growth of international trade and foreign direct investment in Memphis; educating Memphis businesses in conducting business on an international basis; driving economic development through interaction with foreign organizations; and accomplishing this with the help of Memphians with a keen understanding of international business. There are two evening receptions and an educational series presented by the International Business Council each year.

U.S. Department of Commerce - Export Assistance Center

One of dozens of offices run by the U.S. Department of Commerce providing advice and expertise to small businesses on how to export one's products. There are export assistance centers in about 100 American cities and in 80 other countries. Each U.S. Export Assistance Center is staffed by professionals from the SBA, the U.S. Department of Commerce, the U.S. Export-Import Bank, and other public and private organizations. Together, their mission is to provide the help you need to compete in today's global marketplace. The U.S. Export Assistance Center is a one-stop shop, designed to provide export assistance for small- or medium-sized business.

U.S. Commercial Service

The U.S. Commercial Service is the trade promotion arm of the U.S. Department of Commerce's International Trade Administration. U.S. Commercial Service trade professionals in over 100 U.S. cities and in more than 75 countries help U.S. companies get started in exporting or increase sales to new global markets.

Society of International Business Fellows

Founded in 1981, the Society of International Business Fellows (SIBF) is a non-profit business association offering access to an influential network of members and their collective international contacts; a variety of educational programs focused on international commerce and culture; the opportunity to give back through SIBF's Global Network Foundation; and the camaraderie and shared experiences of lifelong friendships. Members are active internationally and share the belief that a keen understanding of history, culture and geopolitics is critical to success in today's global business environment.

Success in today's marketplace is increasingly impacted by the phenomenon of globalization. Through educational programs and access to the world's foremost speakers, SIBF offers members an unparalleled strategic advantage to enhance and support their international business success. Programs have been held all over the world from Cuba to Thailand to Turkey, Montenegro to Mexico and all points between.

Relationships are the cornerstone of SIBF. Members have access to a local group of trusted peers as well as a worldwide network of influential contacts. The sharing of educational experiences and business best practices leads to invaluable relationships with other high-level executives. Through involvement in local, national and international initiatives, members build enduring relationships.

Memphis in May (MIM) International Festival

International Education Program of MIM: Creating a Global Classroom. The Memphis in May International Festival believes that education is an integral part of any festival. International awareness is at the core of the Memphis in May International Festival's commitment to the education of the Mid-South community, children and adults alike. Each year, the area's youth immerse themselves in the culture of our honored country through our curriculum guide, student competitions, international exchanges, and more.

While Memphis in May International Festival fosters the education of an entire community, our focus begins on the youth of the area. Memphis in May's goal: by the time a student graduates from high school, they will have had the opportunity to experience the customs and cultures of 13 different countries from around the world. Each year, Memphis in May accomplishes this goal through an extensive and diverse youth education program offered to every student and school in the Memphis and Shelby County area, including over 200 city and county schools, dozens of private schools, and a very active home school association.

Our award-winning education program would not be possible without the support and assistance of corporate partners and our international friends. Every year, *The Commercial Appeal,* Memphis' major daily newspaper, graciously prints and binds the festival's Curriculum Guide. Educators, artists, and writers in the local community come together and give their time to judge the Festival's numerous educational contests. Memphis in May International Festival has been able to build relationships in the community that allow the education program to continue to grow, thrive and benefit the entire community.

The student Exchange Program of MIM has also been key to the international celebration. The Student Exchange Program provides selected students and chaperon with an all-expense paid, once-in-a-lifetime opportunity to experience the culture of our honored country. Each year students are selected based on communication skills, grades, and community service. Each spring, a group of Memphis in May exchange students travels to Memphis in May's honored country for 10-12 days - enough time to give students a true taste of the country without interfering with their school year. All students stay with selected host families in the host country, attend classes at a host high school, visit famous monuments and landmarks, and experience a different culture firsthand. Prior to travel, preparation sessions are held with emphasis on orientation to the culture and country the students will visit, along with travel details and student responsibilities as Memphis in May ambassadors. The program is offered at no charge to the students or accompanying chaperons. Selected students are encouraged to share their experiences and new knowledge of the honored country with local school and community groups after their return. The Memphis in May Student Exchange Program is open to any 11th or 12th grade student enrolled in a public, private, or authorized home school within Shelby County; the student must be enrolled from August to June of the current school year. Each year Memphis in May brings distinguished guests from the honored country, experts in their respective fields, to share their professional experiences with the business audiences of Memphis.

Dr. Ben Kedia served on the Board of Directors of Memphis in May for three years.

Academy of International Business (AIB)

Dr. Kedia served as Program Chair, Vice President and President of the Academy of International Business-U.S. Southwest.

AIB is the leading association of scholars and specialists in the field of international business. Established in 1959, today, AIB has 3396 members in 77 different countries around the world. Members include scholars from the leading global academic institutions as well consultants, researchers, government and NGO representatives. We welcome individuals and institutions from developing countries, newly industrialized countries, as well as industrialized countries to join AIB. The Academy also has sixteen chapters established around the world to facilitate networking as well as the facilitation and exchange of knowledge at a more local level.

Academy of Management

Dr. Kedia served as Division Chair, Program Chair, and Doctoral Consortium Chair of the International Management Division of the Academy of Management.

The Academy of Management is a leading professional association for scholars dedicated to creating and disseminating knowledge about management and organizations. Founded in 1936 by two professors, the Academy of Management is the oldest and largest scholarly management association in the world. Today, the Academy is the professional home for 18,113 members from 111 nations.

Academy members are scholars at colleges, universities, and research institutions, as well as practitioners with scholarly interests from business, government, and not-for-profit organizations. The Academy of Management is guided by the vision to inspire and enable a better world through our scholarship and teaching about management and organizations and the mission to build a vibrant and supportive community of scholars by markedly expanding opportunities to connect and explore ideas. The Academy's 24 professional divisions and interest groups promote excellence in the established management disciplines that they represent.

Pacific Asian Consortium for International Business Education and Research (PACIBER)

PACIBER was created in 1988 as a consortium of 27 leading universities dedicated to bridging the gap by establishing linkages to promote international business education, research and exchange of information among faculty and students. PACIBER stands as a forum for the exchange of ideas where members can network and learn from one another. Through faculty exchanges and other mutually beneficial alliances, member universities can raise the levels of their business education programs to world class standards.

Consortium for Undergraduate International Business Education

CUIBE is a consortium of schools and universities that have undergraduate International Business programs. The primary objectives of the consortium are to provide its members with an opportunity to benchmark their programs against other member schools and facilitate sharing of best practices in International Business education.

Governor's School for International Studies (U of Memphis)

The Governor's School for International Studies (GSIS) provides a four week immersion into the world around us, including global cultures, languages and perspectives. Moreover, the program provides a rigorous introduction to the field of International Studies, including six credit hours of college coursework.

GSIS offers the opportunity to see far beyond the boundaries of the state and explore and assess the economic, historical and cultural relationships of several countries. Students discuss world issues with political and business leaders. Also they develop their own conclusions and solutions to problems faced by third world nations. Through courses, projects, lectures and discussions, students discover the complexities of international independence. The goals of the curriculum are:

- To develop problem solving skills related to global events
- To develop an appreciation and understanding of other cultures
- To enrich the critical thinking process with an international perspective
- To provide intensive instruction and research experiences in the political, economic and social systems of the world.

Formal courses, supervised individual and group projects, and experimental learning techniques is part of the program. Seminars led by prominent international, national, and local scholars, statesmen, and business executives allow students to gain extensive insight into international relations. In-depth study of languages, customs, lifestyles, and cultures of various nationalities is an integral part of the learning experience.

Foreign Languages and Literature Department (U of Memphis)

Foreign language study is central to the mission of the University of Memphis to educate its students for a diverse and global society. With today's levels of foreign trade, tourism, international business, and international relations, knowledge of other languages and an understanding of other cultures is a must. The Department of Foreign Languages and Literatures offers not only basic language instruction, but also offers advanced work in foreign literatures, linguistics, culture, civilization, and business.

Instruction is offered in 12 languages: Arabic, Chinese, French, German, Greek, Hebrew, Italian, Japanese, Latin, Portuguese, Russian, and Spanish. Students may complete a major with a single-language concentration in French, German, Japanese, Latin, or Spanish, or a two or three-language concentration combining any of the following: Chinese, French, German, Greek, Italian, Japanese, Latin, Portuguese, Russian, and Spanish.

Annual Foreign Language Fair: Memphis-area high school students demonstrate their knowledge of foreign languages and cultures at the annual Foreign Language Fair held at the University of Memphis. The students compete in a variety of contests, including poetry recitation, writing, costumes, folk dance, drama, music, projects, crafts, and a "Culture Bowl." Competitive events are conducted in French, German, Japanese, Latin, and Spanish. The fair is sponsored by the University's Department of Foreign Languages and Literatures.

Confucius Institute (U of Memphis)

The Confucius Institute is a public institute with the goal of promoting Chinese language and culture and supporting local Chinese teaching internationally through affiliated Confucius Institutes around the globe.

Confucius Institutes are established by the China National Office for Teaching Chinese as a Foreign Language, headquartered in Beijing. The University of Memphis is home to the only Confucius Institute in the state of Tennessee and the first in the Mid-South.

In conjunction with its partner institution, Hubei University in China, the Confucius Institute at the University of Memphis promotes understanding of the Chinese language and culture among the people of the United States, develops friendly relations between the U. S. and China, accelerates the expansion of multiculturalism, and provides opportunities for students studying the Chinese language.

The Confucius Institute at the University of Memphis occupies the entire 11th floor of Wilder Tower beginning in early 2009. A statue of Confucius, designed by a local artist, greets visitors to the Institute.

The Confucius Institute at the University of Memphis is closely affiliated with the University's new Asian Studies and International Trade program, whose aim is to provide students with the critical combination of skills that an increasing number of companies seek: international business knowledge, foreign language proficiency, cultural sensitivity and experience abroad. The program was created by an anonymous $1 million donation to the University.

The University of Memphis has long participated in educational exchanges with a number of universities in China, including Hubei University, its partner in the Confucius Institute.

A pilot institute was established in Tashkent, Uzbekistan, in June 2004. The first Confucius Institute opened on November 21, 2004 in Seoul, Korea.

International Education Week (U of Memphis)

International Education Week is a joint initiative of the U.S. Department of State and the U.S. Department of Education. Its aim is to promote programs that prepare Americans to live and work in a global environment and to attract future leaders from abroad to study, learn, and exchange experiences in the United States.

University sponsors are the Student Activities Council, Phi Beta Delta, the International Student Association, the Center for International Programs and Services, the Wang Center for International Business, the Fogelman College of Business and Economics, and the College of Communication and Fine Arts.

Center for International Programs and Services (U of Memphis)

The Center for International Programs and Services is a multi-faceted operation with several offices meeting a variety of needs for the University, starting with the International Student Services staff, who monitor and maintain federal compliance for the university relative to Homeland Security regulations, as well as assisting approximately 1000 foreign scholars and prospective international applicants to the University of Memphis.

Highly visible on campus, the Study Abroad Program is excitedly serving an increasing number of Memphis students going overseas to enhance their education, and our Intensive English for Internationals program is the largest program of its kind in Tennessee, improving the language skills of both resident and visiting non-native speakers.

The Center for International Programs and Services enhances greater international understanding through funding of programs and faculty travel. The Center for International Programs and Services is critically important to the global participation required for the future of Memphis, the Mid-South, and the United States.

The University of Memphis study abroad programs are designed to provide students with the opportunity to combine a rigorous academic program with a cross-cultural learning experience that is not available in the United States. The Center offers semester, academic year and summer programs in over 160 institutions in 40 countries to meet the diverse needs of the U of M student population. The Study Abroad Scholarship is designed to encourage students to study abroad. The University awards scholarships to academically talented students who plan to enroll in an exchange or other approved program in a foreign country. Priority will be given to students in programs which promote the development of international competency, which is defined as the acquisition of a foreign language or extended experience in a foreign culture.

IMBA CLASS of 1995: First Row: Stephen DiLossi, Heidi Wysong, Laurie McSwiggin, Karine Christin, Marion Sorrells, Yen-Chin Chu, Nicole Billeaud, and Pat Taylor (staff). Second Row: Mei-Ying Chuang, Linda Taneff, Jonathan Ballinger, Susanne Nilson, and Dr. Irene Duhaime. Third Row: Dr. Ben Kedia, Tonna Bruce, Ben Clark, Patrick Wilkerson, Roger Walters, Robert Bagby, John Bass, and Jeffrey Whitworth. Fourth Row: Todd Blowers, William White, Waiel Abukhaled, David Edwards, and Dr. Otis Baskin.

IMBA CLASS of 1996: Seated: Emily Roberts, Nichaya Sukpanich, Dianna Bronson, Kerith Wilkes, Serena Moore, Julie Jenkins, Miriam Neill, Melissa Martin, and Katrina Taylor. Standing: Solongowa Borzigin, Padmanaban Subbaraman, Kevin Wood, Fred Jordan, Frank Holloman, Richard Waits, Sanford Shefsky, Zhenyu Yao, Nicolas Von Gunten, Sam Friedman, Sean Click, Tsunehiko Ishikawa, Wisit Wichayacoop, Scarlett Karas, and Sarah Peterson. Not pictured: Alexander Dolaptchiev and Max Painter.

IMBA CLASS OF 1997: Front row: Lei Geng, Walker Carter, Amanda Sheffield, Michelle Alonso, Sangita Yadav, Heather Murray, Jacqueline Broussard, Lara Babaoglu, Voralax Siriratchuwong, Amy Crawford, Soren Rasmussen, Valerie Daffin, and Gregory Steiner. Back Row: David Parker, Vladimir Lisenko, Quynk-Hju Camella Vu, Juan Sacoto, Ivan Irizarry, Mark Geismar, and Ramesh Balakrishnan. Not pictured: Ajay Chawdhry and Srikant Chellappa.

IMBA CLASS OF 1998: Front row: Brenda Schneider, Lee Wiggins, Jacqueline Renaud, Cynthia Meeks, Elizabeth Perry, Woraporn Rattanasampan, Alejandro Ordonez, and Yongmei Hu. Back Row: Jeremy Nelson, Yongbiao Chang, James Cook, Mark Mathison, Donald Stuart Hurst, Jon Carnes, Vincent Gachet-Varlet, Wei Chen, Nathaniel West, Jason Cox, Joseph Anthamatten, Suraj Shrestha, and Curtis Bickers.

IMBA CLASS OF 1999: Front row: Tsunhui Jen, Celine Loeuille, Kornwara Yongrithikul, Sumaddhaya Boonchokhiranmedha, Anne Blewett, Kristin Counts, Annie Cox, Yi Li, and Yoadan Tilahun. Middle Row: Brandon Barry Gee, Peiyu Wang, Brett Ragghianti, Ivan Figueredo, Adolfo Errazuriz, Jennyfer Immanuel, Karen Starkey, Michael Stadler, and Ralph Shaffer. Back Row: Steven Worthington, Anurag Babbar, Jonathan Reid Markle, Jean-Marc Colombel. Alan Shane Helm, Sumit Agarwal, John Luke Perkins, Jeffrey Nelson, Adam Bishop, and John Collins. Not pictured: Abhijit Ahluwalia.

IMBA CLASS OF 2000: Front Row: Jean-Yves Piton, Anna Kalibekova, Maoyun Wang, Shuk Yi Lui, Mei Yee Chui, Nitita Tangjaturonrusmee, Zhijuan Xu, Isabel Melo, Natalia Llamazares, and Carlos Avila. Standing: Erming Tuo, Kimberly McFadden, Matthew Taylor, Bum Joon Ahn, Ramon Ernesto Rivera, Ramon Aguillon, Roberto Leao, Patrick Fisher, Mary Ellen Patton, Carlos Murgas, Nicholas Getaz, Wendy Villafana, Gvido Lilje, and Alexander Grayes. Not pictured: Amit Doshi and Ekaterina Mechitbayeva Fabel.

IMBA CLASS OF 2001: Front row: Olivia Kelly, Tetyana Kostomakha (Bryan), Takako Saiin, Sandra Groschwitz, and Mei Yang. Middle Row: Phillip Devasia, Jared Hemming, Gregory Pauken, Iwona Drozdek, Rhea Lynn Baker, Carolin Voegele, Marcia Steel, Heather Robinette, and Rocio Pelayo. Third row: Dr. Ben Kedia, George (Trey) Anding, Edwin Wang, Jesus Parilla-Recuero, Ray (Trip) Owen, Nirav Momaya, Jonathan Maples, Michal Stepniak, Pranoop Sandhu, Ranjit Banthia, Jerry Miele, and David Walker.

IMBA CLASS OF 2002: Front row: Hiromi Sakashita, Rebekah Anderson, Bland Murphy, Stephanie Hamilton, and Geetika Bansal. Middle row: Nikhil Pande, Ejineiwebi Nwaobi, Frank Masiello, Allison Manning, Andrea Klevan, Mary Ann Gordon, and Lisa Orsland. Back row: Dr. Ben Kedia, Kevin Hallquist, Allison Kern, Jared Barney, Brian Britt, Michael Hartmann, and Roger Bynum.

IMBA CLASS OF 2003: Front row: Yishan Gong, Alexandria Benoit, and Katja Huste. Back row: Carlos Araujo, Shavkat Sultanbekov, Yelena Domashova, Roger Smeltzer, and Marc Sexton.

IMBA CLASS of 2004: Front row: April Duncan, Luan Nation, Anya Lukyanova, Nisha Dave, Youshen Yang, and Brigette Guimond. Middle row: Heather Reed, LaKeshia Rhyne, Shin-Woong Kim, Ruth Curtis, Dr. Ben Kedia, Yun Kim, and Daniela Hlasna. Back row: Ray (Todd) Gaddis, Saurabh Sarkar, Paramvir Sharma, Aymeric Martinoia, Charles Lovings, and Christopher Thompson.

IMBA CLASS OF 2005: Front row: Brett Norman, Xinyan, Wang, Nathan Herr, and Erin Schierer. Second row: Bonnie Mallalieu, Uwe Gneiting, and Limeng Wu and Joseph Litherland. Third row: Leiah Miller, Michael Halper, and Cedric Kolter. Back row: IMBA Staff: Dottie Shelton, Dr. Ben Kedia, Tonna Bruce, and Pat Taylor.

IMBA CLASS OF 2006: Front row: Eric Wooten, Jie Wu, Brian Jones, Samiyah Sattar, and Kelli Kirk. Second row: Mary Ann Portt, Najada Bedini, Sara McWilliams, and William Ryan Gatgens. Third row: Monika Zub, Nikolaus Turner, Svetlana Ganea, and Austin Sledd. Fourth row: IMBA Staff: Tonna Bruce, Dr. Ben Kedia, and Pat Taylor.

IMBA CLASS OF 2007: Front row: Kathryn Newell, Meredith Broadhead, Kosha Mehta, Erica Smith, and Jessica Mohon. Second row: Joshua Wright, Jakub Novak, and Daniel Christian. (Not pictured: Caroline Goodman)

IMBA CLASS OF 2008: Front row: Andrea Suarez, Sneha Kollepara, and Anna Coplon. Second row: John Hassell, Scott Smith, and Sara Williams. Third row: David Comas, Jason De Freitas, and Michael Lyons. Fourth row: IMBA Staff: Dr. Ben Kedia, Dr. P.K. Jain, Barbara Stevenson, and Pat Taylor.

IMBA CLASS OF 2009: Front row: Phleacia Cagle, Erin Redden, Sarah Maurice, and Pat Taylor (Staff). Second row: Archana Jain, Emily Brickell, Jackson Wadsworth, Ryan Weakley, and Vladimir Ambartsoumian. Third row: Mama Younousse Dieng, Brian Beall, Allen Godsey, Di Wang, and Dr. P.K. Jain. Fourth row: Dr. Ben Kedia, Papa Ndiaye, Michael Morawski, Namit Kedia, Daniel Bradford, Jeffrey Smith, Zachary Stafford, and Barbara Stevenson (Staff)

IMBA CLASS OF 2010: Front row: Sara Tanhaee, David Fihn, Flavia Hite, and Courtney Carr Harlow. Second row: Shih-Ting Huang, Angela Meduri, Dennis Morgan, Russell (Gary) Boxill, and Pat Taylor (Staff). Third row: Barbara Stevenson (Staff), Matthew Long, Sean Kerins, Bradley Pope, Ashley Wallace, and Dr. Ben Kedia.

IMBA CLASS OF 2011: First row: Dr. Ben Kedia, Amelia Akpotu, Bethany Woodall, and Kathryn Murphy. Second row: Oksana Ambrozyak, Changjuan Li, and Carey Vitrano. Third row: Charles Cackler, Yingying Song, Ramona Popescu Hong, and Seema Kedia. Fourth row: Pat Taylor (Staff), Clifford Kuntzman, Nathan Moore, and Mark Wlodawski. Not pictured: Kirill Pervun.

IMBA CLASS OF 2012: First Row: Sonal Kukreja, Yuan Lu, and Rachel Yvonne Patterson; Second Row: Kathleen Lauren Adgent, Paige Kathryn Bigham, Pat Taylor (Staff); Third Row: Matthew Glenn Farmer and Bjorn Latvala Bjorholm; Dr. Balaji Krishnan, Dr. Ben Kedia. Not pictured: Fang Lei

Class	Student Name	Company Name	Location	Track
1995	N. Billeaud	Smith & Nephew	Orthez, France	French
1995	M. Sorrells	Smith & Nephew	Orthez, France	French
1995	L. Taneff	Kazed S.A	Montpellier, France	French
1995	J. Whitworrth	Kazed S.A	Montpellier, France	French
1995	B. Clark	Magnet-Schultz	Memmingen,Germany	German
1995	S. Nilson	STECA	Memmingen,Germany	German
1995	P. Wilkerson	Hans Kolb Wellpappe	Memmingen,Germany	German
1995	W. Abukhaled	Industria del Alcali	Monterrey, Mexico	Spanish
1995	T. Blowers	State Govt of Nuevo Leon	Monterrey, Mexico	Spanish
1995	D. Edwards	Protexa/Pepsi Co.	Monterrey, Mexico	Spanish
1995	L. Tirado	Protexa/Texaco	Monterrey, Mexico	Spanish
1995	R. Walters	Buckman Labs	Champinas, Brazil	Spanish
1995	W. White	Am Cham	Monterrey, Mexico	Spanish
1995	K. Christin	Wang's International	Memphis, TN	US
1996	S. Click	Mutelle Force Sud	Montpellier, France	French
1996	A. Dolaptchiev	IMAJE	Bourg-Les, France	French
1996	F. Holloman	CEFPF	Paris, France	French
1996	S. Moore	SICAME	Pompadour, France	French
1996	N. V. Gunten	Smith & Nephew	Orthez, France	French
1996	K. Wilkes	Mutuelle Force Sud	Montpellier,France	French
1996	E. Roberts	Hypo Bank	Munich, Germany	German
1996	S. Shefsky	Robert Bosch GmbH	Munich, Germany	German
1996	K. Taylor	F. Willich GmbH	Dortmund,Germany	German
1996	K. Wood	Bertelsmann,GmbH	Gutersloh,Germany	German
1996	D. Bronson	MS Carriers/Trans. Easo	Monterrey, Mexico	Spanish
1996	S. Friedman	Am Cham, Mexico	Mexico City, Mexico	Spanish
1996	J. Jenkins	Am cham Guadalajara	Gaudalajara,Mexico	Spanish
1996	F. Jordan	Industria del Alcali	Monterrey, Mexico	Spanish
1996	S. Karas	York-Mexico	Monterrey, Mexico	Spanish
1996	M. Martin	Cerveceria Cuauhtemoc	Monterrey, Mexico	Spanish
1996	M. Painter	Smith & Nephew	Mexico City, Mexico	Spanish
1996	S. Peterson	MS Carriers/Trans. Easo	Monterrey, Mexico	Spanish
1996	R. Waits,II	Am Cham-Mexico	Monterrey, Mexico	Spanish
1996	S. Borzigin	Sedgwick James	Memphis, TN	U.S
1996	T. Ishikawa	Wright Medical Tech.	Memphis, TN	U.S
1996	M. Neill	Wang's International	Memphis, TN	U.S
1996	P. Subbaraman	Thomas & Betts	Memphis, TN	U.S
1996	N. Sukpanich	Maybelline,Inc	Memphis, TN	U.S
1996	W. Wichayacoop	Brother Industries	Memphis, TN	U.S

Class	Student Name	Company Name	Location	Track
1997	L. Babaoglu	AXIOHM	Montrouge, France	French
1997	W. Carter	Smith & Nephew	Orthez, France	French
1997	V. Daffin	Mutuelle Force Sud	Montepellier, France	French
1997	H. Murray	J.F Hillebrand	Beaune-Vignolles, Fr.	French
1997	C. Quynh-Nhu Vu	Eurasante	Lille, France	French
1997	S. Yadav	Eurasante	Lille, France	French
1997	M. Alonso	Robert Bosch GmbH	Leinfelden, Germany	German
1997	G. Steiner	Bertelsmann,GmbH	Gutersloh, Germany	German
1997	J. B.-Taylor	MS Carriers/Trans. Easo	San Mateo, Mexico	Spanish
1997	I. Irizarry	Industria del Alcali	Garcia, Mexico	Spanish
1997	D. Parker	La Veneciana,SA	Madrid, Spain	Spanish
1997	A. Sheffield	Smith & Nephew	Mexico City, Mexico	Spanish
1997	R. Balakrishnan	Dobbs International	Memphis, TN	U.S
1997	A. Chawdhry	Federal Express	Memphis, TN	U.S
1997	S. Chellappa	Cummins Engines Co	Memphis, TN	U.S
1997	V. Lisenko	International Paper	Memphis, TN	U.S
1997	S. Rasmussen	Sofamor Danek	Memphis, TN	U.S
1997	J. Sacoto	Sedgwick James Inc	Memphis, TN	U.S
1997	V. Siriratchuwong	United Techn.,Carrier	Memphis, TN	U.S
1998	M. Mathison	Babcock & Wilcox	Beijing, China	Chinese
1998	J. Carnes	Smith & Nephew	Orthez, France	French
1998	J. Cox	Mutuelle Force Sud	Montpellier, France	French
1998	J. Renaud	C.R.R.P	Lille, France	French
1998	L. Wiggins	Federal Express	Brussels, Belgium	French
1998	J. Cook,Jr	VEW Energie	Dortmund, Germany	German
1998	V. Gachet-Varlet	Jon Vaillant GmbH	Remscheid, Germany	German
1998	J. Nelson	Pavone Inform. Systeme	Paderborn, Germany	German
1998	E. Perry	Robert Bosch GmbH	Stuttgart, Germany	German
1998	N. West	VEW Eurotest	Dortmund, Germany	German
1998	J. Anthamatten	Smith & Nephew	Mexico City, Mexico	Spanish
1998	C. Bickers	IBM	Guadalajara, Mexico	Spanish
1998	S. Hurst	Industria del Alcali	Monterrey, Mexico	Spanish
1998	C. Meeks	Vitro Groupo	Monterrey, Mexico	Spanish
1998	B. Schneider	Vitro Groupo	Monterrey, Mexico	Spanish
1998	Y. Chang	Brookfield	Memphis, TN	U.S
1998	W. Chen	Sedgwick	Memphis, TN	U.S
1998	Y. Hu	Smith & Nephew	Memphis, TN	U.S
1998	A. Ordonez	Sedgwick	Memphis, TN	U.S
1998	W. Rattanasampan	Sofamor Danek	Memphis, TN	U.S

Class	Student Name	Company Name	Location	Track
1999	A. Bishop	Shenzhen United Bus.	Shenzhen, China	Chinese
1999	A. Cox	A.O Smith Water Heater	Nanjing, China	Chinese
1999	A. Blewett	Smith & Nephew	Orthez, France	French
1999	B. Gee	AVS Azur	Perols, France	French
1999	L. Perkins	Schweppes	Paris, France	French
1999	S. Helm	Misselbeck Formenbau	Ingolstadt, Germany	German
1999	R. Shaffer	Servmark	Ingolstadt, Germany	German
1999	K. Starkey	Audi	Ingolstadt, Germany	German
1999	J. Collins	Smith & Nephew	Mexico City, Mexico	Spanish
1999	K. Counts	Thomas & Betts	Monterrey, Mexico	Spanish
1999	R. Markle	Vitro Groupo	Monterrey, Mexico	Spanish
1999	J. Nelson	Thomas & Betts	Monterrey, Mexico	Spanish
1999	B. Ragghianti	IBM	Guadalajara, Mexico	Spanish
1999	M. Stalder	Vitro Groupo	Monterrey, Mexico	Spanish
1999	S. Worthington	Alcatel Telecom	Madrid, Spain	Spanish
1999	S. Agarwal	Delta Beverage	Memphis, TN	U.S
1999	A. Ahluwalia	Sofamor Danek	Memphis, TN	U.S
1999	A. Babbar	Federal Express	Memphis, TN	U.S
1999	S. Beaver	Orgill Inc	Memphis, TN	U.S
1999	J-M. Colombel	BFI,Inc (a subs. of Avnet)	Memphis, TN	U.S
1999	A. Errazuriz	Thomas & Betts	Memphis, TN	U.S
1999	I. Figueredo	United Agri Products	Memphis, TN	U.S
1999	J. Imanuel	Sedgwick	Memphis, TN	U.S
1999	T. Jen	Sofamor Danek	Memphis, TN	U.S
1999	Y. Li	JMGR,Inc.	Memphis, TN	U.S
1999	C. Loeuille	Sofamor Danek	Memphis, TN	U.S
1999	Y. Tilahun	Sofamor Danek	Memphis, TN	U.S
1999	P. Wang	Memphis Group	Memphis, TN	U.S
1999	K. Yongrithikul	Dobbs International	Memphis, TN	U.S
2000	B.J Ahn	Sino World Sincerity Adv.	Beijing, China	Chinese
2000	N. Getaz	Chamber of Commerce	Greenoble, France	French
2000	A. Grayes	Servmark	Ingolstadt, Germany	German
2000	M. Taylor	Misslbeck	Ingolstadt, Germany	German
2000	P. Fisher	Smith & Nephew	Mexico City, Mexico	Spanish
2000	K. McFadden	Thomas & Betts	Monterrey, Mexico	Spanish
2000	C. Murgas	Varco-Pruden Buildings	Monterrey, Mexico	Spanish
2000	E. Patton	IBM	Jalisco, Mexico	Spanish
2000	W. Villafana	Trevino and Associates	Monterrey, Mexico	Spanish
2000	R. Aguillon	Cummins Powercare	Memphis, TN	U.S

Class	Student Name	Company Name	Location	Track
2000	A. Doshi	Delta Beverage	Memphis, TN	U.S
2000	A. Kalibekova	Smith & Nephew	Memphis, TN	U.S
2000	R. Leao	United Agri Products	Memphis,TN	U.S
2000	G. Lilje	The Pallet Factory	Memphis,TN	U.S
2000	N. Llamazares	United Agri Products	Memphis,TN	U.S
2000	S. Lui	Federal Express	Hongkong, China	U.S
2000	E. Fabel	Thomas & Betts	Memphis, TN	U.S
2000	I. Melo	Dobbs International	Memphis, TN	U.S
2000	J.-Y. Piton	Sofamor Danek	Memphis, TN	U.S
2000	R. Rivera	Varco-Pruden Buildings	Memphis, TN	U.S
2000	N. Tangjaturonrusmee	Sofamor Danek	Memphis, TN	U.S
2000	E. Tuo	Thomas & Betts	Memphis, TN	U.S
2000	M. Wang	Federal Express	Memphis, TN	U.S
2000	Z. Xu	Sofamor Danek	Memphis, TN	U.S
2001	E. Wong	A.O Smith Water Heater	Nanjing, China	Chinese
2001	G. Anding	Steelcase Stafor	Strasbourg, France	French
2001	R. L. Baker	Dauphin Affichage	Strasbourg, France	French
2001	Rocio Pelayo	Place Des Vosges	Strasbourg, France	French
2001	H. Robinette	Multiples	Strasbourg, France	French
2001	M. Steele	Altir Technologies	Strasbourg, France	French
2001	G. Pauken	Audi	Ingolstadt,Germany	German
2001	J. Maples	International Paper	Tokyo, Japan	Japanese
2001	D. Walker	VP Buildings	Monterrey, Mexico	Spanish
2001	R. Banthia	Pepsi Americas	Memphis, TN	U.S
2001	P. Devasia	Continental Traffic Sys.	Memphis, TN	U.S
2001	I. Drozdek	Leggett & Platt,Inc	Memphis, TN	U.S
2001	S.Groschwitz	Cummins,Inc	Memphis, TN	U.S
2001	T. Kostomakha	VP Buildings	Memphis, TN	U.S
2001	N. Momaya	Meritex Logistics	Memphis, TN	U.S
2001	J. Parrilla	Gategourmet	Memphis, TN	U.S
2001	T. Saiin	Cummins,Inc	Memphis, TN	U.S
2001	P. Sandhu	VP Buildings	Memphis, TN	U.S
2001	M. Stepniak	General Electric	Erie, PA	U.S
2001	C. Voegele	Thomas & Betts	Memphis, TN	U.S
2001	M. Yang	Carrier Corporation	Memphis, TN	U.S
2001	O. Kelly	Sonata Software Ltd	Bangalore, India	World Region
2001	J. Miele	WIPRO	Bangalore, India	World Region
2001	R. Owen	WIPRO	Bangalore, India	World Region
2002	F. Masiello	A.O. Smith Water Heater	Nanjing, China	Chinese

Class	Student Name	Company Name	Location	Track
2002	M. A. Gordon	Georgia Pacific	Strasbourg, France	French
2002	K. Hallquist	Millipore	Strasbourg, France	French
2002	J. Barney	Media Saturn	Ingolstadt, Germany	German
2002	R. Bynum	Messe Munchen GmbH	Ingolstadt,Germany	German
2002	M. Hartmann	BDO Consulting	Cologne, Germany	German
2002	A. Klevan	Messe Munchen GmbH	Ingolstadt,Germany	German
2002	A. Kern	Smith & Nephew	Tokyo, Japan	Japanese
2002	S. Hamilton	Grupo IMSA	Monterrey, Mexico	Spanish
2002	A. Manning	Cemex	Monterrey, Mexico	Spanish
2002	B. Murphy	Enertec	Monterrey, Mexico	Spanish
2002	E. Nwaobi	VP Buildings	Monterrey, Mexico	Spanish
2002	L. Orsland	Enertec	Monterrey, Mexico	Spanish
2002	G. Bansal	VP Buildings	Memphis, TN	U.S
2002	N. Pande	Gategourmet	Memphis, TN	U.S
2002	H. Sakashlta	Smith & Nephew	Memphis, TN	U.S
2002	B. Britt	Infosys	Bangalore, India	World Region
2003	Carlos Araujo	United Agri Products	Memphis, TN	U.S
2003	A. Benoit	Gategourmet	Memphis, TN	U.S
2003	Y. Domashova	VP Buildings	Memphis, TN	U.S
2003	Y. Gong	Cummins power care	Memphis, TN	U.S
2003	K. Huste	Sofamor Danek	Memphis, TN	U.S
2003	M. Sexton	Smith,Kline & Beechum	Munich, Germany	German
2003	R. Smeltzer	VP Buildings	Monterrey, Mexico	Spanish
2003	S. Sultanbekov	Dunavant Enterprises	Memphis, TN	U.S
2004	R. Curtis	Steritech,ECPS,S.A	Strasbourg, France	French
2004	B.Guimond	Destination Travel Agy.	Strasbourg, France	French
2004	C. Lovings	Leipa Company	Schrobenhausen, Ger.	German
2004	L. Nation	Leipa Company	Schrobenhausen, Ger.	German
2004	C.Thompson	Panasonic	Osaka, Japan	Japanese
2004	N. Dave	Cummins	Memphis, TN	U.S
2004	D. Hlasna	Cummins	Memphis, TN	U.S
2004	F. Kim	Coco Cola Enterprises	Memphis, TN	U.S
2004	Y. Kim	Gategourmet	Memphis, TN	U.S
2004	A. Lukyanova	Nike	Memphis, TN	U.S
2004	A. Martinoia	Aerospace Products Intl	Memphis, TN	U.S
2004	S. Sarkar	Medtronic	Memphis, TN	U.S
2004	P. Sharma	Cummins	Memphis, TN	U.S
2004	A. Thorsdottir	Morgan Keegan	Memphis, TN	U.S
2004	Y. Yang	Cummins	Memphis, TN	U.S

Class	Student Name	Company Name	Location	Track
2004	T. Gaddis	Garvan O'Doherty group	Derry, Ireland	World Region
2004	H. Reed	Perfecseal Limited	Derry, Ireland	World Region
2004	L. Rhyne	University of Ulster	Derry, Ireland	World Region
2005	J. Litherland	LORD,S.A	Mundolsheim, France	French
2005	L. Miller	Destination Travel Agency	Strasbourg, France	French
2005	C. Kolter	ALDI GmbH & Co	Geisenfield, Germany	German
2005	M. Halper	Panasonic	Osaka, Japan	Japanese
2005	B. Norman	Almidones, Mexicanos	Guadalajara, Mexico	Spanish
2005	B. Mallalieu	Cemex	Monterrey, Mexico	Spanish
2005	E. Schierer	Cemex	Monterrey, Mexico	Spanish
2005	A. Troy	Cemex	Monterrey, Mexico	Spanish
2005	U. Gneiting	Medtronic	Memphis, TN	U.S
2005	X. Wang	Mallory Alexander Lgsts	Memphis, TN	U.S
2005	L. Yu	Cummins	Memphis, TN	U.S
2005	N. Herr	Perfecseal Limited	Derry, Ireland	World Region
2005	D. Weaver	Federal Express	London, England	World Region
2006	S. McWilliams	Chamber of Commerce	Strasbourg, France	French
2006	E. Wooten	Panasonic	Osaka, Japan	Japanese
2006	R. Gatgens	Cemex	Monterrey, Mexico	Spanish
2006	A. Sledd	Federal Express	Monterrey, Mexico	Spanish
2006	N. Turner	Cemex	Monterrey, Mexico	Spanish
2006	N. Bedini	Medtronic	Memphis, TN	U.S
2006	S. Ganea	Medtronic	Memphis, TN	U.S
2006	J. Wu	Cummins	Memphis, TN	U.S
2006	M. Zub	Aerospace Products Intl	Memphis, TN	U.S
2006	B. Jones	University of Ulster	Derry, Ireland	World Region
2006	K. Kirk	NORIBIC	Derry, Ireland	World Region
2006	M. A. Portt	CRESCO	Derry, Ireland	World Region
2006	S. Sattar	University of Ulster	Derry, Ireland	World Region
2007	S. Voller	Council of Europe	Strasbourg, France	French
2007	E. Smith	ALDI GmbH & Co	Geisenfield, Germany	German
2007	J. Wright	Servmark	Munich, Germany	German
2007	D. Christian	Kurimoto	Osaka, Japan	Japanese
2007	R. Ausman	Glassfiber	Monterrey, Mexico	Spanish
2007	M. Broadhead	Federal Express	Monterrey, Mexico	Spanish
2007	K. Newell	Sigma Alimentos	Monterrey, Mexico	Spanish
2007	C. Goodman	Cummins	Memphis, TN	U.S
2007	K. Mehta	Cummins	Memphis, TN	U.S
2007	J. Novak	Autozone	Memphis, TN	U.S

Class	Student Name	Company Name	Location	Track
2008	J. Hasselle	KPMG	Munich,Germany	German
2008	M. Lyons, Jr.	Fujitsu	Osaka, Japan	Japanese
2008	D. Comas	Sapienta Consejeria	Monterrey, Mexico	Spanish
2008	S. Smith	Federal Express	Monterrey, Mexico	Spanish
2008	S. Williams	IUSACELL	Monterrey, Mexico	Spanish
2008	J. De Freitas	Medtronic	Memphis, TN	U.S
2008	S. Kollepara	FedEx	Memphis, TN	U.S
2008	A. Suarez	Cummins	Memphis, TN	U.S
2008	A. Coplan	Cresco Trust	Derry, Ireland	World Region
2009	V.Ambartsoumian	Kele, Inc.	Memphis, TN	U.S.
2009	B. Beall	Congressman Jo Bonner	Washington D.C.	Spanish
2009	D. Bradford	Fujitzu	Osaka, Japan	Japanese
2009	E. Brickell	EUREX Marketing	Germany	German
2009	P. Cagle	Edward Jones Invest.	Memphis, TN	World Region
2009	M. Dieng	Well Child	Memphis, TN	U.S.
2009	A. Godsey	Vesuvius Mexico	Monterrey, MX	Spanish
2009	A. Jain	Kele, Inc.	Memphis, TN	U.S.
2009	N. Kedia	Thyssen Krupp Elevators	Germantown, TN	U.S.
2009	P. Ndiaye	Aerospace Products Intl	Memphis, TN	U.S.
2009	S. Maurice	Verizon	Memphis, TN	World Region
2009	M. Morawski	Cargill	Memphis, TN	U.S.
2009	E. Redden	Alsace Intl	Strasbourg, France	French
2009	Z. Stafford	UPS	Memphis, TN	World Region
2009	J. Wadsworth	AutoZone	Memphis, TN	World Region
2009	D. Wang	CE-BIO	Olive Branch, MS	U.S.
2009	R. Weakley	Raymond James Invest.	Memphis, TN	World Region
2010	R. Boxill	Cummins	Memphis, TN	U.S.
2010	E. Czarra	U.S. Dept. of State	Paris, France	French
2010	D. Fihn	K. Osamu & Hashimoto's Tax	Osaka, Japan	Japanese
2010	C. C. Harlow	ALSAC-St. Jude	Memphis, TN	French
2010	F. Hite	Mallory Alexander	Memphis, TN	U.S.
2010	S-T. Huang	Outlets at Vicksburg	Vicksburg, MS	U.S.
2010	S. Kerins	Mercado Global	Panajachel, Guatemala	Spanish
2010	M. Long	Titan Indus.-Bangalore	Bangalore, India	World Region
2010	A. Meduri	Mark Merchandising-Avon	NYC, New York	World Region
2010	D. Morgan	ARES Systems Group	Vicksburg, MS	World Region
2010	B. Pope	Fujitsu	Osaka, Japan	Japanese
2010	S. Tanhaee	Marco	Monterrey, MX	Spanish
2010	A. Wallace	International Paper	Chile	Spanish

Class	Student Name	Company Name	Location	Track
2011	A. Akpotu	Kele, Inc.	Memphis, TN	French
2011	O. Ambroziak	Cummins, Inc.	Memphis, TN	U.S.
2011	C. Cackler	Waddell & Reed Finl Adv.	Memphis, TN	Spanish
2011	S. Kedia	FedEx	Memphis, TN	World Region
2011	C. Kuntzman	Reto Juvenil Internacional	Costa Rica	Spanish
2011	C. Li	Phia Salon	Columbus, OH	U.S.
2011	N. Moore	AutoZone	Memphis, TN	World Region
2011	K. Murphy	Dow Chemical	Midland, MI	World Region
2011	K. Pervun	Aginsky Consulting Grp.	Portland, OR	U.S.
2011	R. P. Hong	First TN Bank/Cummins	Memphis, TN	U.S.
2011	Y. Y. Song	FedEx/UBS Fin. Services	Memphis, TN	U.S.
2011	C. Vitrano	Celtic, Intl	Baton Rouge, LA	World Region
2011	M. Wlodawski	World Expo-Deloitte, Touche	Shanghai, China	Chinese
2011	B. Woodall	DHL Global Forwarding	Memphis, TN	World Region
2012	K. Adgent	FedEx	Memphis, TN	Spanish
2012	P. Bigham	Sole4Soul	Nashville, TN	Spanish
2012	B. Bjorholm	Nikkou Shoukai	Japan	Japanese
2012	M. Farmer	FedEx		German
2012	S. Kukreja	International Paper	Memphis, TN	U.S.
2012	F. Lei	UBS Financial Services	Memphis, TN	U.S.
2012	Y. Lu	FedEx	Memphis, TN	U.S.
2012	R. Patterson	NTT West	Osaka, Japan	Japanese
2012	J. Reese	FedEx	Memphis, TN	World Region
2012	S. Reese	FedEx	Memphis, TN	Chinese

CLASS	COMPANY OF EMPLOYMENT	CITY, STATE	COUNTRY
1996	Accuride	Evansville, IN	USA
1996	EMIDS	Nashville, TN	USA
1996	FedEx Services	Memphis, TN	USA
1996	Nashville State Community College	Nasville, TN	USA
1996	Pricewaterhouse Coopers	Boston, MA	USA
1996	Standard Chartered Bank	New York, NY	USA
1997	Finding Fosbury	Soborg	Denmark
1997	Pricewaterhouse Coopers, LLP	Kingsport, TN	USA
1998	Sunshine Enterprises	Memphis, TN	USA
1998	U.S. Drug Enforcement Admin.	Monterrey	Mexico
1998	Viking Range Corporation	Greenwood, MS	USA
1999	BP	Houston, TX	USA
1999	Colliers International	Nashville, TN	USA
1999	GE Energy	Frisco, TX	USA
1999	Panama Land Futures	Panama City	Panama
1999	The Clorox Company	Oakland, CA	USA
2000	Arcadia Corporation	Memphis, TN	USA
2000	FedEx Services	Monument, CO	USA
2000	Franklin Templeton	Brooklyn, NY	USA
2000	Medtronic	Memphis, TN	USA
2000	Xonka	Guadalajara	Mexico
2001	Accenture	Chicago, IL	USA
2001	Dish Hospitality	Mumbai	India
2001	Explora Chile, S.A.	Santiago	Chile
2001	FedEx Trade Networks	Memphis, TN	USA
2001	Goodrich	San Diego, CA	USA
2001	Med Trans Corporation	Lewisville, TX	USA
2002	Deview Electronics	Dallas, TX	USA
2002	Diebold, Inc	Greensboro, NC	USA
2002	FedEx Services	Memphis, TN	USA
2002	Opin Kerfi Ehf.	Reykjavik	Iceland
2002	Perceptive Software	Liberty, MO	USA
2003	FedEx Services	Memphis, TN	USA
2003	FTN Financial / First TN Bank	New York, NY	USA
2003	Vision Commercial Real Estate	Bedford, TX	USA
2005	BridgePoint Medical	Irvine, CA	USA
2005	The Boeing Company	Seattle, WA	USA
2006	Caesars Entertainment	Las Vegas, NV	USA
2006	Canadian Tire Corporation	Toronto, ON	Canada
2006	Constellation Energy	Baltimore, MD	USA
2006	Intermundo Media LLC	Boulder, CO	USA
2007	FedEx Services	Memphis, TN	USA
2007	International Paper	Memphis, TN	USA
2008	Genco/ATC	Memphis, TN	USA
2009	Methodist Le Bonheur Healthcare	Memphis, TN	USA
2010	AutoZone	Memphis, TN	USA
2010	Paychex /Import/Export Start- Up	Memphis, TN	USA
2011	FedEx Services	Memphis, TN	USA
2011	Nike	Memphis, TN	USA

AUGUSTINE LADO was born and raised in Sudan. Educated at the University of Khartoum, Lado came to the United States in 1986 to earn his master's degree at Arkansas State and PhD in strategic business management the University of Memphis in 1992. Lado joined the Clarkson Business School faculty in 2002. Lado's research expertise lies in global business strategy: how companies can successfully navigate the pitfalls of "going global" through savvy leadership, organizational structure, information technology, and strategic alliances and partnerships. "But even the best corporate structure and supply-chain software in the world doesn't mean much if it's not implemented by the right people, the right staffing," says Lado. The knowledge, skills and cultural understanding that make up the core competencies of a business are embedded in "human systems." In Lado's Global Business Strategy class, students work in groups to develop a business plan and make a winning pitch to would-be investors. The students are challenged to design products, production methods and supply-chain networks that reflect the economic, environmental and social concerns in emerging economies such as Brazil, Russia, India and China.

SUKONO SOEBEKTI obtained the Doctoral Degree in Management at the University of Memphis in 1995. He holds an engineering degree from Bandung Institute of Technology, Indonesia, the leading institute of technology in the country. His MBA degree was from The University of Southern California – IBEAR Program. In 1998 he became the fourth President of PPM Institute of Management in Jakarta, the largest management education and development institute in Indonesia. He successfully led the institution in the hard times during the deep Asian Economic Crisis in 1998. In 2000, he became the first Chairman of the board of management of IICD (the Indonesian Institute for Corporate Directorship). IICD, which main mission is to internalize good corporate governance practices in Indonesia was founded by Mr Soebekti, together with 11 other colleagues from prominent universities in Indonesia. At the moment, IICD is being nominated by the IFC and the Global Corporate Governance Forum as one of the Good Corporate Governance Center of Excellence representing the Asia Pacific region. He resides in Jakarta with his wife, Happy, two children and one granddaughter.

ANANDA MUKHERJI is a Professor of Management at Texas A&M International University in Laredo, Texas, USA. He joined the university in 1998. He completed his Ph.D. in Business Administration from The University of Memphis, USA, in 1998. His dissertation chair was Dr. Ben Kedia and the topic was "Internal capabilities and external relationships: Their impact on international strategy, control, and performance." Earlier, he had completed his masters in Management and Industrial Relations from Xavier Labour Relations Institute, India, in 1979 and obtained his B.A. in Economics (Honours) from St. Xavier's College, India, in 1977. His research interests are in strategic management, entrepreneurship, competitive strategies, international business, risk and return, and agency theory. His research has been published in *Competitiveness Review, International Business Review, Journal of Business Research, Journal of Business Strategies, Journal of Managerial Issues, Journal of Socio-Economics, Journal of World Business,* and *Management International Review,* among others. He also regularly presents at the conferences of the Academy of Management and the American Society for Competitiveness.

PAULA DANSKIN ENGLIS is Professor of Management at the Campbell School of Business, Berry College and is Research Fellow at the Dutch Institute for Knowledge Intensive Entrepreneurship (Nikos) at the University of Twente, The Netherlands. Dr. Englis received a Bachelor of Science in Economics with honors and a Master in Business Administration from the University of Tennessee at Chattanooga. She earned her Ph.D. in Business Administration from the University of Memphis in 2000. Dr. Englis' research focuses on entrepreneurship and knowledge management with an international emphasis including application in born global firms and family businesses. Articles based on her research have been published in a number of leading journals including *Academy of Management Review, Business Horizons, Entrepreneurship Theory & Practice, Entrepreneurial Executive, Family Business Review, Journal of Knowledge Management, Journal of Small Business Management, Journal of World Business* and *Management International Review.* Dr. Englis is also chair of the Department of Management. She founded and heads the Entrepreneurship Program at Berry College.

CLAY DIBRELL is an Associate Professor of Management at The University of Mississippi. He earned his Ph.D. from The University of Memphis in 2000 where he majored in Strategic Management and minored in International Business. His research is at the intersection of strategy and international business with a focus on the role of entrepreneurs and families in business processes and the competitiveness of firms in global markets. His studies have examined strategies and processes related to firms' competitiveness in different contexts (e.g., transition economies) and industries (e.g., natural resource) and entrepreneurial behaviors (e.g., innovativeness) in small- to medium-sized firms. His research has been published in leading academic journals including *Entrepreneurship Theory & Practice, Journal of Small Business Management, Family Business Review, Journal of Family Business Strategy, Journal of Business Research, Small Business Economics, Journal of World Business*, and *Management International Review*. He has taught entrepreneurship, strategic management, and international business courses at the undergraduate, MBA, doctorate, and/or EMBA levels in the US, Europe, and Australia. Additionally, he serves as an associate editor for the Journal of *Family Business Strategy*, as well as on the editorial boards of the *Family Business Review* and *Journal of World Business*.

LILIANA PÉREZ-NORDTVEDT is an Associate Professor of Strategic Management at the University of Texas at Arlington. She received her Ph.D. from the University of Memphis in 2005. Dr. Pérez-Nordtvedt also has a B.S. in Industrial Engineering from the Universidad de los Andes (Bogotá, Colombia) and an M.B.A. from Indiana University of Pennsylvania. Her work appears in many journals including *Organization Science, Journal of Management Studies, Journal of Business Venturing, Human Resource Management, Journal of International Management, International Business Review, Journal of Small Business Management, Journal of Global Business Research* and *Competitiveness Review*. She has published book chapters in the *Handbook of International Management Research* (B.J. Punnett and Oded Shenkar, eds.) and *Multinational Corporations and Global Poverty Reduction* (S. Jain, ed.). Her current research interests include organizational entrainment, multinational organizational learning and knowledge transfer.

SOMNATH LAHIRI received his Ph.D. in Business Administration from the University of Memphis in 2007. Prior to coming to the US, he obtained a bachelor's degree in Civil engineering and a post-graduate diploma in management, both from Indian universities. He has served as a practicing engineer for about 13 years in private and public sector organizations in India. Somnath's current teaching and research interests are in the areas of strategic management, international management, and international business. His works have appeared or have been accepted for publication in the *Asia-Pacific Journal of Management, Business Horizons, European Business Review, European Management Journal, International Business Review, Journal of International Management, Journal of World Business, Management International Review* and *Thunderbird International Business Review* among several others. Somnath has received the Illinois State University Research Initiative Award and the Best Reviewer Award of the Academy of International Business. He has also been a co-recipient of the Best Paper Award in Emerging Economies Track of the Academy of International Business. Somnath lives with his wife, Susmita, and son, Soumit, in Normal, Illinois. In his leisure time he listens to music and plays ping-pong with his son.

DEBMALYA MUKHERJEE is an Assistant Professor at The University of Akron, USA. Debmalya earned a Bachelor of Law degree from University of Calcutta (India), and an MBA from Ohio University. He completed his doctoral studies as a research associate at the Robert Wang Center, University of Memphis in 2008. His research interests concern emerging economy firms, offshoring, interorganizational relationship issues, and international strategic alliances. Debmalya's works have appeared or have been accepted in *Journal of Management Studies, Journal of Business Research, European Management Journal, Management Decision, Asia Pacific Journal of Management, Journal of World Business, European Business Review* and *Leadership and Organizational Development Journal,* among others. Debmalya also serves on the editorial review board of *Journal of World Business* and *Leadership and Organizational Development Journal.* He received both the Research and Teaching Excellence Awards from the College of Business Administration of the University of Akron in 2012. This is the first time that any faculty member has received both awards in the same year. Debmalya lives in Akron, Ohio with his wife, Amrapali and son, Ayushman.

NOLAN GAFFNEY is an Assistant Professor of Strategic Management at the University of North Texas. He primarily teaches Administrative Strategy in the MBA program, but also helps lead yearly summer study abroad trips. He attained his Ph.D. at the University of Memphis in 2012. During his four years in the Wang Center and under the guidance of Ben Kedia, he developed an internationally focused Strategic Management research program, specifically on the institutional, cultural, and competitive drivers of Emerging Market Multinational Enterprises outward foreign direct investment decisions. This promising research program has already led to scholarly publications, numerous academic conference presentations, and serves as the basis of a promising research pipeline. Prior to entering the Ph.D. program, Nolan earned his MBA at the University of Cincinnati in 2008 and his undergraduate degree in Logistics & Transportation at the University of Tennessee in 2003. His research interest in International Management stems from his time working for a highly diversified international transportation company, which gave him a tremendous amount of exposure to and experience working in a globalized world.

JACK CLAMPIT is a current Ph.D. Candidate under Ben Kedia at the Robert W. Wang Center for International Business (CIBER). His research focuses on the impact of country-level institutions on business, including an examination of distal links such as institutional antecedents on the front end and societal outcomes on the back end. His dissertation focuses on informing the institutional and cultural distance constructs by shifting emphasis from simple linear distance between countries to fit between countries and firm level goals. Under Dr. Kedia's guidance, he has already won multiple Best Paper and Best Reviewer awards at various international conferences, has published several studies in books and top tier international business journals (e.g., *Management International Review*), and has several more studies either under, or soon to be under, review at top research outlets (e.g., *Journal of Management Studies, Journal of International Business Studies, Academy of Management Review*). Upon graduation, he plans to continue the legacy of Wang Center-produced researchers, either abroad or at a top research institution in the U.S.

THE UNIVERSITY OF MEMPHIS®

FOGELMAN COLLEGE OF BUSINESS AND ECONOMICS

International Business BBA Program

Wang Center for International Business
The University of Memphis
220 Fogelman Executive Center
330 Innovation Drive
Memphis, TN 38152-3130

Telephone: (901) 678-3499

International Business BBA: Your Bridge to a Rewarding Future

Why should you choose the INBS BBA program?

Are you interested in succeeding in the global marketplace?

Does a desire to meet new people while studying in a foreign country motivate you?

If so, you should consider choosing **International Business** as your major/minor. Acquiring foreign language skills and an understanding of foreign cultures will equip you to take full advantage of opportunities in the modern global economy. Firms in fields such as logistics, IT, marketing, and management consulting are seeking graduates with internationally oriented training. The INBS program can also prepare you for graduate education.

Curriculum:

- Broad, interdisciplinary curriculum allows you to choose courses in business, foreign language, and social studies that build on the foundation of general education and business core courses.
- Concentrate on Economics, Finance, Logistics/Supply Chain Management, Marketing Management—or mix and match.

INTERNATIONAL BUSINESS PROGRAM

FOR UNDERGRADUATE STUDENTS

157 MAJORS IN 2012

- Foreign languages offered include French, Italian, Spanish, German, Russian, Japanese, and Arabic.

How valuable is Study Abroad, and how can you afford it?

Students who participate in a **Study Abroad** program . . .

- Gain a deeper understanding of a foreign culture and region.

- Improve their language skills through everyday activities, such as shopping, using public transportation, and talking with residents.

- Gain insights into the operations of foreign firms and governments through site visits to businesses and institutions in the host country.

The INBS BBA program manager will provide you with up-to-date information on Study Abroad programs that are designed especially for International Business students.

International Business majors are eligible for competitive scholarships offered by the Wang Center for International Business.

What are the options for Internships?

Adding an internship to your course work provides valuable hands-on training that complements your classroom learning. International Business students may apply for internships available through the Fogelman

College of Business and Economics. The INBS BBA program manager also seeks new internship opportunities at Memphis area firms that are engaged in international trade and advertises these positions to students.

Where can you meet other INBS BBA majors/minors?

The **Society of International Business**

Students (SIBS) is made up of both undergraduate INBS BBA students and graduate students in the International MBA Program and is operated by and for the students.

Meeting information is posted on the INBS website: http://www.people.memphis.edu/~wangctr/Pages/Undergrad_IB_Program.htm

How do you get started?

Contact the INBS BBA program manager to learn more about the program and receive **academic advising** tailored to your needs. This service helps you to design a program of study that matches your interests in business, foreign language, and area studies.

> Wang Center for Int'l Business
>
> 220 Fogelman Executive Center
>
> Tel: 901-678-3499
>
> E-mail: ptaylor@memphis.edu

INTERNATIONAL BUSINESS PROGRAM
FOR UNDERGRADUATE STUDENTS *(continued)*

1. **Casey Beck**: Salamanca, Spain (June 3-30, 2000)
2. **Bethany Jo Woodall:** (May 2003)
3. **Luis A. Yuan:** (May 2003)
4. **Erin McKenna:** Spain (June 2004)
5. **Joseph Weekly:** University of San Jose in Costa Rica, (June-July 2005)
6. **Keith Duff:** Univ. of San Jose in Costa Rica (Summer 2005)
7. **Felicia Hill:** Univ. of San Jose in Costa Rica (Summer 2005)
8. **Whitney Douglas:** Spain (July 2005)
9. **Luke Hill:** Japan (Aug. 2004–May 2005)
10. **Daniel Bradford:** Japan (Sept. 2004–June 2005)
11. **Clifford Kuntzman:** Univ. of San Jose, Costa Rica (June 30-July 30, 2006)
12. **Bernard Sherrod:** Univ. of San Jose, Costa Rica (June 30-July 30, 2006)
13. **C B Luke Hill:** Sport & Culture in the Global Marketplace, London, UK (July 16-29, 2006)
14. **Claire Millman:** Institut Français des Alpes in Annecy, France (June 2006)
15. **Emily Lawrence:** Univ. of San Jose in Costa Rica (June 30-July 30, 2006)
16. **Kathryn Murphy:** Madrid, Spain (June – July 2007)
17. **Clifford Kuntzman:** Salamanca, Spain (June 2007)
18. **Richard Du:** Osaka University of Economics, (Sep. 2006 – July, 2007)
19. **Justin Weekly:** U. of Costa Rica (June 27-July 28, 2008); Monterrey, Mexico (July 29-Dec. 10, 2008)
20. **Jacqueline Craft:** Barcelona, Spain, CEA Program (May 30-June 27, 2008)
21. **Meredith Ray:** London, U.K. (July 13-26, 2008)
22. **Adrian Ishee:** Buenos Aries, Argentina (Summer 2009)
23. **Silu Wang:** Study Japanese language and culture in Osaka, Japan (2009)
24. **Rachael Redfearn:** Study Spanish language and culture in Argentina (2009)
25. **Brian Booker:** Study Japanese at Tokyo Univ. in Tokyo, Japan (2009-10)
26. **Jeffrey Gagne:** Shanghai University, China (Aug. 24-dec. 21, 2010)
27. **Amber Curtis:** Monterrey, Mexico (Jan 5-May 20, 2010)
28. **David Reeves:** University of Surrey, London, UK (July 4-17, 2010)
29. **Amber Hagewood:** University of Surrey, London, UK (July 4-17, 2010)
30. **Jonathan Williams**: University of Surrey, London, UK (July 4-17, 2010)
31. **Lucas Chinn:** Osaka University of Economics, Japan (May 10-June 2, 2010)
32. **Alvara Palacia:** Alicante, Spain (Feb. 2-April 30, 2010)
33. **Jeremy Smothers:** Costa Rica (June 28-July 31,2010)
34. **Angel Shah:** University Pontificia de Salamanca, Spain (June 1-26, 2010)
35. **Silu Wang:** Fudan University, Shanghai, China (Fall semester 2010)
36. **Manica Buenaventura**: University of Murcia, Spain (Sept. 1-July 15, 2010)
37. **Kaitlynn Lee:** Eichstaett, Germany (July 14-Aug. 16, 2011)
38. **Britnee Peters:** Salamanca, Spain (June 3-30, 2011)
39. **Elizabeth Yen:** Shanghai University, China (Feb. 8-June 2011)
40. **Ingrid Merritt:** Lille Catholic University, France (June 2-July 2, 2011)
41. **Janelle Arguijo:** Catholic University, Germany (April – August 2011)
42. **Ciari Arrington:** London, UK (July 10-23, 2011)

Year	Company	Language	Length	Participants
1991	Federal Express	Bus. French I & II	8 & 13 weeks	36
1992	Cylix	Bus. French I & II	13 weeks ea.	17
	PSI	Business French I	13 weeks	5
	VVP America	Business Spanish	13 weeks	12
1993	Mid South Milling	Business Spanish I	13 weeks	19
	Helena Chemical	Business Spanish I	13 weeks	15
1994	Midland Financial Co.	Business Spanish I	13 weeks	11
1995	Varco-Pruden	Business Chinese I	13 weeks	15
1996	Varco-Pruden Bldgs.	Portuguese I	14 weeks	11
	Promus Hotel Corp.	Business Spanish I	14 weeks	5
	Maybelline, Inc.	Business French I	14 weeks	11
	Cummins Engine	Business Spanish I	14 weeks	15
	Thomas & Betts	Business Spanish I	14 weeks	12
	Regional Medical Ctr.	Business Spanish I	14 weeks	13
1997	Sparks Companies, Inc.	Spanish I	14 weeks	10
	Cummins Engine	Spanish I	14 weeks	15
	Decca, Inc.	Spanish I	14 weeks	6
1998	Regional Medical Center	Spanish	14 weeks	15
	Varco-Pruden	Spanish	14 weeks	12
	Sheraton Casino & Hotel	French	2 half days	22
	Mphis-Shelby Co Health	Spanish I	14 weeks	15
	U.S. Pretrial Services	Spanish I	14 weeks	15
	LeBonheur	Spanish I	14 weeks	15
	Varco-Pruden Bldgs.	Spanish I (a&b)	14 weeks ea.	30
	Baxter Health Co.	Spanish I	14 weeks	15
	Cummins Engine	Spanish II	14 weeks	15
	Autozone	Spanish I	14 weeks	15
	Sparks Companies, Inc.	Spanish I & II	14 weeks ea.	20
1999	RiceCO	Spanish II	14 weeks	5
	Cummins Engine	Beginning Spanish	14 weeks	17
	Cummins Engine	Intermed. Spanish	14 weeks	9
	W. TN Health Ed. Ctr.	Beginning Spanish	2 days	52
	Victim's Assistance Ctr.	Spanish II	14 weeks	17
2000	AALAS	Beginning Spanish	7 weeks	12
	ALSAC-St. Jude	Beginning Spanish	14 weeks	15
	ALSAC-St. Jude	Spanish II	14 weeks	12
53 COMPANIES		**845 PARTICIPANTS**		

HENRY A. KISSINGER

Henry A. Kissinger, chairman of Kissinger Associates, an international consulting firm, served as Secretary of State and Assistant to the President for National Security Affairs under President Nixon. In 1983, he was appointed by President Reagan to chair the National Bipartisan Commission on Central America. Winner of the Nobel Peace Prize in 1973, Dr. Kissinger was also awarded the Presidential Medal of Freedom (the nation's highest civilian award) in 1988, and the Medal of Liberty in 1986. As a prime mover in international relations, he has a unique perspective on events in the world today. He has written numerous books and articles on United States foreign policy, international affairs and diplomatic history. His syndicated column appears in leading U. S. newspapers and in over 40 foreign countries.

WILLIAM E.BROCK

William E. Brock, President of The Brock Group, a firm he started in 1989, was U. S. Secretary of Labor from 1985 to 1987, and served on the Economic Policy Council and the President's Task force on Regulatory Relief. Brock served in the U. S. Senate from 1970 to 1977 and was named U. S. Trade Representative in 1981. In that capacity he was the President's chief trade advisor and international trade negotiator, and also chaired the cabinet-level Trade Policy Committee. Brock is active nationally and internationally on major forums dealing with 1992, European and Pacific Rim issues, and the politics of trade and infrastructure.

RICHARD WRIGHT

Richard Wright is first secretary for trade and commercial affairs at the Delegation of the Commission of the European Communities. Since taking up his post in Washington in January, 1988, he has been responsible for monitoring EC-US trade and commercial relations. He has worked for the Commission for nine years, of which seven years have been with the Directorate General for External Relations. Mr. Wright was a member of the EC's negotiating team on several major issues and represented the Community on several important dispute settlement panels.

JAMES L. BARKSDALE

James L. Barksdale, Executive Vice Presiden and Chief Operations Officer for Federal Express Corporation, is responsible for the daily operations of the world's largest full-service all cargo airline. In the eight years since Barksdale assumed his current positio the company has grown from $1 billion to more than $7 billion in revenue and has expanded its operations to more than 119 countries in North and South America, Europe, Australia, the Middle East and the Far East.

DAVID GERGEN

David Gergen, Editor-at-Large, *U. S. News & World Report*, was White House Communication Director for President Ronald Reagan. He is a regular analyst for The MacNeil/Lehrer News Hour and a regular commentator on National Public Radio's "All Things Considered." Recently, The London Observer called him "Washington's leading insider-journalist."

FOUAD M. ALAEDDIN

Fouad M. Alaeddin, Partner, Arthur Andersen & Co., Riyadh, Saudi Arabia, is Managing Partner of all of Arthur Andersen's Middle East operations. He serves as advisor and consultant to numerous U. S. and foreign-based multinational companies operating in that part of the world.

WASHINGTON SYCIP

Washington SyCip, Senior Partner, Arthur Andersen & Co., Manila, is chairman and founder of the SGV Group, the largest accounting and management consulting firm in East Asia. He presently serves as Chairman of the Board of Trustees and Board of Governors of the Asian Institute of Management, Phillipines, and on the international advisory boards of numerous U. S. multinational companies operating

MEMPHIS: SEIZING THE GLOBAL OPPORTUNITY

The Arthur Andersen International Business Symposium

May 17, 1990

Presented In Cooperation With The Robert Wang Center For International Business At Memphis State University And The Memphis Area Chamber Of Commerce

ARTHUR ANDERSEN

MEMPHIS: SEIZING THE GLOBAL OPPORTUNITY

THE ARTHUR ANDERSEN INTERNATIONAL BUSINESS SYMPOSIUM

Presented in Cooperation with the Robert Wang Center
for International Business at Memphis State University
May 17, 1990

THOMAS PETERS

Tom Peters, founder of The Tom Peters Group, is recognized as one of the most incisive and thought-provoking business analysts of our time. As coauthor of *In Search of Excellence* and *A Passion for Excellence*, author of *Thriving On Chaos: Handbook for a Management Revolution*, and as a prolific contributor to the business press and broadcast media, Peters has virtually rewritten the basic principles of management practice and international market competition. Through his appearances before hundreds of public and private sector audiences, and through his collection of best-selling audiotapes, Mr. Peters has upended traditional thinking and turned his challenge of business orthodoxy into a worldwide revolution.

JOHN E. ROBSON, DEPUTY SECRETARY OF THE U.S. TREASURY

The Honorable John E. Robson has spent a distinguished career in both the public and private sectors. He was appointed Deputy Secretary of the Treasury, the number two position in the department, by President George Bush on May 15, 1989. Prior to this appointment, he served as dean and professor of management at Emory University's School of Business and Administration, CEO of G.D. Searle & Co., chairman of the Civil Aeronautics Board, general counsel and then Under Secretary of the U.S. Department of Transportation, and a consultant with the Bureau of the Budget.

BEN J. WATTENBERG

Ben J. Wattenberg is a senior fellow at the American Enterprise Institute, well-known radio and television commentator, contributing editor of *U.S. News & World Report*, syndicated columnist, and author of numerous books including *The Birth Dearth, The Good News Is The Bad News Is Wrong, The Real America*, and a new book titled, *The First Universal Nation: Leading Indicators and Ideas About the Surge of America at Home and Abroad*. He also co-wrote two widely-read books, *The Real Majority* and *This U.* _ senior editor of *The American Enterprise* magazine, and has been an advisor to a number of U.S. presi_

GEORGE T. SHAHEEN

George T. Shaheen has combined exemplary professional skills with four-year success story at Andersen Consulting. Named Managing P_ 1989, he steers the work of over 18,000 professionals as Andersen C_ meet the challenges of the new world order. In 1990, he was named_ University's Krannert Graduate School of Management, as well as t_ Nu Fraternity.

DAVID F. KININMONTH

As Regional Manager for the New Zealand Trade Development Board, David F. Kininmonth is his country's top trade official in the U.S. His previous postings include directorships of trade policy and industrial development for the New Zealand Department of Trade and Industry, secretary to the U.S.S.R.-New Zealand Trade Agreement, and numerous high level government positions with responsibility for development of markets around the world.

BRIAN D. SMITH

Brian D. Smith is currently Partner-in-Charge of Arthur Andersen's practice in Central and Eastern Europe, and coordinator of its audit and business advisory services in Europe, Africa, and the Middle East. He previously served as Partner-in-Charge of the London audit practice and Managing Partner of the Worldwide Audit and Business Advisory practice.

JAY MARTIN

Jay Martin spent a short career in Georgia as a teacher and door-to-door salesman of pots and pans before moving to Memphis in 1969 to found National Safety Associates. From a desk in his living room and $500 in borrowed money, he has built a business which *Inc.* magazine recently listed as the twenty-second fastest growing private company in the United States. Named Tennessee Exporter of the Year in 1989, NSA projects current year net sales of $350 million from its manufacturing and distribution operations in the U.S. and abroad.

NELLIE K_

Nellie K. M. Fo_ _g office and a sp_ _ong, the People's R_ _y participant in _c Rim investments, an_ Legislative Council.

RICHARD E. BELL

Richard E. Bell is president and chief executive officer of Riceland Foods, Inc., a Fortune "500" list member. Before joining Riceland in 1977, Bell served as Assistant Secretary of Agriculture for International Affairs and Commodity Programs in the Nixon and Ford administrations, president of the U.S. Department of Agriculture's Commodity Credit Corporation, and as one of the principal negotiators of the first long-term grain agreement with the Soviet Union.

DR. BEN L. KEDIA

Dr. Ben L. Kedia serves as director of the Robert Wang Center for International Business at Memphis State University, and also holds the Robert Wang Chair of International Business at the Center. Known nationally for his international trade research and curriculum development, he recently spearheaded a successful effort to obtain a $270,000 U.S. Department of Education grant to strengthen the international programs at MSU and Southern Illinois University.

COMPETING IN THE GLOBAL MARKETPLACE

THE ARTHUR ANDERSEN INTERNATIONAL BUSINESS SYMPOSIUM

May 23, 1991

COMPETING IN THE GLOBAL MARKETPLACE

THE ARTHUR ANDERSEN INTERNATIONAL BUSINESS SYMPOSIUM

Presented in Cooperation with the Robert Wang Center for International Business at Memphis State University
May 23, 1991

Announcing the

¥ $

CHINA

ECONOMIC SUMMIT

December 8-9, 1994
Nashville, Tennessee

Sponsored by the Tennessee Department of
Economic and Community Development, with
cooperation from The Wang Center for International
Business, University of Memphis.

The China Economic Summit will bring the world's
largest market, and one of the most underdeveloped, to
Tennessee. For two days, some of the United States and
China's leading economic minds will be in Nashville to
discuss ways to take advantage of the growing business
opportunities in the People's Republic of China.

If you or your company does business in China...
or wants to... you need to be in Nashville
December 8-9, 1994.

It will open new doors.

CHINA ECONOMIC SUMMIT
Nashville, Tennessee

Sponsored by the Tennessee Department of Economic and
Community Development, with cooperation from the Wang
Center for International Business, University of Memphis
December 8-9, 1994

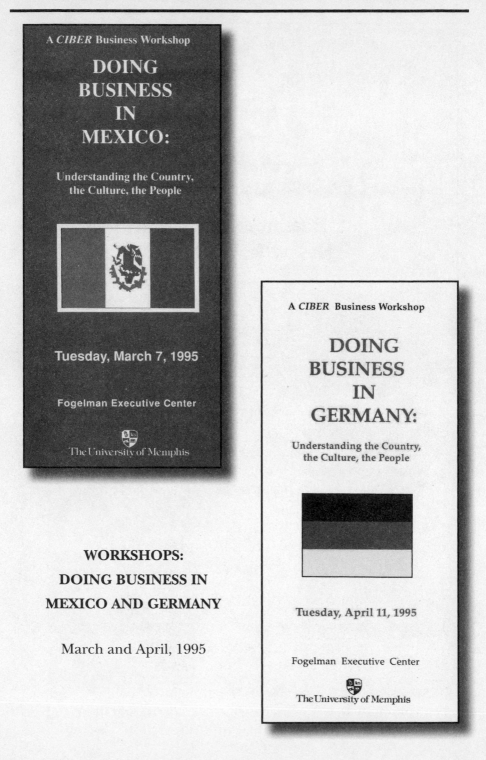

A *CIBER* Business Workshop

DOING BUSINESS IN MEXICO:

Understanding the Country, the Culture, the People

Tuesday, March 7, 1995

Fogelman Executive Center

The University of Memphis

A *CIBER* Business Workshop

DOING BUSINESS IN GERMANY:

Understanding the Country, the Culture, the People

Tuesday, April 11, 1995

Fogelman Executive Center

The University of Memphis

WORKSHOPS:

DOING BUSINESS IN MEXICO AND GERMANY

March and April, 1995

SWEDISH AIRLINE EXECUTIVES DELEGATION
October 4-8, 1995

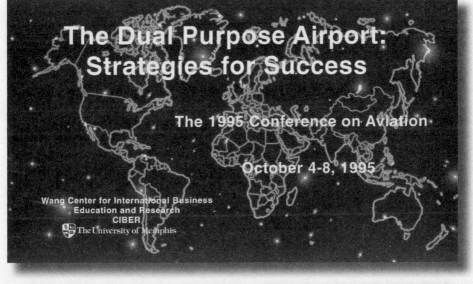

THE DUAL PURPOSE AIRPORT: STRATEGIES FOR SUCCESS
October 4-8, 1995

China Machinery and Automotive Industrial Delegation

AGENDA
November 18-20, 1996

Tuesday, November 19

8:30-10:00 a.m.	Tour of Cummins Engine, Inc.
	William (Bill) Shuman, Director for International Marketing
	Dave Hardin, Marketing Manager
	Yu Guoping (Edmund), Financial Analyst

10:00-11:15 a.m.   Tour of Memphis Distribution Center, Cummins Engine, Inc.
Dave Hardin, Marketing Manager
Yu Guoping (Edmund), Financial Analyst

11:45 a.m.   Luncheon, Owen Brennan's Restaurant
Hosted by Mr. Hardin

1:00-2:30 p.m.   Wang's International, Inc.
Mrs. Susie Wang, Executive Vice President

2:30 p.m.   Depart for University of Memphis

3:00-5:00 p.m.   Wang Center for International Business
Dr. Ben Kedia, Director
Judy Scales, Assistant Director
Dr. Ting Ho, Chief Economist, Federal Express Corporation
Jim Powell, International Finance Exchange
Dr. Robert Radway, Vector International (New York City)
John Threadgill, Memphis Area Chamber of Commerce

Wednesday, November 20

8:00 a.m.   Depart for Varco-Pruden

8:30-10:00 a.m.   Varco-Pruden Buildings International
Kris Hahn, VP International, Asian Service Manager
Jim Drake, Senior Vice President, VP International
Sam Love, Director of Systems, VP International
Jingwei Zhang, Engineering Project Leader, VP International

3:00 p.m.   Depart for Detroit

CHINA MACHINERY AND AUTOMOBILE
INDUSTRIAL DELEGATION
November 18-20, 1996

HIS EXCELLENCY NITYA PIBULSONGGRAM
AMBASSADOR TO THE U.S. ROYAL THAI EMBASSY

(Left) Judy Scales, Assistant Director, Wang Center;
Ambassador Nitya Pibulsonggram;
Ree Russell, U.S. Department of Commerce
1996

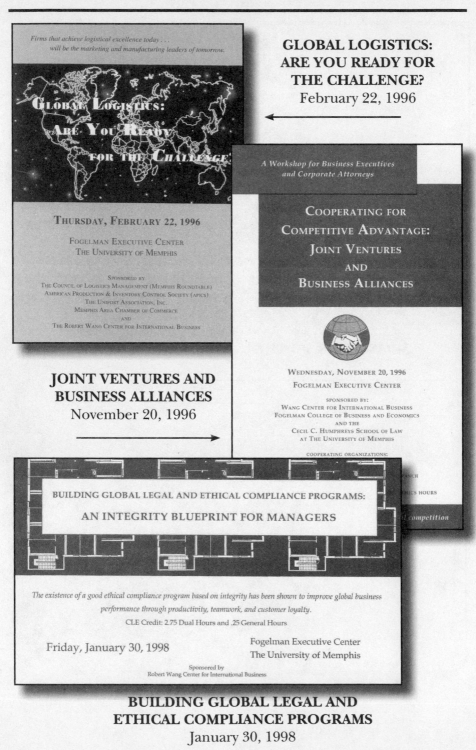

**GLOBAL LOGISTICS:
ARE YOU READY FOR
THE CHALLENGE?**
February 22, 1996

**JOINT VENTURES AND
BUSINESS ALLIANCES**
November 20, 1996

**BUILDING GLOBAL LEGAL AND
ETHICAL COMPLIANCE PROGRAMS**
January 30, 1998

Brief Information about the delegation from Qingdao Textile Corporation:[1]

1. Brief background information about QD Textile Corporation:

It was established in 1951. It has 72 enterprises (some established in 1920's), one Textile University, one research institute and one hospital with total of 120,000 employees. The business involves in spinning, weaving, knitting, wool-spinning & weaving, dyeing, finishing, reprocessing, synthetic fiber producing, garment manufacturing and textile machinery manufacturing.

2. Delegation members:

Name	Sex	Unit	Position
Wang, lei	M	QD Textile Corporation	General manager
Zhang, Zhengwei	M	QD Textile supply and Marketing Corporation	General manager
Yin, Guopu	M	Department of Planning and Development	Director
Cai, Guanxin	M	Department of Overseas Trading	Interpreter
Kong, Xingde	M.	Qingdao No. 4 Cotton Textile Mill	Director
Song, Xusheng	M	Qingdao No. 3 Cotton Textile Mill	Director
Bi, Jinde	M	Finance and Accounting Office	Manager
Wang, Jianhua	F	Department of Economy & Trade	Director
Pan, Yuanyi	F	Qingdao Hua-jin real Estate Group	Deputy general manager
Zheng, Lihua	M	Qingdao Canvas Mill	Director

3. Duration of the visit: 14 days, from March 19 to April 2, 1997.

4. Purpose of the visit:

1). Visit American textile plants to experience the textile industries and learn the newest development in the production from spinning to apparel, fashion design, dyeing, and equipment.
2). Seek cooperation in new products, new technologies to compete in international market.
3). Establish a network for textile retail and wholesale markets.
4). Establish a network for receiving orders of textile production from American companies.
5). Learn new development of internet for promoting textile production and searching suppliers and services.
6). Visit Hudson for a die cutting system
7). Visit a division of DuPont, their joint-venture partner
8). Visit a division of Japanese Company for a Jet-spinning machinery.
9). Visit cotton suppliers for direct network for exporting cotton to China.
10). Set up an agent for purchasing new and used textile equipment.

QINGDAO TEXTILE DELEGATION
1997

GLOBAL EXECUTIVE NETWORK

Doing Business in Brazil:
Trade and Investment Opportunities

An international forum linking business executives from Brazil, Memphis and the Mid-South region.

May 29-30, 1997
Memphis, Tennessee, USA

DOING BUSINESS IN BRAZIL:
TRADE AND INVESTMENT OPPORTUNITIES
May 29-30, 1997

BRAZILIAN DELEGATION
May 29-30, 1997

Chinese Delegation from Cotton Industry
Hosted by
WANG CIBER
September 1998

Tang Mingzhen
Jiangsu Province Department of Agriculture

Gu Bingfang
Zhangjianggang City Cotton Center

Gu Bingfang
Zhangjianggang City Cotton Center

Xu Qinsheng
Taicang Cotton Farm

Cui Yifu
Dongtai Cotton Farm

Zhou Caiqing
Gaoyou Cotton Group Co.

Chen Lichang
Siyang Cotton Farm

CHINESE
DELEGATION
FROM COTTON
INDUSTRY

September 1998

DELEGATION
The Peoples Government of Hexi District
Tianjin, China
October 15, 1998

1. Mr. Shen Jiacong
   Standing Vice President of Hexi District
   Tianjin, China

2. Mr. Sun Xuelin
   Director
   Tianjin Hexi Commission of Foreign Economic Relations
   and Trade
   Tianjin, China

3. Ms. Guan Sufen
   Chairman and Board President
   Tianjin Jianshan Lianhua Industry and Commerce Group

4. Mr. Shi Yunping
   General Manager
   Tianjin Yinyu Industry and Commerce Co.

5. Mr. Zhang Yanjing
   Deputy General Manager
   Tianjin Xinlianhua Energy Development Co., Ltd/

THE PEOPLES
GOVERNMENT
OF HEXI
DISTRICT
TIANJIN, CHINA

October 15, 1998

**DOING BUSINESS
WITH CHINA
IN THE 21ST
CENTURY**

March 25, 1999

**Impact of Culture on
Doing Business
in Asia**

FDX Seminar Agenda
March 3, 1999

8:00 a.m.   Continental Breakfast

8:30 a.m.   *Culture: Changing the Way
We Do Business*
Dr. Ben L. Kedia

9:45 a.m.   *Chinese Business Culture (Part I)*
Dr. Rosalie Tung

10:45 a.m.   Break

11:00 a.m.   *Chinese Business Culture (Part II)*
Dr. Rosalie Tung

12:30 p.m.   Lunch in Executive Dining Room

1:45 p.m.   *Japanese Business Culture*
Mr. Len Parker

3:15 p.m.   Break

3:30 p.m.   *Business Travel in Asia:
Putting Culture to Work*
Dr. Rosali...
Mr. Len P...
Dr. Ben L...

4:30 p.m.   Adjournmer...

**E-COMMERCE
E-EXPLOSION!
IS YOUR BUSINESS
E-READY?**

March 2, 2000

E-Commerce E-Xplosion!

Is Your Business E-Ready?

Thursday 2 March 2000

A dynamic one-day forum designed to explore
the opportunities, trends and challenges that
E-Commerce presents to business.

Wang Center for International Business
The University of Memphis

Richard Celeste

Naresh Chandra

Larry G. Tanning

Vivek Paul

David Bronczek

Larry Gordon

Ben L. Kedia

U.S.-India Info Tech Conference
May 10-12, 2000   Memphis, TN USA
AGENDA

Thursday, May 11

7:30 AM	Continental Breakfast
8:30 AM	*Welcome* **Ben L. Kedia, Director, Wang Center** **The University of Memphis**
8:45 AM	*A Profile of India* **(Video Introduction)**
9:00 AM	*India Today* **The Honorable Richard Celeste** **U.S. Ambassador to India** **The Honorable Naresh Chandra** **Indian Ambassador to U.S.** **Questions from Audience**
10:00 AM	Break
10:15 AM	*IT in the 21st Century: Implications for U.S. Business* **Larry G. Tanning, Chairman and CEO** **Tanning Technology (NASDAQ)** **Questions from Audience**
11:00 AM	*India's Technology Resources & Opportunities for U.S. Firms* **Vivek Paul, CEO and Managing Director** **Wipro** **Questions from Audience**
12:00 Noon	*Lunch and Special Guest Speaker* **David Bronczek, CEO** **FedEx Corporation**
1:30 PM Panel:	*Expe...* Mode...
2:45 PM	Brea...
3:00 PM Panel:	*Capa...* Mode...
4:00 PM	*An I...*
4:30 PM	*Closi...*

From Gurus to . . . Gigabytes!

India's Informa tion Technology:
A 21st Century Resour ce for U.S. Companies

U.S. - India Information Technology Conference
10-12 May 2000   Memphis, TN U.S.A.

High quality,
talented manpower
and reasonable costs make India
a destination of choice for U.S. firms
wanting to outsource key IT projects.

FedEx Corporation
Wang Center, University of Memphis
Government of India, Indian Embassy
Confederation of Indian Industries (CII)
Memphis in May and Memphis Area Chamber

INDIA'S INFORMATION TECHNOLOGY: A 21ST CENTURY RESOURCE FOR U.S. COMPANIES

May 10-12, 2000

The Impact of the Seven Revolutions: Looking Out to the Year 2025

1:30 pm
Thursday, February 3

Fogelman Executive
Conference Center
University of Memphis

PRESENTED BY

SOCIETY OF INTERNATIONAL
BUSINESS FELLOWS (SIBF)

AND THE

WANG CENTER FOR
INTERNATIONAL BUSINESS

THE UNIVERSITY OF
MEMPHIS.

WITH
SPONSORSHIP SUPPORT FROM

Buckman
LABORATORIES

JACKSON
Jackson Products, Inc.

STANFORD GROUP COMPANY

MALLORY ALEXANDER
INTERNATIONAL LOGISTICS
Confidence worldwide

Regions Bank

Morgan Keegan
Morgan Keegan & Company, Inc.
Members New York Stock Exchange. SIPC

Memphis Regional Chamber

The "Seven Revolutions" is a challenge to leaders — a challenge to think seriously about events that are over the horizon and a challenge to formulate and carry out policies in the near term in order to effect longer-range consequences.

Erik R. Peterson, senior vice president and director of the Global Strategy Institute at the Center for Strategic and International Studies (CSIS), will make the thought provoking Seven Revolutions presentation which identifies and analyzes the major forces shaping the world through the year 2025 — demographic growth, resource management, technology innovation and diffusion, development and distribution of knowledge, economic integration, the nature and mode of conflict, and the challenge of governance.

Headquartered in Washington, D.C., CSIS is a private, nonpartisan organization dedicated to providing world leaders with strategic insights on, and policy situations to, current and emerging global issues.

- **Population**
- **Resources**
- **Technology**
- **Information**
- **Integration**
- **Conflict**
- **Governance**

SEVEN REVOLUTIONS
Looking Out to the Year 2025...
...and the major forces shaping the world.

THE UNIVERSITY OF
MEMPHIS.

REGISTRATION FORM ➡

THE IMPACT OF THE SEVEN REVOLUTIONS:
LOOKING OUT TO THE YEAR 2025

February 3, 2005

Business Opportunities Seminar

Successfully Exploring and Exporting to Asian Markets

April 6, 2005
The University of Memphis,
Fogelman Executive Conference Center

Billions of consumers live in Asia. Where are the best opportunities for your company and how can you seize them? This seminar will give you the information and tools you need to successfully enter and succeed in a specific market or the larger region. U.S. manufacturers and service providers should plan to attend in order to get industry sector intelligence, make contacts, and learn about valuable export promotion resources.

At this seminar, you'll:

* Receive updates on current events, market prospects, and the economic situation of the region

* Learn how to successfully negotiate the business cultures of these markets

* Gain knowledge of available resources, assistance, and marketing activities in the region

* Meet one-on-one with Senior Commercial Officers (SCOs) of the U.S. Commercial Service—trade experts who are on the ground in key markets around the world—from Australia; New Zealand; China; Hong Kong; Indonesia; Japan; Korea; Malaysia; Philippines; Singapore; Taiwan; Thailand; Vietnam; and the Asia-Pacific Economic Cooperation, a forum for facilitating economic growth in the Asia-Pacific region

* Visit the FedEx Resource Center and meet FedEx transportation and logistic professionals

Who should attend?

The CEOs, owners, and decision makers of U.S. manufacturing and service companies interested in making or increasing sales in Asia should plan to attend this seminar.

Asia Now—Exporting to Asia Just Got Easier.

Register now

Event:	Asia Now: Successfully Exploring and Exporting to Asian Markets
When:	Wednesday, April 6, 2005 from 8:00 am – 5:00 pm
Where:	The University of Memphis, Fogelman Executive Conference Center, 330 Innovation Drive, Memphis, TN 38152-3115.
Registration:	To register for this timely seminar and schedule your private, individual one-on-one counseling sessions, register on-line at: buyusa.gov/asianow/sco_meeting.html, or call Jeanne Tutor at 901-678-2805
Cost:	$75 per person (if registration made before April 1st) $85 at the door. Fee includes lunch.
Presenters:	Mike Ducker, Executive Vice President, FedEx (invited)
	Ann Bacher, Regional Director East Asia Pacific, U.S. Commercial Service
	Senior Commercial Officers from the U.S. Commercial Service, East Asia Pacific Region
Brought to you by:	• FedEx • Memphis Chamber of Commerce • Memphis World Trade Club • Regional Chamber Forum • University of Memphis • U.S. Commercial Service • Council of Logistics Management • Memphis District Export Council

DISTRICT EXPORT COUNCIL

THE UNIVERSITY OF MEMPHIS.

FedEx

CSCMP

ASIA NOW: BUSINESS OPPORTUNITIES SEMINAR

SUCCESSFULLY EXPLORING AND EXPORTING TO
ASIAN MARKETS

April 6, 2005

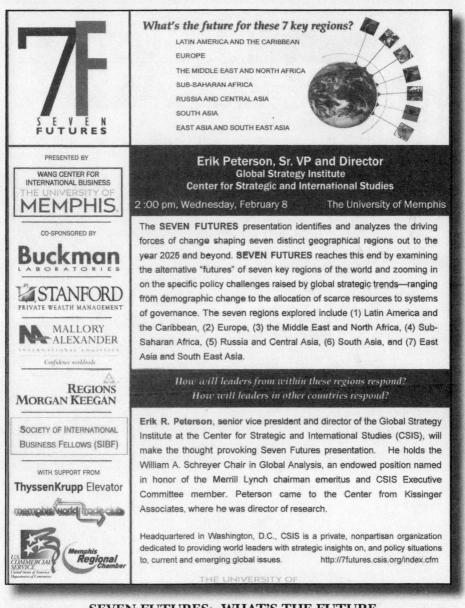

**SEVEN FUTURES: WHAT'S THE FUTURE
FOR THESE 7 REGIONS?**

LATIN AMERICA AND THE CARIBBEAN * EUROPE * MIDDLE EAST AND
NORTH AFRICA * SUB-SAHARAN AFRICA * RUSSIA AND CENTRAL ASIA *
SOUTH ASIA * EAST ASIA AND SOUTH EAST ASIA

February 8, 2006

DOING BUSINESS IN EMERGING MARKETS: CHINA AND INDIA

June 17, 2008

The Way Out of Economic and Financial Crisis: Lessons and Actions

- Plan to Attend -	You are invited to be our guest for a live webcast featuring the **Bank of Japan Governor Masaaki Shirakawa**. Governor Shirakawa will address the current global economic crisis and offer lessons from Japan's recent experience.

Thursday, April 23
11:30 am—1:30 pm

Room 385,
Fogelman College
of Business &
Economics

Light Lunch and
Parking Pass
Provided

U.S.-JAPAN
INNOVATORS
NETWORK
CONNECT • COLLABORATE • CATALYZE

THE UNIVERSITY OF
MEMPHIS.

Speaker: Masaaki Shirakawa, Governor, Bank of Japan
Presider: William R. Rhodes, Chairman & President, Citibank
Date: Thursday, April 23
Agenda: 11:30   Light Lunch
12:00   Webcast Presentation by Governor Shirakawa
1:00   Q&A

Location: Room 385, Fogelman College of Business & Economics
(Corner of Innovation Drive and Central)

Parking: Parking Garage (Innovation Drive); Parking pass provided
Lunch: Light Lunch available
RSVP: Please e-mail: abcole@memphis.edu by Monday, April 20

SPONSORED BY

National Association of Japan-America Societies
Washington, D.C. 20036

Wang Center for International Business (CIBER)
Fogelman College of Business & Economics

THE WAY OUT OF ECONOMIC AND FINANCIAL CRISIS: LESSONS AND ACTIONS

MASAAKI SHIRAKAWA
GOVERNOR, BANK OF JAPAN

April 23, 2009

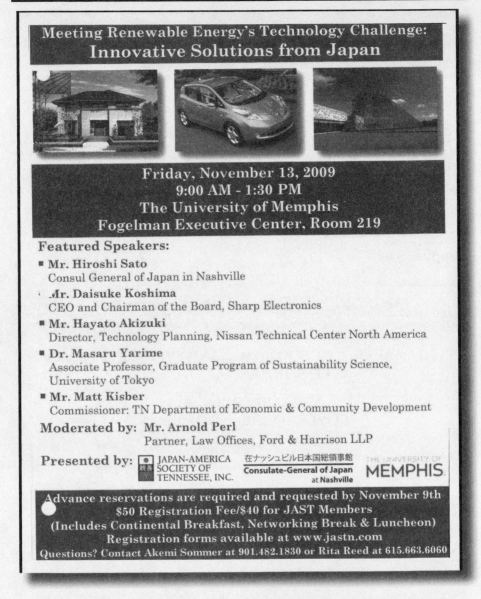

MEETING RENEWABLE ENERGY'S TECHNOLOGY CHALLENGE: INNOVATIVE SOLUTIONS FROM JAPAN

November 13, 2009

INTERNATIONAL BUSINESS COUNCIL

TOPIC

Doing Business in Spain/IBC Update

The Trade Commission of Spain in the United States oversees trade and investment opportunities between the state of Tennessee and Spain. During this presentation, Trade Commissioner Mario Buisan will discuss synergies between both regions, discuss Spain's key industry sectors, and update the group on assistance available to companies interested in entering the Spanish market.

SPEAKER

Mario Buisán,
Trade Commissioner of Spain

DATE/TIME

TUESDAY, NOVEMBER 30, 2010
MEMPHIS MARRIOTT HOTEL
4:00 p.m. - 4:30 p.m.
IBC UPDATE
4:30 p.m. - 5:00 p.m.
Presentation by Spanish Trade
5:00 p.m. -6:00 p.m.
Reception

This event is complimentary for Chamber members.
Please RSVP to brenda Montgomery 901-543-3541

**DOING BUSINESS
IN SPAIN**
November 20, 2010

**MEMPHIS AND
INDIA: TRADE
DEVELOPMENT**

November 27, 2010

GREATER MEMPHIS CHAMBER
INTERNATIONAL BUSINESS COUNCIL
Presents

india fest

Memphis and India – Trade Development
Export and Investment Opportunities

Featuring
Deputy Chief of Mission Ambassador Arun K. Singh
Embassy of India
and
Memphis-based companies doing business in India

Friday, August 27, 2010
9:00 a.m. – 1:00 p.m.
Lunch Included

Hilton Hotel Memphis
939 Ridge Lake Boulevard

Admission: $25 for Chamber Members and $35 for Non-Members
Register: bmontgomery@memphischamber.com or 901-543-3541

FedEx® Express

INVEST IN MEMPHIS

INTERNATIONAL BUSINESS COUNCIL
of the Greater Memphis Chamber

INVEST IN MEMPHIS

introduces
TAKING YOUR BUSINESS GLOBAL
May 6, 2010

EXPORT UNIVERSITY

101 – Exporting As a Business Growth Strategy

President Barak Obama has set as a goal to dramatically increase exports from the United States within the next five years. For any company not solely engaged in general retailing, exporting should be a significant component of your business growth strategy.

Export University 101 is the first in a planned series of seminars occurring over the next several months. In this first seminar key components of the export process essential to success in exporting will be examined and explained. Beyond this the goal is not only to tell you how to export but also to connect you to various sources for assistance. In addition

participants will receive several resources to take home with them including books & guides, and other resources.

Registration: 8:30 a.m.
Program Seminar:
9:00 a.m. – 11:45 a.m.

tunisia

Memphis in May International Festival, Inc.℠

MEMPHIS IN MAY
INTERNATIONAL FESTIVAL 2010

Lunch with the Ambassador of Tunisia to the United States
HABIB MANSOUR
Lunch 12:00 noon – 1:00 p.m.

TAKING YOUR BUSINESS GLOBAL

May 6, 2010

MEMPHIS MULTI MODAL CONFERENCE

May 11-12, 2010

CYBER SECURITY EXPO

October 7, 2011

1989-2012

CIBER Advisory Council composed of key business executives and academics. Promotion of the international agenda of the Fogelman College and the U of Memphis by facilitating coordination of the Wang CIBER (Council meeting held annually in October)

1989

"The Challenge of Doing Business in the Soviet Market," (Conference, Nov 3)

1990

"Memphis: Seizing the Global Opportunity," Arthur Andersen International Business Symposium, Keynote Speakers: Henry A. Kissinger, Former Secretary of State under President Nixon, and James L. Barksdale, COO, Federal Express Corporation, (Conference, May 17)

"Doing Business with East Asia and the Pacific," (Seminar, February 8)

1991

"U.S. Competitiveness in the Global Marketplace," Arthur Andersen International Business Symposium, Keynote Speakers: Thomas J. Peters, Founder of the Tom Peters Group, and John E. Robson, Deputy Secretary of the U.S. Treasury under President George Bush, (Conference, October 4-5)

"U.S.-Mexico-Canada Free Trade Agreement," (Seminar, April 26)

"Building Business Partnerships with Japan," (Workshop, March 21)

"Competing in the Global Marketplace," (Conference, May 23)

"Strategic Decisions: Business in the Soviet Union," (Workshop, November 7)

1992

"Doing Business with Germany," (Workshop, February 6)

"NAFTA," (Conference, May 26)

"Doing Business in a Global Village: European Overview," (Seminar for FedEx Managing Directors, July 15)

"Business Ethics," (Symposium, September 25)

1993

"TQM Pitfalls and Prescriptions," (Workshop, April 5)

"Russian Business Delegation," (Breakfast Meeting, May 17)

"AMA's Conference on Competitiveness: Rethinking the Organization," (Oct. 3)

"Corporate Implementation of Business Ethics," (October 8)

"Diversity: Managing For Strategic Advantage—Skills for a Global Market," (October 26-28)

"Doing Business with Mexico and Canada: After the Vote," (Workshop, Dec 2)

1994

"Global Interdependence: The U.S. and the Third World," (National Teleconference produced by Old Dominion University, February 10)

"Marketing in the Central and Eastern Europe for Marketing and Sales Executives," (March 14)

"Competing for Order Flow," International Securities (Workshop, Mar 24-25)

"Exporting Under NAFTA," Co-sponsored with Federal Express and USDOC
    (Conference, March 15)
"Successful International Negotiation Skills," Co-sponsored by TN Small
    Business Development Center, Memphis Area Chamber of Commerce,
    Mid-South Exporters' Roundtable, Memphis World Trade Club,
    USDOC/ITA (Symposium, April 7)
"TQM on Campus for Global Competitiveness," Co-sponsored by APICS (A
    Summer Academic Workshop, July 28)
"Relationship between European Community and Eastern Europe," (Seminar
    for Board of Directors, Economic Club of Memphis, September 9)
"Seminar for Managing Directors, FedEx Corp.," (September 22)
"From Being Guard to Global Integrator: The Role of New International
    Manager," (Speech at Rotary Club of Germantown, October 3)
"International Business Network Project: Seminar Series in International
    Business," Co-sponsored with University of Southern Mississippi
    (October 19-20)
"Management Workshop," High-level delegation of 20 Chinese Government
    and Business Representatives from Shanghai, China (Oct. 25 – Nov. 3)
"NAFTA Conference," (November 1)
"German Reunification from American Perspective," Co-sponsored by World
    Affairs Council (November 1)
"China Economic Summit: Prospects and Opportunities," Co-sponsored by
    TN Department of Economic and Community Development, Nashville,
    TN (December 8-9)

1995

"Developing a Global Mind-Set," (Managing Seminar for FedEx Directors, Feb. 23)
"Doing Business in Mexico: Understanding the Country, the Culture and the
    People," (Workshop, March 7)
"Doing Business in Germany: Understanding the Country, the Culture, and
    the People," (Workshop, April 11)
"On Becoming a Global Manager," (Videotapes for FedEx, June 22)
"Doing Business in Europe: A Focus on Market Structure and Foreign
    Exchange," (Workshop, August 1)
"Managerial Challenge of Globalization," (Seminar for Managing Directors at
    FedEx Corp., August 4)
"The Dual Purpose Airport: Strategies for Success," (International Aviation
    Workshop, October 4-8)

1996

"Global Logistics: Are You Ready for the Challenge?" (Conference, Feb. 22)
"Cooperating for Competitive Advantage: Joint Ventures and Business
    Alliances," Co-sponsored with Cecil C. Humphreys School of Law,
    University of Memphis (Workshop, November 20)
"China Machinery and Automotive Industrial Delegation," (Workshop, Nov.18-20)

1997

"The Future of U.S.-China Relations," Co-sponsored with World Affairs
    Council of Memphis (Seminar, February 28)

"Poland: The Politics and Economies of Transition," Gregosz Kolodo, First Deputy Prime Minister and Minister of Finance, Co-sponsored by World Affairs Council of Memphis (Seminar, March 3)

"Regime Shift: Japanese Politics in a Changing World Economy," Co-sponsored with World Affairs Council of Memphis (Seminar, March 6)

"Fifth Annual East-West Conference: Int'l Management and Marketing," Co-sponsored with TN Board of Regents (Conference, Mar 13-1-6)

"Delegation from Qingdao Textile Corporation, China," (Workshop, March 19-April 2)

"Brazil: Economic Stabilization and Reform Under the Plano Real," Co-sponsored with World Affairs Council (Seminar, April 28)

"Linking the Americas: NAFTA and the Free Trade of the Americas," Co-sponsored with U.S. State Department and World Affairs Council of Memphis (Town Hall Meeting, May 15)

"Brazil: Business and Trade Opportunities for Mid-South Firms," Co-sponsored with American Consulate General in Sao Paulo, Brazil and USDOC (Trade Conference, May 29-30)

"Robert Wang: Portrait of a Memphis Hero," (Reception, July 24)

"Doing Business in South and Sub-Saharan Africa: The Real Deal!" (Mid-South Africa Consortium, September 16)

1998

"Building Global Legal and Ethical Compliance Programs: An Integrity Blueprint for Managers" (Workshop, January 30)

"The China-Hong Kong Reintegration: Challenges and Prospects," Dr. Ming K. Chan, Hoover Institution, Stanford University (Seminar, Feb. 12)

"The European Union: Europe's Response to a New Era of Global Economics," Camille Becker, Belgium (Seminar, March 24)

"Sixth Annual International Trace Conference," Co-sponsored with TN Board of Regents (Nashville, TN, April 5-8)

"The Impending Year 2000: IT Challenges, Strategies, and Solutions," Co-sponsor with SCB Computer Technology Inc. (Conference, July 13)

"Delegation from Chinese Cotton Industry," (Workshop, September)

"Delegation from The Peoples Government of Hexi District," (Workshop, Oct. 15)

1999

"Doing Business with China in the 21st Century," Featuring Dr. Shi Yonghai, President, Chinese Academy for International Trade and Economic Cooperation, Co-sponsored with FedEx (Executive Forum, March 25)

"Impact of Doing Business in Asia," (Seminar, March 3)

"Tenth Anniversary of Robert Wang Center," (Forum, September 8)

2000

"India's Information Technology: A 21st Century Resource for U.S. Companies," Co-sponsored with FedEx Corp., Government of India-Indian Embassy, Confederation of Indian Industries (CII), Memphis in May and Memphis Area Chamber (Conference, May 10-12)

"E-Commerce E-Xplosion! Is Your Business E-Ready?" Co-sponsored with ACCESS LLC, FedEx Corp., Management Information Systems-University of Memphis (Seminar, March 2)

"Seminar on Asian Cultures and Business Practices," Sponsored by FedEx
    Express (Aug 17- Sept 1, Oct 22-27)

2001

"New Opportunities in the Global Economy: The Ninth Annual East-
    West International Business Conference," Co-sponsored with World
    Trade Magazine, USDOC, TN Board of Regents, State of TN ECD, US
    SBA, Appalachian Regional Comm., Memphis & New Orleans Port
    Authorities, Butler Snow Attys, US Chamber of Commerce (Seminar,
    April 9-10)
"Seminar on European Cultures and Business Practices," Sponsored by FedEx
    Express (Jan 28- Feb 2; Sept 16-21)
"Seminar on Latin American Cultures and Business Practices," Sponsored by
    FedEx Express (Oct 28-Nov 2)

2002

"Seminar on Latin American Cultures and Business Practices," Sponsored by
    FedEx Express (Jan 13-18)
"Seminar on Asian Cultures and Business Practices," Sponsored by FedEx
    Express (March 24-29, July 14-19)
"Seminar on European Cultures and Business Practices," Sponsored by FedEx
    Express (Sept 15-19)

2003

"Seminar on European Cultures and Business Practices," Sponsored by FedEx
    Express (Jan 26-31)
"Seminar on Latin American Cultures," Sponsored by FedEx Express (Mar 16-21)
"International Export Letter of Credit Seminar," Co-sponsored with Wachovia
    Bank, U.S. Commercial Service, TSBDC, Forward Logistics Services, and
    Global Marketing Support Services. (June 18)
"China Product Safety Regulations: Coping with China Compulsory
    Certification (CCC) Quality Mark," Co-sponsored with District Export
    Council, Int'l Trade Ctrr-TSBDC, Mid-South Quality-Productivity Ctr.,
    Memphis World Trade Club, Greater Memphis Assoc. for Quality (Aug 6)
"Seminar on Middle Eastern Cultures and Business Practices," Sponsored by
    FedEx Express (Aug 3-7; Sept 14-18)
"Leveraging China: A Southern Strategy for American Business," Co-
    sponsored with US Commercial Service and International Business
    Council of Memphis Chamber (Breakfast Seminar, November 17)
"Practical Strategies for Negotiating Cross-Culturally," Co-sponsored with US
    Commercial Service and International Business Council of Memphis
    Chamber (Breakfast Seminar, November 21)

2004

"Planes, Trains, and Trucks: Learn About NAFTA," Co-sponsored with US
    Commercial Service and International Business Council of Memphis
    Chamber (Breakfast Seminar, January 29)
"Creating Spectacular Performance at Work," Co-sponsored with
    International Business Council (Breakfast Seminar, February 27)
"Seminar on Latin American Cultures," Sponsored by FedEx Express (Mar 18-21)

"Everything New is Old Again: Change at the New York Stock Exchange," Co-sponsored with FedEx, Memphis Society of Financial Analysts, and Economics Club of Memphis (Breakfast Seminar, April 9)

"Seminar on European Cultures and Business Practices," Sponsored by FedEx Express (April 26-31)

"Seminar on Asian Cultures and Business Practices," Sponsored by FedEx Express (Sept 13-16, Oct 11-14)

2005

"The Impact of the Seven Revolutions: Looking Out to the Year 2025," Featuring Erik R. Peterson, Sr. VP and Director, Global Strategy Institute at CSIS. Co-sponsored with Buckman Laboratories, Society of International Business Fellows, Jackson Products, Stanford Group Co., Mallory Alexander, Regions Bank-Morgan Keegan, Memphis Regional Chamber. (Seminar, February 3)

"Asia Now: Successfully Exploring and Exporting to Asian Markets," Co-sponsored with District Export Council, FedEx, CSCMP. Featuring Senior Commercial Officers from Australia, New Zealand, China, Hong Kong, Indonesia, Japan, Korea, Malaysia, Philippines, Singapore, Taiwan, Thailand, Vietnam, (Business Opportunities Seminar, April 6)

"Seminar on Asian Cultures and Business Practices," Sponsored by FedEx Express (April 18-21, Sept 12-15)

"Seminar on European Cultures and Business Practices," Sponsored by FedEx Express (Oct 17-20)

2006

"Seven Futures of Latin America & Caribbean, Europe, Middle East & North Africa, Sub-Saharan Africa, Russia & Central Asia, South Asia, East Asia & South East Asia," Featuring Erik R. Peterson, Sr. VP and Director, Global Strategy Institute at CSIS. Co-sponsored with Buckman Lab., Mallory Alexander, Regions Morgan Keegan, Society of Int'l Business Fellows, Stanford, ThyssenKrupp Elevator, Memphis World Trade Club, Memphis Regional Chamber, US Commercial Service (Seminar, Feb 8)

"Seminar on Latin American Cultures," Sponsored by FedEx Express (Mar 6-9)

"Seminar on Asian Cultures and Business Practices," Sponsored by FedEx Express (March 27-30; Sept 18-21; Oct 2-5)

2007

"Global Business in the Flat World," (Presentation to FedEx executives, Feb. 15)

"Memphis Multi-Modal Conference," Co-sponsored with Memphis World Trade Club and others (March 27-28)

"Seminar on Asian Cultures and Business Practices," Sponsored by FedEx Express (March 26-29; Sept 24-27; Oct 15-18)

2008

"Memphis Multi-Modal Conference," Co-sponsored with Memphis World Trade Club and others (March 19-20)

"Doing Business in Emerging Markets: China and India," Co-sponsored with Buckman Laboratories, Evans & Petree Attys., Mallory Alexander, Memphis Business Journal, Primacy, Society of International Business Fellows, International Business Council, Memphis World Trade Club, (Breakfast Seminar, June 17)

2009

"Meeting Renewable Energy's Technology Challenge: Innovative Solutions from Japan," Featuring Bank of Japan Governor Masaaki Shirakawa, Co-sponsored with Japan-American Society of TN, Inc., Consulate-General of Japan (Nashville), (Seminar, November 13).

"The Way Out of Economic and Financial Crisis: Lessons and Actions," Co-sponsored with National Association of Japan-America Societies (Washington DC). (Webcast, April 23).

"Cyber Security Expo," Co-sponsored with FedEx, CISCO, Symantec, Act Online, FedEx Institute of Technology, U of Memphis' Center for Information Assurance (Conference, October 15)

2010

"Memphis and India: Trade Development," Co-sponsored with Memphis in May, FedEx Express, Greater Memphis Chamber, (Presentation, August 27)

"Taking Your Business Global: Tunisia," Co-sponsored with International Business Council, Memphis in May International Festival, Inc., (Export Seminar, May 6)

"Memphis Multi Modal Conference," Co-sponsored with Memphis World Trade Club, International Port of Memphis, CSX Intermodal, Canada, Cargo Business, Intermodal Cartage Co, BNSF Railway, CBRE/Memphis, M.G. Maher, Union Pacific, Delta, Avalon, Norfolk Southern, Smith & Nephew, *Memphis Business Journal*, Greater Memphis Chamber, (Seminar, May 11-12)

"Doing Business with Spain/IBC Update," Co-sponsored with Greater Memphis Chamber. Featuring Mario Buisan, Trade Commissioner of Spain, (Workshop, November 30)

2011

"Doing Business in Belgium: In the Heart of Europe," Co-sponsored with Memphis World Trade Club (May 5)

"Sustainable Real Estate, Co-sponsored with Economic Club and Urban Land Institute (Conference, March 24-26)

"U.S. and India Trade Development: Export and Investment Opportunities," Sponsored with Memphis Chamber (Presentation, November)

"China: The New Frontiers for Export," Co-sponsored with International Business Council, Memphis Chamber (January 25)

"Cyber Security Expo," Co-sponsored with U of Memphis Center for Information Assurance (October 7).

"TN Trade Program," Co-sponsored with Memphis Chamber, (December 7)

2012

"Mid-South Aerotropolis Conference," Sponsored by FedEx and Elvis Presley Enterprises, Inc., (April 10)

"Doing Business with the Philippines," Co-sponsored with International Business Council and Memphis in May, (May 10)

Discover the New Europe!

Faculty Study Abroad

Antwerp Belgium

Integration and Unification
of the European Union

May 14-24, 2006

FACULTY STUDY ABROAD IN ANTWERP, BELGIUM
CIBER SPONSORS: 1994 - 2006

Brigham Young University
Florida International University
Michigan State University
Purdue University
Texas A&M University
University of Colorado Denver

University of Connecticut
University of Florida
University of Kansas
University of Maryland
University of Memphis
University of Wisconsin

Discover the New Europe!

Faculty Study Abroad

Strasbourg France

Integration and Unification of the European Union

May 10-21, 2009

FACULTY STUDY ABROAD IN STRASBOURG, FRANCE
CIBER SPONSORS: 2007-2009

Brigham Young University

Florida International University

Purdue University

Texas A&M University

University of Colorado Denver

University of Connecticut

University of Kansas

University of Maryland

University of Memphis

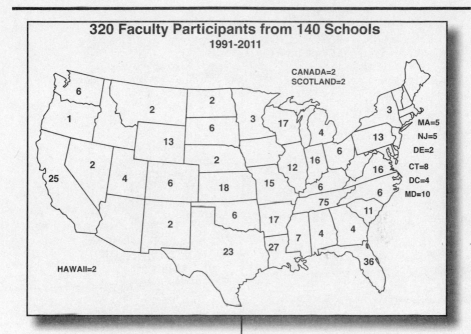

320 Faculty Participants from 140 Schools
1991-2011

CANADA=2
SCOTLAND=2

MA=5
NJ=5
DE=2
CT=8
DC=4
MD=10

HAWAII=2

ALABAMA A&M UNIVERSITY
   Mohammad Robbani
ANGELO STATE UNIVERSITY
   Kurt Buerger
   Norman Sundermann (2)
ARKANSAS COLLEGE
   Cassie Crieghton
ARKANSAS STATE UNIVERSITY
   Clint Relyea
BARRY UNIVERSITY
   Charles Rarick
   Greg Winter
BELMONT UNIVERSITY
   Bradley Dean Childs
   Marilyn Young
BOWLING GREEN STATE UNIVERSITY
   Sherry Sullivan
BRIGHAM YOUNG UNIVERSITY
   Nile Hatch
BUTLER UNIVERSITY
   Bela Florenthal
CALIFORNIA STATE UNIVERSITY, CHICO
   Glenn M. Gomes (2)
   James M. Owens (2)
CALIFORNIA STATE UNIV., SACRAMENTO
   Amin A. Elmallah
   Ming-Ting Mike Lee
   Nobuaki Namiki
   Peter A. Sharp
CENTRAL WASHINGTON UNIVERSITY
   Hugh Spall

   Gary P Mahan
GEORGIA SOUTHERN UNIVERSITY
   Leslie B. Fletcher
GRAMBLING STATE UNIVERSITY
   Gary Poe
HARRIS STOWE STATE UNIVERSITY
   Peter Ndoma-Ogar
HENRY FORD COMMUNITY COLLEGE
   William H. Harvey
HOWARD UNIVERSITY
   Lorenzo Morris
JAMES MADISON UNIVERSITY
   Diane Riordan
   Newell Wright
JOHN CARROLL UNIVERSITY
   John C. Soper
KANSAS STATE UNIVERSITY
   Lori Bergen
LA SIERRA UNIVERSITY
   Prudence Pollard
LOUISIANA STATE UNIV. AT EUNICE
   Joan L. Hernandez
LOUISIANA TECH UNIVERSITY
   Gene Johnson
LOYOLA UNIVERSITY NEW ORLEANS
   Michael M. Pearson
MACOMB COMMUNITY COLLEGE
   Cheryl Sypinewski
MARY WASHINGTON COLLEGE
   Margaret Ray

MEREDITH COLLEGE
    Rebecca J. Oatsvall
METROPOLITAN ST. COLLEGE OF DENVER
    Jerry D. Boswell
    Laszlo Pook
MIAMI-DADE COMMUNITY COLLEGE
    Ivan F. Figeuroa
    Blanca R. Ortega
MINOT STATE UNIVERSITY
    James Ondracek
MISSISSIPPI COLLEGE
    Sandra B. Parks
MISSOURI SOUTHERN STATE UNIV.
    Terry Marion
MISSOURI WESTERN STATE COLLEGE
    Dale Kreuger
MONTANA STATE UNIV.-NORTHERN
    Barbara Anne Zuck
MONTCLAIR STATE UNIVERSITY
    C Jayachandran
MURRAY STATE UNIVERSITY
    Roger C Schoefeldt
NEW MEXICO STATE UNIVERSITY
    Richard Adkisson
NEW ORLEANS UNIVERSITY
    Joseph R Razek
NICHOLS COLLEGE
    Louise Nordstrom
    Edward G. Warren (2)
NORTH CAROLINA A&T UNIVERSITY
    William Amponsah
No. GEORGIA COLLEGE AND ST. UNIV.
    Elisabeth Jane Teal Holman
NORTHEAST LOUISIANA UNIVERSITY
    Tom R Lee
    David Loudon
    Donna Luse
    C. William McConkey
    Paul Nelson
    Jerry L. Wall
NORTHERN ILLINOIS UNIVERSITY
    Madan Annavarjula
    Courtney Shelton Hunt
    Tanuja Singh
OKLAHOMA STATE UNIVERSITY
    Ron Miller
PELLISSIPPI STATE
    E. Ely Driver
    Phyllis Driver
PEPPERDINE UNIVERSITY
    Bruce Buskirk (2)
    Clifford E. Darden
    Mark Mallinger
    David Smith

    Terry Young
PEPPERDINE UNIV. GRAZIADIO SCHOOL
    Evan Anderson
    Nikolai Wasilewski
PITTSBURG STATE UNIVERSITY
    Arthur Fischer (2)
    Bienvenido Cortes
    Henry Crouch
PNC BANK, PITTSBURGH
    Clayton "Jamie" Keefer
PRAIRIE VIEW A&M UNIVERSITY
    David Kruegel
PURDUE UNIVERSITY
    Joan Allatta
PURDUE UNIVERSITY CALUMET
    C. Pat Obi
    Radford University
    Deborah S. Cook
    Nancy L Meade
RHODES COLLEGE
    Kelly E. Fish
    Marshall E. Mahon
    Charles C. Orvis
    John M. Planchon (2)
    Katheryn Wright
ROCKHURST COLLEGE
    Merle E. Frey
ROCKHURST UNIVERSITY
    Brian D. Frtizpatrick
    Gail Hoover
RUTGERS UNIVERSITY
    Arthur Klinghoffer
    Judith Klinghoffer
SAINT LOUIS UNIVERSITY
    Janikan Supanvanij
SAN DIEGO STATE UNIVERSITY
    Kenneth Marin
SEATTLE UNIVERSITY
    Carl Obermiller
SONOMA STATE UNIVERSITY
    Robert Girling
SOUTH CAROLINA STATE UNIVERSITY
    David Jamison
So. ILLINOIS UNIV. AT CARBONDALE
    Lars Larson
    Geoffrey S. Nathan
    Jesus A Ponce de Leon
    Arun Rai
    Rich Rivers
    John Summey
    Chuck Stubbart
    Robert C. Waldron
    Margaret E. Winters
ST LOUIS UNIVERSITY
    James E. Fisher

ST. CLOUD STATE UNIVERSITY
  Thom J. Belich
  P.N. SubbaNarasimha
ST. MARY'S UNIVERSITY
  Kamlesh T. Mehta
  Richard Menger
SUNY COLLEGE BUFFALO
  Michael Littman
  Jeff Strieter
TARLETON STATE UNIVERSITY
  Elizabeth Ball
  Dena Johnson
TENNESSEE STATE UNIVERSITY
  Vaidotas Lukosius
  J. Byron Pennington
TENNESSEE TECHNOLOGICAL UNIV.
  Rena C. Ellzy
TEXAS A& M UNIVERSITY
  Ursula Y. Alvarado
  Paul Busch
  James Kolari
  Steven W McDaniel
  Michael W. Putsay
  Dave Syzmanski
THE UNIV. OF ALABAMA IN HUNTSVILLE
  Chris W. Paul II
THE UNIVERSITY OF MEMPHIS
  Kenneth Austin
  Emin Babakus
  Carol Beinstock
  Rabi Bhagat
  Delano Black
  Robert Blanton
  William Carpenter
  Quentin Chu
  David H. Ciscel
  T Bettina Cornwell
  Barbara D. Davis
  Peter S. Davis
  Thomas O. Depperschmidt
  Clifton V. Dixon
  Irene Duhaime
  John Forth Gnuschke
  Charles Hall
  Ben Kedia
  Kenneth Holland
  Mathew W Jewett
  Phillip T. Kolbe
  Constatine Konstans
  Hsiang-te Kung
  George H. Lucas
  James M. Lukawitz
  John Malloy
  Robert M. O'Halloran

  Sidney McPhee
  W T Mealor Jr.
  Satish Mehra
  C S Pyun
  James P. Rakowski
  Rose Rubin
  Tracy Smith
  William T. Smith
  Robert V. Smythe
  J David Spiceland
  Tom Stafford
  Peter K. Tat
  Robert R. Taylor
  Pochara Theearthorn
  William J. Thompson
  Howard S Tu
  Jeanne Tutor
  Terry Umbreit
  Charles Williams
THE UNIV. OF WISCONSIN-MADISON
  Mason A. Carpenter
  Linda Gorshels
TOWSON STATE UNIVERSITY
  Shohreh A. Kaynama
TRUMAN STATE UNIVERSITY
  Adrien Presley
UNIVERISTY OF NEBRASKA AT OMAHA
  Mary Landholt
UNIVERISTY OF SW LOUISIANA
  Patricia A Lanier
UNIVERSITY OF AKRON
  Tim Wilkinson
UNIV. OF ARKANSAS AT LITTLE ROCK
  Marian Crawford
  Mark Dorfman
  Julie J. Gentry
  Garard Halpern
  Vicky A. King
  Andrew Terry
  Ashvin P. Vibhakar
UNIVERSITY OF ARKANSAS PLINE BLUFF
  Kawmena A. Cudjoe
UNIVERSITY OF BALTIMORE
  Richard Trotter
UNIVERSITY OF CALGARY
  Steve G. Sutton
UNIVERSITY OF CENTRAL ARKANSAS
  Lillian C. Parrish
  Bill Seyfried
UNIVERSITY OF CENTRAL FLORIDA
  Pamela S. Lewis
UNIVERSITY OF CENTRAL OKLAHOMA
  Darrell Ford

UNIVERSITY OF CINCINNATI
Charles H. Matthews
UNIVERSITY OF COLORADO
Elizabeth Cooperman
Barbara Ericsson
UNIVERSITY OF COLORADO AT BOULDER
Kenneth R. Gordon
UNIVERSITY OF COLORADO, DENVER
Blair Gifford
Lori Willard
UNIVERSITY OF CONNECTICUT
Kathleen Dechant
Karen File
Shantaram P Hegde
Mohamed Hussein
Suresh Nair
Narasimhan Srinivasan
Mark Youndt
UNIVERSITY OF EVANSVILLE
Christine McKeag
UNIVERSITY OF FLORIDA
Haldun Aytug
Joel Cohen
Sahin Selcuk Erenguc
Arnold A. Heggestad
John L. Kramer
John Kraft
Sandra S. Kramer
Amie Kreppel
Larry Alan Di Matteo
Virginia G. Maurer
W. Andrew McCollough
Terry McCoy
Gary McGill
Anand Paul
Selwyn Piramuthu
Stanley K. Smith
Carol Taylor West
UNIVERSITY OF GLASGOW
Maurizio Carbone
UNIVERSITY OF HAWAII AT MANOA
Jayna Reynon
UNIVERSITY OF INCARNATE WORD
Randall G. Bowden
Patricia L. Burr
Michael Mulnix
Seth K. Parker
UNIVERSITY OF KANSAS
Joyce Claterbos
Allen Ford
Charles E. Krider
Douglas May
Margaret Schomaker
Catherine Schwoerer

Daniel Spencer
Thomas Weiss
UNIVERSITY OF LOUISVILLE
Okbalghi Yohannes
UNIVERSITY OF MARYLAND
Mannika Barros-Carrero
JoAnne Hinshaw
Wolfgang Jank
Shreevardhal Lele
Clarence J Mann
UNIVERSITY OF MISSOURI
Jenice Stewart
UNIVERSITY OF MISSOURI-ST. LOUIS
Betty Warburton Vining
UNIVERSITY OF NEVADA
Glen Atkinson
UNIVERSITY OF NEW ORLEANS
Steven R. Clinton
Dinah Payne
Milton M. Pressley
UNIVERSITY OF NOTRE DAME
Samuel S. Gaglio
John W. Houck
Robert W. Williamson
UNIVERSITY OF OKLAHOMA
Richard Tersine
UNIVERSITY OF PITTSBURGH
Ericka Doreen Hernández Carrera
Shirley Cassing
Jacqueline Saslawski
Monique Jacqueline Van Damme
UNIVERSITY OF PORTLAND
Martha Rhea
UNIVERSITY OF SOUTH CAROLINA
Richard Heiens
Marsha Shelburn
UNIVERSITY OF SOUTH DAKOTA
Thomas L. Davies
Diane Hoadley
Audhesh K. Paswan
Charles Roegiers
Robert Rosacker
UNIVERSITY OF SOUTHERN MISSISSIPPI
David M Hunt
UNIVERSITY OF SOUTHWESTERN
LOUSIANA
Lewis R. Gale IV
Kerry D. Carson
Paula P. Carson
UNIVERSITY OF TAMPA
Barbara Ross Wooldridge
UNIVERSITY OF TENNESSEE, KNOXVILLE
Terry Esper
Funda Sahin

Wendy Tate
Shichun Xu
UNIVERSITY OF TENNESSEE AT MARTIN
B. Wayne Kemp
UNIV. OF THE DISTRICT OF COLUMBIA
Nikolai Victorovich Ostapenko
UNIVERSITY OF WASHINGTON
April Atwood
UNIVERSITY OF WISCONSIN
Jude Rathburn
UNIVERSITY OF WISCONSIN- LACROSSE
Leticia Pena
UNIVERSITY OF WISCONSIN-GREEN BAY
Alla Wilson
UNIVERSITY OF WISCONSIN-MADISON
Hollis Ashbaugh
UNIV. OF WISCONSIN-MILWAUKEE
Jorge A. Gonzalez, Jr.
UNIV. OF WISCONSIN-STEVENS POINT
Richard R Ruppel
UNIV. OF WISCONSIN-WHITEWATER
G.M. Naidu
UNIV. OF SOUTH CAROLINA- AIKEN
Niren Vyas

UTAH STATE UNIVERSITY
Alison Cook
John R. Cragun
VANDERBILT UNIVERSITY
David Parsley
VIRGINIA COMMONWEALTH UNIVERSITY
Charles M. Byles
Van R. Wood
VIRGINIA UNION UNIVERSITY
Patricia Ann Murray
WASHBURN UNIVERSITY
Teresita S Leyell
Kanalis A. Ockree
WINTHROP COLLEGE
Tomiesenia Wiles
WOFFORD COLLEGE
Dennis Wiseman

TOTAL FACULTY
PARTICIPANTS = 320

FDIB-Globalization Seminars
June 7-10, 2012
The University of Memphis

- Intro to International Business
- International Accounting
- International Finance
- Global Supply Chain Management
- International Marketing
- International Management

Apply by April 30, 2012 for the early registration fee of $1395
A limited number of $250 scholarships are available!

PROGRAM INFORMATION: memphis.edu/wangctr   CONTACT: abcole@memphis.edu

The FDIB-Globalization Seminars are designed to help business faculty bring international context into the classroom and to expand teaching and research skills.

Each seminar is built around a comprehensive *coursepack* to support and demonstrate the globalization of business. These course materials will be available to seminar participants.

- course outlines   - reference materials
- case studies   - experiential exercises
- powerpoint slides

6 FDIB-GLOBALIZATION SEMINARS*

Introduction to International Business:
Michael Pustay, Texas A&M University
Mike Peng, University of Texas at Dallas

NEW! International Accounting:
Lee Radebaugh, BrighamYoung University
Carolyn M Callahan, University of Memphis

International Finance:
Kirt Butler, Michigan State University
Hakan Saraoglu, Bryant University

Global Supply Chain Management:
Tomas Hult, Michigan State University
Ernest Nichols, The University of Memphis

International Management:
Jeffrey A Krug, Loyola University New Orleans
Ben L. Kedia, The University of Memphis

International Marketing:
S. Tamer Cavusgil, Georgia State University
Attila Yaprak, Wayne State University

Participants attend one seminar.

Agenda

Thursday, June 7
5:30 PM   Welcoming Reception
7:15 PM   Overview of Global Economic Transformation by Dr. Ben L. Kedia

Friday, June 8 (Concurrent Seminars)
8:30 AM   FDIB-Globalization Seminars
- Intro to International Business
- International Accounting
- International Finance
- International Management
- International Marketing
- Global Supply-Chain Management
12:00 PM Lunch
1-5:00 PM FDIB-Globalization Seminars

Saturday, June 9
8:30 AM   FDIB-Globalization Seminars
12:00 PM Lunch
1-5:00 PM FDIB-Globalization Seminars

Sunday, June 10
8:30 AM   Workshops (Concurrent Workshops)
- Research
- Pedagogy
- Grant Opportunities
11:30 AM Lunch
Program Concludes

Sponsored by
UNCFSP-Institute for International Public Policy and CIBERs* at Duke University, Georgia State University, Michigan State University and University of Memphis, plus the Center for Global Business at University of Texas, Dallas.

*Centers for International Business Education and Research designated by the U.S. Department of Education.

FDIB-GLOBALIZATION SEMINARS

CIBER SPONSORS (1991-2012)

Duke University
Florida International University
Georgia Institute of Technology
Georgia State University
Michigan State University

Texas A&M University
The Ohio State University
University of Florida
University of Kansas
University of Memphis
University of Wisconsin

University of Texas, Dallas and UNCFSP-IIPP

SPEAKERS AND SEMINAR LEADERS

INTRO TO INTERNATIONAL BUSINESS SEMINAR (1992-2012)

Dr. Otis W. Baskin, University of Memphis
Dr. O. C. Ferrell, University of Memphis
Dr. Jeffrey Krug, University of Memphis
Dr. Subhash C. Jain, University of Connecticut
Dr. Vinod Jain, University of Maryland
Dr. Mike Peng, University of Texas, Dallas
Dr. Michael Pustay, Texas A&M University

INTERNATIONAL ACCOUNTING (2010-2012)

Dr. Carolyn Callahan, University of Memphis
Dr. Lee Radebaugh, Brigham Young University

INTERNATIONAL FINANCE (1992-2014)

Dr. Raj Aggarwal, John Carroll University
Dr. Gordon Bodnar, Johns Hopkins University
Dr. Kirt Butler, Michigan State University
Dr. Cheol Eun, Georgia Institute of Technology
Dr. Phillip Kolbe, University of Memphis
Dr. Hakan Saraoglu, Bryant University
Dr. Pochara Theerathorn, University of Memphis

INTERNATIONAL MANAGEMENT (1992-2012)

Dr. Rabi Bhagat, University of Memphis
Dr. Mason Carpenter, University of Wisconsin
Dr. Ben L. Kedia, University of Memphis
Dr. Jeff Krug, Loyola University of New Orleans
Dr. Sumit K. Kundu, Florida International University
Dr. Arie Lewin, Duke University
Dr. Hans Schollhammer, Univ. of California, Los Angeles

INTERNATIONAL MARKETING (1992-2012)

Dr. Emin Babakus, University of Memphis
Dr. S. Tamer Cavusgil, Georgia State University
Dr. Bettina Cornwell, University of Memphis
Dr. Francis Ulgado, Georgia Institute of Technology
Dr. Peter B. P. Walter, University of Arkansas
Dr. Attila Yaprak, Wayne State University

GLOBAL INFORMATION TECHNOLOGY (2000-2001)

Dr. Tor Guimaraes, TN Technological University
Dr. Prashant Palvia, University of Memphis
Dr. Steven J. Simon, Florida International University

GLOBAL E-BUSINESS (2002-2006)

Dr. Mark A. Jamison, University of Florida
Dr. Kissan Joseph, University of Kansas
Dr. Virginia Mauer, University of Florida
Dr. Robert Thomas, University of Florida

GLOBAL SUPPLY CHAIN MANAGEMENT (2005-2012)

Dr. Tomas Hult, Michigan State University
Dr. Ernie Nichols, Jr. University of Memphis
Dr. Anthony Ross, MIchigan State University

GEOGRAPHIC AREA STUDIES(1994)

Dr. Roderic A. Camp, Tulane University
Dr. M. Donald Hancock, Vanderbilt University

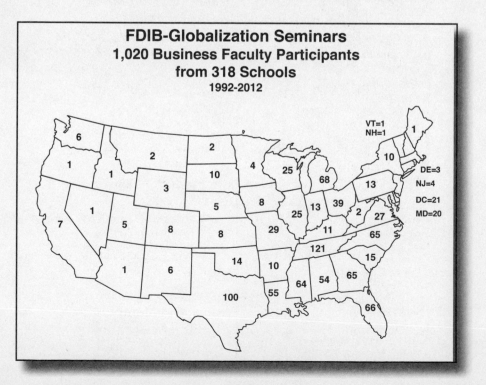

FDIB-Globalization Seminars
1,020 Business Faculty Participants
from 318 Schools
1992-2012

A & M COMMERCE
    Janet Walker
ADAMS STATE COLLEGE
    Jay Weiner
AIR FORCE ACADEMY
    Brian Walker
ALABAMA A&M UNIVERSITY
    Augustine Dike
    Chris Enyinda
    Marsha Griffin
    Rohit Jain
BARBARA JONES
    Halima Qureshi
    Eric Rahimian
    Mohammad Robbani
    Andrea Tillman
ALABAMA STATE UNIVERSITY
    Brenda Autry
    Le-Quita Booth
    Gow-Cheng Huang
    Xueyu Cheng
    Jae Choi
    Sun Gi Chun
    Jean Crawford
    Charlie Hardy
    Janel Bell Haynes
    Kamal Hingorani
    Walter Montgomery
    Robert McNeal
    Tammy Prater
    La `Shaun Seay
    Kim Smith
    Percy Vaughn Jr.
    Jiin Wang
    Don Woodard
    Susan Young-Coleman
ALBANY STATE UNIVERSITY
    Everett Cordy
    Alireza Dorestani
    Jonathan Elimimian
    Yousef Jahmani
    Bingguang Li
    Michael Rogers
    Hassan Said
    Don Snyder
    Chiou Wang
ALCORN STATE UNIVERSITY
    Wille Anderson
    Marcharie Chambliss
    Clyde Posey (2)
    Lisa Micicih
    A. Benedict Udemgba
ANGELO STATE UNIVERSITY
    James Wilkins

Anhui University
    Qian Gao
ANHUI UNIVERSITY
    Qian Gao
APPALACHIAN STATE UNIVERSITY
    Pennie Bagley
    Betty Coffey
    Tracy Reed
ARKANSAS STATE UNIVERSITY
    Alan Campbell
    David Kern
    Laddie Logan
    John Mello
    Sarath Nonis
    Richard Taylor
ARKANSAS TECH UNIVERSITY
    Kevin Mason
AUBURN UNIVERSITY
    William Foxx
    Philip Gregorowicz
    Carel Ligeon
    Lesley Mace
    Jeffery Periatt
    Gwinyai Utete
BALDWIN-WALLACE COLLEGE
    Thomas Donahue
    Peter Rea
    Malcolm Watson
BALL STATE UNIVERSITY
    Jatinder Gupta (2)
    Erdogan Kumou
    Rathin Rathinasamy
    Srinivasan Sundaram
BELMONT ABBEY COLLEGE
    William Van Lear
BELMONT UNIVERSITY
    Howard Cochran, Jr.
BETHUNE-COOKMAN UNIVERSITY
    Sussan Aysar
    Susan Baxter
    Gina Beckles
    Aubrey Long (2)
    Michael Santonino
    William J. Ziegler
BIRMINGHAM SOUTHERN COLLEGE
    Shirley Schooley
BLOOMSBURG UNIVERSITY
    David Heskel
BLUEFIELD STATE COLLEGE
    Albert Berkoh
BOSTON COLLEGE
    Catherine Lerme
BOWIE STATE UNIVERSITY
    Fiseha Eshete (3)

James Dixon (Sr.)
Jongdoo Lee
Granville Sawyer
Regina Tawah
BOWLING GREEN STATE UNIVERSITY
Man Zhang
BRIGHAM YOUNG UNIVERSITY
Brooklyn Derr
Gary Mckinnon
Grant McQueen
Kristie Seawright
Steven Thorley
Buena Vista University
Scott Anderson
Steve Remington (2)
Carroll University
Dennis Debrecht
Gary Olsen
Richard Penesky
Greg Shultz
CENTRAL CONNECTICUT STATE UNIV.
Joseph Fung
CENTRAL MICHIGAN UNIVERSITY
David Sprague
CENTRAL MISSOURI STATE UNIV.
Dennis Krumwiede
CENTRAL STATE UNIVERSITY
Charles Anderson
Firooz Ghavami
Edwige Sery (2)
Charles Showell
CENTRAL WASHINGTON UNIVERSITY
Joseph Bradley
Greg Cant
Megan Sellick
CHICAGO STATE UNIVERSITY
Zafar Bokhari
Linnae Bryant
Wolanyo Kpo (2)
Rooseveit Martin (2)
Vincent Osaghae
CHRISTIAN BROTHERS UNIVERSITY
Bonnie Fancher
Jana Kvzmicki
Cayce Lawrence
Frank Marion
John Megley, III
Claire Nash
Ernest Nordtvedt
Don Nyonna
Patricia Papachristou (2)
Sarah Pitts
Kristin Prien (2)
Michael Ryan

CLARK ATLANTA UNIVERSITY
Mohammad Bhuiyan (2)
Rajul Gokarn
Siriyama Herath
Mohammad Latif
Marlissa Phillips
Zelealem Yiheyis
John Young
CLEMSON UNIVERSITY
Sri Sridharan
CLEVELAND STATE UNIVERSITY
Andrew Gross
COLLEGE OF SAN MATEO
Janice Willis
COLLIN COLLEGE
Barbara Palmer
COLORADO STATE UNIVERSITY
Susan Athey
Charles Butler
Joe Cannon
Jennifer Coats
Jim McCambridge
Cherie O'Neil
COLUMBUS STATE COMM. COLLEGE
Wesley Blyth
Bud Cohan
Jack Popovich
Mary Vaughn
CREIGHTON UNIVERSITY
Stephen Hutchens
DALTON STATE COLLEGE
Donna Mayo (2)
Rita Moore
Laura Rose
DAYTONA STATE COLLEGE
Michael Avery
DELAWARE STATE UNIVERSITY
Bridget Anakwe
Constant Beugre
Nandita Das
Nancy Ning
Nanda Viswanathan (2)
DELTA STATE UNIVERSITY
Renee Foster (2)
Val Hinton
Gokhan Karahan
Eckward McKnight
Randall Pearcy
John Quon
Ashley Soliz
Vicki Webster
Jennifer Ziegelmayer
DILLARD UNIVERSITY
Richard Baucum

Edgar Chase
Christian Fugar
Richard Igwike (2)
Susan Kadlec
Anthony Pinder
DRURY COLLEGE
Clifton Petty
Duke University
Billie Maciunas
EAST TENNESSEE STATE UNIVERSITY
Ugur Yavas
EASTERN ILLINOIS UNIVERSITY
Aline Arnold
Barbara Kemmerer
Nancy Marlow
EASTERN KENTUCKY UNIVERSITY
Richard Powers
Carolyn Siegel
EASTERN MICHIGAN UNIVERSITY
Al Diallo
Elif Persinger
ELIZABETH CITY STATE UNIVERSITY
Yan Jin
Debjani Kanjilal
Alex Ogwu
Ngozi Oriaku
Narendra Sharma
Kungpo Tao
ELON COLLEGE
Helen Currie
Katherine Kort
Brian Nienhaus
Ken Paul
Herb Schuette
ELON UNIVERSITY
Catherine Chiang
EMBRY RIDDLE AERONAUTICAL UNIV.
Cindy Greenman
EMORY UNIVERSITY
Jagdish Sheth
ESCOLA SUPERIOR DE COMERCE INT'L
Marta Segura-bonet
FAYETTEVILLE STATE UNIVERSITY
Boris Abbey
Khalid Dubas
Pamela Jackson
Baeyong Lee
Fazlul Miah
Shahnawaz Muhammed
Donatus Okhomina
Dothang Truong
Thomas Williams
Craig Wishart
FEDERAL EXPRESS
Donna Price

FERRIS STATE UNIVERSITY
Richard Hewer
FLORIDA A&M UNIVERSITY
Charles Evans
Joycelynn Finley-Hervey
Roscoe Hightower
Aretha Hill
Angela Lewis
Angela Murphy
Augustine Nwabuzor
Johnston Osagie
Daaim Shabazz (2)
Annette Singleton
J Sutterfield
FLORIDA INSTITUTE OF TECHNOLOGY
Tim Muth
FLORIDA INTERNATIONAL UNIVERSITY
Karlene Cousins
FLORIDA MEMORIAL COLLEGE
Johnnie Adams
Edwin Goldberg
Rita Koyame
Robert Labadie (3)
Bilal Makkawi
FLORIDA MEMORIAL UNIVERSITY
Abbass Entessari (2)
Eddie Hand
William Lucky
Debra Perkins (3)
FLORIDA SOUTHEASTERN UNIVERSITY
Joseph Kilpatrick
FLORIDA SOUTHERN UNIVERSITY
David Grossman
FORT HAYS STATE UNIVERSITY
Ralph Gamble
FORT VALLEY STATE UNIVERSITY
Regina Ivory Butts
Paul Hatchett
Aretha Hill
Marian Terrell
FREED-HARDEMAN UNIVERSITY
Jim Shelton
Tamie Sorrell
Dwayne Wilson
GEORGIA COLLEGE & STATE UNIV.
Nate Bennett
Sally Humphries
GEORGIA SOUTHERN UNIVERSITY
Constance Campbell
Nancy Wagner
GEORGIA STATE UNIVERSITY
Ronald Barden
Jacobus Boers
Wade Danis

Gautam Goswami
Ihsen Ketata
David Nachman
Marta White (2)
GLASSBORO STATE COLLEGE
Robert Lynch
GOVERNORS STATE UNIVERSITY
Anthony Andrews
Dashan Cui
David Green
Olumide Ijose
Susan Ji
Evelina Mengova
John Simon
Feng Tian
Jun Zhao
GRAMBLING STATE UNIVERSITY
Marc Cadet
Semere Haile (2)
Mahmoud Haj
Ghebre Keleta (2)
Alethea Lindsay
Obonnaya (John) Nwoha (3)
Gary Poe (2)
Cheryl Vaicys
GRAND CANYON UNIVERSITY
Ryan Lunsford
GRAND VALLEY STATE UNIVERSITY
Lawrence Blose
Rita Grant
Carol Sanchez
GREENSBORO COLLEGE
Alexander Kondeas
GROVE CITY COLLEGE
Jeremy DalleTezze
Laura Havrilla
HAMPTON UNIVERSITY
Priscilla Aaltonen
Kanata Jackson
Terri Kirchner
Nicoleta Maghear
Edwin Makamson (2)
Patrick Simanjuntak
Susanne Toney
Lida Zarrabi
HARRIS STOWE UNIVERSITY
Charles Sykes (2)
HARRISBURG AREA COMM. COLLEGE
Marcia Hajduk
HARRIS-STOWE STATE UNIVERSITY
Richarlene Beech
Joyce Eisel
Robert Kamkwalala
Johndavid Kerr

Peter Ndoma-Ogar
Charles Sykes
Fatemeh (Fara) Zakery
HENDERSON STATE UNIVERSITY
Anita Williams
Hendrix College
Karen Oxner
HINDS COMMUNITY COLLEGE
Renee Akers
Janice Duncan
Dick Robertson
Tom Shepherd
Renee Summers
HINDS COMM. COLLEGE, RANKIN
Clair Helms
HOWARD UNIVERSITY
Micah Crump
Maru Etta
Jin-Gil Jeong
Masoud Kavoossi
Narendra Rustagi
HUNTINGDON COLLEGE
Samir Moussalli
HUSSON COLLEGE
Barry Lin
HUSTON-TILLOSTON UNIVERSITY
Jaenean Davis-Street
IDAHO STATE UNIVERSITY
Philip Nitse
ILLINOIS STATE UNIVERSITY
Barbara Ribbens
INDIANA STATE UNIVERSITY
Robert Green
INDIANA UNIVERSITY OF NORTHWEST
Surekha Rao
IOWA WESTERN COMM. COLLEGE
James Ficek
ITESM, CAMPUS GUADALAJARA
Alejandro Allera
Eileen Daspro
Alejandro De Santiago
JACKSON STATE UNIVERSITY
Steve Agahro
JOHANNES KEPLER UNIV. OF LINZ
Katharina Hofer (2)
JOHNSON C. SMITH UNIVERSITY
Sunday Ndoh
James Nguyen
Yvette Russell
Alfred Smith
Perumal Thirumurthy
JONES COUNTY JUNIOR COLLEGE
Joe Mauldin
Debbie Moseley

Charlotte Williams
KANSAI GAIDAI UNIVERSITY
Samuel Doss
KANSAS STATE UNIVERSITY
Marne Arthaud-Day
Kimberly Charland
Janis Crow
Li-tzang (Jane) Hsu
Esther Swilley
Sabine Turnley
KENNESAW STATE COLLEGE
Susan Carley
KENNESAW STATE UNIVERSITY
Virginia Ingram
KENT STATE UNIVERSITY
Mike Mayo
KEPLER UNIVERSITY
Petra Kuehr
KYUNG HEE UNIVERSITY
Ho-hyung Lee
LAMBUTH COLLEGE
Wilburn Lane, Jr.
LANGSTON UNIVERSITY
Michael Hamilton (2)
Hossein Sarjeh Payma
Noopur Singh
Solomon Smith
LANSING COMMUNITY COLLEGE
Bill Motz
LEMOYNE-OWEN COLLEGE
Sharon Bush
Amitava Chatterjee
Harold Curnutte
Austin Emeagwai
Sam Kazali
Dean Kruger
Reoungeneria McFarland
LEWIS UNIVERSITY
Robert Atra (2)
LINCOLN UNIVERSITY
Robert Allen
William Dadson
Ganga Ramdas
Oswald Richards (2)
Harry Washington
LIPSCOMB UNIVERSITY
William Ingram
LIVINGSTON UNIVERSITY
Ken Tucker
LONDON MILLENIUM COLLEGE
Olawale Olanrewaju
LONG ISLAND UNIVERSITY
Steven Chang
LOUISIANA TECH UNIVERSITY
Sean Dwyer

Larry Jarrell
Anthony Jurkus
LOYOLA UNIVERSITY, NEW ORLEANS
Pamela Van Epps
LYNN UNIVERSITY
Ralph Norcio
LYON COLLEGE
Cassie Creighton
Atul Mitra
MAKERERE UNIVERSITY
Warren Byabashaija
Julius Kakuru
Joseph Ntayi
MANHATTAN COLLEGE
Frederick Greene
MANKATO STATE UNIVERSITY
Li Zhang
MARSHALLTOWN COMM. COLLEGE
George Johnson
MEREDITH COLLEGE
Ying Liao
Merrill Lynch
Thomas Williams
METHODIST COLLEGE
Jeffrey Zimmerman
MICHIGAN STATE UNIVERSITY
Humaira Mahi
Stewart Miller
Sarah Singer
MIDDLE TENNESSEE STATE UNIVERSITY
Kenneth Tillery
MIDWESTERN STATE UNIVERSITY
Yoshikazu Fukasawa
John Martinez
Roy Patin
Phil Wilson
MILLSAPS COLLEGE
Edward Ryan, Jr.
MINOT STATE UNIVERSITY
Deanna Klein
MISSISSIPPI COLLEGE
Frank Hood (2)
Kevin Pauli
Patty Saliba
MISSISSIPPI GULF COAST CM. COL.
Amy Chataginer
Lisa Courtney
Jack Gazzo
Troy Guider
Nancy Higdon
Megan Parkman
MISSISSIPPI STATE UNIVERSITY
Paul Grimes (2)

Joseph Peyrefitte
Richard Still (2)
MISSISSIPPI VALLEY STATE UNIVERSITY
A. Chowdhury (2)
Tadesse Mengistu (4)
Rajanikanth Naraseeyappa
Naraseeyappa Rajanikanth
MISSOURI SOUTHERN ST. COLLEGE
Nii Adote Abrahams
Janet Buzzard
Suzanna Long
Chris Moos
MISSOURI SOUTHERN STATE UNIVERSITY
Maria Bejan
Henri Coeme
Terry Marion
MISSOURI WESTERN STATE COLLEGE
Carol Roever
MONMOUTH UNIVERSITY
James Smith
MONTANA STATE UNIV., BILLINGS
Tim Brotherton
Rakesh Sah
MONTCLAIR STATE COLLEGE
Chandana Chakraborty
Zaman Zamanian
MONTCLAIR STATE UNIVERSITY
Edward Bewayo
Nadeem Firoz
Chueng-kue Hsu
C. Jayachandran
Mark Kay
Richard Lord
Glenville Rawlins
Farahmand Rezvani
Diane Schulz
Gladys Torres-Baumgarten
MOREHOUSE COLLEGE
Hosein Abghari
Siavash Abghari
Keith Hollingsworth
Emmanuel Onifade
Glenwood Ross
Teloca Sistrunk (2)
MORGAN STATE UNIVERSITY
Rodney Stump
MORRIS BROWN COLLEGE
Robert Adams
Anna Anderson
Ciyata Coleman
Howard Cooper
Reginald Cosby
Guy Johnson
Julu Kothapa
Godwin Onyeaso

Benjamin Strickland
Gloria Tate
Herbert Watkins
MURRAY STATE UNIVERSITY
Louis Cheng
Betty Driver
Sandra Jeanquart
Bonnie Mcneely
Fred Miller
Roger Schoenfeldt
Tommy Stambaugh
NEW MEXICO STATE UNIVERSITY
Maria De Boyrie
Carl Enomoto
Gerald (Jerry) Hampton
Ashish Mahajan
Benjamin Taylor
NIAGARA UNIVERSITY
Peggy Choong
NORFOLK STATE UNIVERSITY
Jim Chen
V Dondeti
Bidhu Mohanty
Christopher Ngassam
Bhagaban Panigrahi
Denise-Margaret Thompson
Allan Unseth
Mohamed Youssef
Enrique Zapatero (2)
NORTH CAROLINA A&T STATE UNIV.
Betty Brewer
Basil Coley
Linda Coley
Kathryn Dobie (2)
Susan Houghton
Kimberly McNeil (2)
Japhet Nkonge
Brandis Phillips
George Stone
Danielle Winchester
NORTH CAROLINA CENTRAL UNIV.
Deirdre Guion
Raj Iyengar
Javad Kargar
Robert Moffie
Mark Rosso
Malavika Sundararajan
NORTH DAKOTA STATE UNIVERSITY
Matthew Walker
NORTH GEORGIA COL.& ST. UNIV.
Jeffrey Foreman
NORTH HARRIS COLLEGE
Ronald Foshee

NORTHEAST LOUISIANA UNIVERSITY
 Robert Eisenstadt
NORTHERN ILLINOIS UNIVERSITY
 James Johnson
 Chang Liu
NORTHERN STATE UNIVERSITY
 Hillar Neumann
 Anthony Urbaniak
OAKLAND COMMUNITY COLLEGE
 Vincent Deni
 Gary Grant
 Kathleen Lorencz
 Michael Smydra (2)
OAKLAND UNIVERSITY
 Addington Coppin
OKLAHOMA CITY UNIVERSITY
 Irvine Clarke, III
 Patrick Fitzgerald (2)
 Michael Frew
 Gordon Gray
 Jeri Jones
 David May
 Ronnie Shaw
 Jonathan Willner (2)
OLD DOMINION UNIVERSITY
 Joan Mann
OLIN ORDINANCE
 Dean Bartles
PALM BEACH ATLANTIC UNIVERSITY
 Ann Langlois (2)
 Edgar Langlois
PALMER U. OF NEBRASKA, KEARNEY
 David Palmer
PEPPERDINE UNIVERSITY
 David Ralph
 John Richardson
PHILDELPHIA UNIVERSITY
 Cathy Rusinko
POLK COMMUNITY COLLEGE
 Maria Lehoczky
PRAIRIE VIEW A & M UNIVERSITY
 Gin Chong
 Omprakash Gupta
 Kishwar Joonas
 Emmanuel Opara
 Rahim Quazi
 Munir Quddus
 Sudhir Tandon
 Jian Yang
PROVIDENCE COLLEGE
 Deirdre Bird
 Pamela Sherer
PUBLIC UTILITY RESEARCH CENTER
 Mark Jamison

PURDUE UNIVERSITY
 Padmapriya Francisco
RHODES COLLEGE
 Pamela Church
RICHLAND COLLEGE
 Larry Lehman
RIDER UNIVERSITY
 Joy Schneer
ROCKHURST UNIVERSITY
 Brian Fitzpatrick
RUST COLLEGE
 Sheela Bhagat
 Richard Frederick
 Himanshu Mishra
 Chigbo Ofong
 Sujata Sinha
SAGINAW VALLEY STATE UNIVERSITY
 Danilo Sirias
SAINT AUGUSTINE'S COLLEGE
 Marcel Ngambi
 David Washington
SAINT JOSEPH'S UNIVERSITY
 Alfredo Mauri
SAINT LEO COLLEGE
 Thomas Wilson
SALISBURY STATE UNIVERSITY
 Catherine Beise
 Kashi Khazeh
SAM HOUSTON STATE UNIVERSITY
 John Newbold
SAN DIEGO STATE UNIVERSITY
 Karen Ehrhart
SAVANNAH STATE UNIVERSITY
 Anshu Arora
 Suman Niranjan
 Jun Wu
SEATTLE UNIVERSITY
 Meenakshi Rishi
SHINKOH TECHNOLOGIES, INC.
 Fred Tennant
SOUTH CAROLINA STATE UNIVERSITY
 Hector Butts (2)
 Hanas Abdul Cader
 Keli Feng
 David Jamison (2)
 Jaejoo Lim
 Guohua Ma
 Innocent Nkwocha
 Kathy Quinn
 Ellen Robinson
 Marion Sillah
 Renu Singh
 Cleveland Thomas
SOUTHEAST MISSOURI STATE UNIVERSITY
 Deborah Beard

SOUTHERN ARKANSAS UNIVERSITY
James Clark
SOUTHERN CONNECTICUT ST. UNIV.
Ellen Frank
SOUTHERN ILLINOIS UNIVERSITY
John Fraedrich (2)
Jesus Ponce De Leon (2)
Timucin Ozcan
Andrew Szakmary (2)
Raymond Wacker (2)
SO. ILLINOIS UNIV., EDWARDSVILLE
Ali Kutan
SOUTHERN NEW HAMPSHIRE UNIV.
Mahboubul Hassan
SOUTHERN UNIVERSITY A&M COLLEGE
Donald Andrews
Mary Darby
Ghirmay Ghebreyesus (2)
Stephen Jaros
Andrew Muhammad
Jose Noguera
Saviour Nwachukwu
Mysore Ramaswamy
Gregory Spann
SOUTHERN UNIV. AT NEW ORLEANS
David (Ghasem) Alijani
Marjorie Fox
Adrine Harrell-Carter
Frank Martin
Muhammed Miah
J. Steven Welsh
Ashagre Yigletu
SOUTHERN UNIV., BATON ROUGE
Sung No
SOUTHERN UNIVERSITY/LSU
Joseph Omonuk
SOUTHWEST TEXAS STATE UNIV.
Jose Trinidad
ST. AMBROSE UNIVERSITY
Patrick O'Leary
ST. EDWARD'S UNIVERSITY
Eugene Lambert, Jr.
R. Gary Pletcher
ST. JOHN'S UNIVERSITY
Nejdet Delener
Samir Fahmy
ST. LOUIS CM. COL.-FORREST PARK
Nicholas Peppes
ST. MARY'S UNIVERSITY
Dianna Coker
Julie Dahlquist
Brooke Envick
Richard Priesmeyer
Gregory Roth

Kent Royalty
Richard Szecsy (2)
Jim Welch
Orion Welch (4)
STATE TECHNICAL INST., MEMPHIS
Oluwatoyin Adesipe
Thurston Shrader (2)
STATE U. OF NEW YORK, GENESEO
Nader Asgary
STEPHEN F. AUSTIN STATE UNIV.
Joe Ballenger
Samuel Jones
SUFFOLK COUNTY COMM. COLLEGE
Dorothy Laffin-Wright
SUFFOLK UNIVERSITY
Sungmin Ryu
TALLADEGA COLLEGE
Kadhim Al-Alwan
Emmanuel Chijioke
Michael Taku
TARLETON STATE UNIVERSITY
Brigitte Barbier
Rusty Freed
Walter Kendall
Linda LaMarca
Sue Lewis
Randy McCamey
Sankar Sundarrajan
Beverly Turner
TEMPLE UNIVERSITY
Tanvi Kothari
TENNEESSEE STATE UNIVERSITY
Dharmendra Dhakal
John Hasty
Joel Jolayemi
David King (3)
Xiaoming Li
Vaidotas Lukosius
Nelson Modeste
Francisca Norales
Hollis Price, Jr.
Jeffrey Siekpe
Sharon Thach
TENNESSEE TECHNOLOGICAL UNIV.
Tor Guimaraes
Julie Pharr
Bob Wood
TEXAS CHRISTIAN UNIVERSITY
Rob Rhodes
Gregory Stephens
TEXAS SOUTHERN UNIVERSITY
Donald Bond
Mayur Desai (2)
David Hansen

Burke Mathes
Kwadwo Ofori-Brobbey (2)
Lucy Ojode
Kamala Raghavan
Kizhanatham Ramaswamy
Marion Smith
TEXAS STATE UNIVERSITY
Gail Zank
TEXAS TECH UNIVERSITY
Alan Whitebread
THE COLLEGE OF NEW JERSEY
Sharyn Gardner
TRINITY COLLEGE
Eric Grosse
TROY UNIVERSITY
Mary Catherine Colley
TULANE UNIVERSITY
Roderic Camp
TUSKEGEE UNIVERSITY
William Cheng
Jerome Duncan
Anthony Freeman
Mark Freeman
Elaine Fuller
Benjamin Newhouse (2)
Earnell Seay
Lee Simmons
Eric Smith
Jingyo Suh
Leo Upchurch
U.S. AIR FORCE ACADEMY
Toby Edison
UNBSJ
Emin Civi
UNCF SPECIAL PROGRAMS CORP.
Nicholas Bassey
UNION BANK OF SWITZERLAND
Jack Tatom
UNION GRADUATE COLLEGE
Alan Bowman
UNION UNIVERSITY
Darin White
UNIVERSITY OF ALABAMA
Chad Hilton
Helenka (Lenka) Nolan
UNIV. OF ALABAMA, HUNTSVILLE
Yeqing Bao
James McCollum
Ravi Patnayakuni
Cynthia Ruppel
UNIVERSITY OF ARKANSAS
David Douglas
Hassan Hefzi
Larry Perry

UNIV. OF ARKANSAS, FAYETTEVILLE
Michael Carter
UNIV. OF ARKANSAS, FORT SMITH
Robert Sell
UNIV. OF ARKANSAS, LITTLE ROCK
David Blevins
Peter Walters
UNIV. OF ARKANSAS, PINE BLUFF
Lawrence Awopetu
Serena Brenneman
Kwamena Cudjoe
Eddie Hand (2)
Carla Martin (2)
Joon Park
Peter Wui
UNIV. OF CALIFORNIA, LOS ANGELES
Hans Schollhammer
UNIVERSITY OF CENTRAL OKLAHOMA
Tom Trittipo
UNIVERSITY OF CINCINNATI
Roger Chiang
UNIVERSITY OF DALLAS
David Higgins
UNIVERSITY OF DAYTON
Victor Forlani (2)
UNIVERSITY OF EVANSVILLE
Martin Fraering
LaShone Gibson
UNIVERSITY OF FLORIDA
Jiyoung Hwang
Jayashree Mahajan
UNIVERSITY OF GUAM
Kim Duck Shin (2)
UNIVERSITY OF HOUSTON
Jonathan Du
Xavier Gomez
Linda Hayes
Ursula Kettlewell
Jun-Yeon Lee
Yong Lee
June Lu
Asghar Nazemzadeh
Ron Salazar
Ron Sardessai
David Satava
Rajan Selvarajan
Chun-Sheng Yu
Ziad Swaidan
Joseph Ur
James Walton
UNIV. OF HOUSTON, CLEAR LAKE
L. Harrison-Walker
UNIV. OF ILLINOIS, SPRINGFIELD
Adil Mouhammed

UNIVERSITY OF LEEDS
Keith Glaister
UNIVERSITY OF LOUISIANA, LAFAYETTE
David Chretien (3)
UNIVERSITY OF MARYLAND
Jane Ross
U. OF MARYLAND, EASTERN SHORE
Julius Alade
Nagy Habib
Dandeson Panda
U. OF MASSACHUSETTS, DARTMOUTH
Richard Golen
UNIVERSITY OF MEMPHIS
Laura Alderson
Kenneth Austin
Eric Brey
Jack Clampit
Virginia Danehower
Peter Davis
Nolan Gaffney
Maria Gondo
Somnath Lahiri
Scott Mooty
Deb Mukherjee
Ivan Muslin
Prashant Palvia
Sam Ranganathan
R. Southern
Ronald Wilkes
UNIV. OF MICHIGAN, ANN ARBOR
Thomas Hemphill
UNIVERSITY OF MICHIGAN, FLINT
Erin Cavusgil
Joseph McGaugh (2)
UNIV. OF MINNESOTA, DULUTH
Jannifer David
UNIV. OF MINNESOTA, DULUTH
Praveen Aggarwal (2)
UNIVERSITY OF MISSISSIPPI
Jace Baker
Delvin Hawley
Hugh Sloan, Iii
Kirk Wakefield
UNIVERSITY OF MISSOURI, ROLLA
Morris Kalliny
UNIVERSITY OF MISSOURI, ST. LOUIS
Elizabeth Vining
UNIVERSITY OF NEW ORLEANS
Dinah Payne
UNIVERSITY OF NORTH ALABAMA
Santanu Borah (2)
UNIVERSITY OF NORTH TEXAS
Nancy Spears
UNIVERSITY OF NORTHERN IOWA
Karthik Iyer

UNIVERSITY OF NORTHWEST
William Nelson
UNIVERSITY OF PITTSBURGH
Dung Nguyen
UNIVERSITY OF PORTLAND
Howard Feldman
UNIVERSITY OF PUERTO RICO
Maria Amador-Dumois
Jorge Ayala
Evaldo Caborrouy
Julian Hernandez-Serrano
Elena Martinez
Victor Mojica
Rosa Reyes
Hector Rios-Maury
Graciela Roig
Yolanda Ruiz
Maritza Soto
Israel Vazquez
UNIVERSITY OF SOUTH DAKOTA
Janet Buelow
Lynn Muller (3)
Bijay Naik
Audhesh Paswan
Charles Roegiers
James Weisel
UNIVERSITY OF SOUTH FLORIDA
Cindy Bean
UNIV. OF SOUTHERN MISSISSIPPI
George Carter
James Mcquiston
Farhang Niroomand
Edward Nissan
UNIV. OF SOUTHWESTERN LOUISIANA
Joel Authement
Patricia Lanier
Bento Lobo
Hudson Rogers
UNIVERSITY OF TAMPA
Marca Bear
Velma McCuiston (2)
William Rhey
UNIVERSITY OF TENNESSEE
Robert Jones
Rodney Runyan
UNIV. OF TENNESSEE, CHATTANOOGA
Howard Finch
Mark Mendenhall
Judy Nixon
Omid Nodoushani
Docia Rudley
Marsha Scheidt
UNIVERSITY OF TENNESSEE, MARTIN
Bob Figgins

Mahmoud Haddad
Mary Lemons
Ed Timmerman
UNIV. OF TEXAS PAN AMERICAN
Cynthia Brown
UNIVERSITY OF TEXAS, EL PASO
John Pettit, Jr.
Janet Omundson
UNIVERSITY OF TEXAS, TYLER
Barbara Wooldridge (2)
U. OF THE DISTRICT OF COLUMBIA
Paul Bachman
Jian Hua
Charlie Mahone
William White
U. OF THE INCARNATE WORD, TEXAS
J .T. Norris
UNIVERSITY OF THE VIRGIN ISLANDS
Aurelia Donald
Marie Hermann
Lonnie Hudspeth (2)
Solomon Kabuka
Aubrey Washington
UNIVERSITY OF WASHINGTON
Mike Giambattista
UNIV. OF WASHINGTON, TACOMA
Tracy Thompson
UNIVERSITY OF WISCONSIN
Jon Fields
Kelly Nowicki
Sampathkumar Ranganathan
Scott Swanson
Lila Waldman
UNIV. OF WISCONSIN MILWAUKEE
Hong Ren
UNIV. OF WISCONSIN EAU CLAIRE
Dawna Drum
UNIV. OF WISCONSIN LA CROSSE
Nicole Gullekson
Leticia Pena
UNIV. OF WISCONSIN, MILWAUKEE
Sali Li
En Mao
UNIV. OF WISCONSIN, WHITEWATER
John Chenoweth
Amy Coon
Yezdi Godiwalla
Richard James
Marilyn Lavin
K. Parboteeah
Louise Tourigny
VANDERBILT UNIVERSITY
M. Hancock

VENTURA COLLEGE
Jeffery Stauffer
VIRGINIA COMMONWEALTH UNIV.
Charles Byles
Frank Franzak
Otis Jarvis
VIRGINIA STATE UNIVERSITY
Yao O. Amewokunu
Elin Cortijo-Doval
David Coss
Lynette Hammond
Steve Holeman
Junsang Lim
Bryan Menk
VIRGINIA TECH
John Pinkerton
WAKE FOREST UNIVERSITY
Anton Pujol
WASHBURN UNIVERSITY
Aron Levin
WASHTENAW COMMUNITY COLLEGE
William Grimes
WAYNE STATE COLLEGE
Gerald Conway (2)
WEBSTER UNIVERSITY
Barrett Baebler (2)
Dave Brennan
Jim Evans
Steve Hinson (2)
Jeff Holdeman
Brad Scott
WEIDNER UNIVERSITY
Myroslaw Kyj
WEST CHESTER UNIVERSITY
Hung Chu
WEST VIRGINIA UNIVERSITY
Karen Denning
WESTERN IOWA TECH COMM. COL.
Edward Sibley
WESTERN KENTUCKY UNIVERSITY
Douglas Fugate
Patricia Todd
WESTERN MICHIGAN UNIVERSITY
Kuriakose Athappilly (2)
Nancy Schullery
WIDENER UNIVERSITY
Ahmad Salam
WILLIAM JEWELL COLLEGE
Deborah Scarfino
WINSTON SALEM STATE UNIVERSITY
Susita Asree
Monica Cain
William Carden
Moula Cherikh

Alice Etim
Suresh Gopalan
Robert Herring
Thomas Jones
Nikolaos Karagiannis
Alican Kavas
Melissa Mann
Notis Pagiavlas
Beth Schneider
Kathy Stitts
Edward Zajicek

WRIGHT STATE UNIVERSITY
Peter Carusone
Nicolas Gressis

WRIGHT STATE U., LAKE CAMPUS
Alan Chesen
W. Demmy

XAVIER UNIVERSITY
James Bartkus
Harold Bryant
Cary Caro
Steven Cobb

Richard Peters
Jamal Rashed
Beth Wilson
Robert Zimmerman

XAVIER UNIVERSITY OF LOUISIANA
Mark Quinn
Candice Roche
Shael Wolfson

YORK COLLEGE
Max Kline

YOUNGSTOWN STATE UNIVERSITY
Birsen Karpak (2)
William Vendemia

TOTAL BUSINESS FACULTY PARTICIPANTS = 1,020

NUMBER OF SCHOOLS = 318

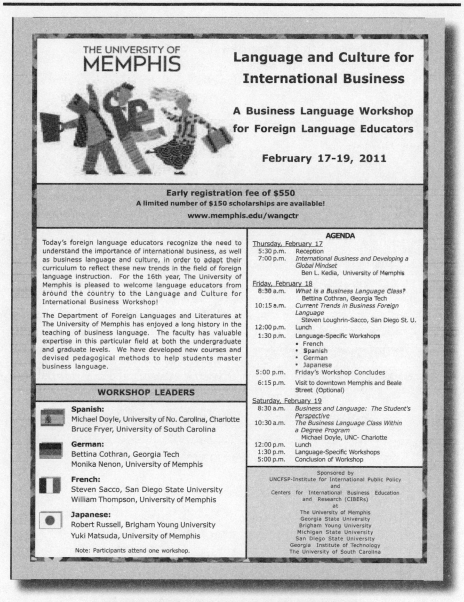

THE UNIVERSITY OF
MEMPHIS

Language and Culture for International Business

A Business Language Workshop for Foreign Language Educators

February 17-19, 2011

Early registration fee of $550
A limited number of $150 scholarships are available!
www.memphis.edu/wangctr

Today's foreign language educators recognize the need to understand the importance of international business, as well as business language and culture, in order to adapt their curriculum to reflect these new trends in the field of foreign language instruction. For the 16th year, The University of Memphis is pleased to welcome language educators from around the country to the Language and Culture for International Business Workshop!

The Department of Foreign Languages and Literatures at The University of Memphis has enjoyed a long history in the teaching of business language. The faculty has valuable expertise in this particular field at both the undergraduate and graduate levels. We have developed new courses and devised pedagogical methods to help students master business language.

WORKSHOP LEADERS

Spanish:
Michael Doyle, University of No. Carolina, Charlotte
Bruce Fryer, University of South Carolina

German:
Bettina Cothran, Georgia Tech
Monika Nenon, University of Memphis

French:
Steven Sacco, San Diego State University
William Thompson, University of Memphis

Japanese:
Robert Russell, Brigham Young University
Yuki Matsuda, University of Memphis

Note: Participants attend one workshop.

AGENDA

Thursday, February 17
5:30 p.m.   Reception
7:00 p.m.   *International Business and Developing a Global Mindset*
            Ben L. Kedia, University of Memphis

Friday, February 18
8:30 a.m.   *What Is a Business Language Class?*
            Bettina Cothran, Georgia Tech
10:15 a.m. *Current Trends in Business Foreign Language*
            Steven Loughrin-Sacco, San Diego St. U.
12:00 p.m. Lunch
1:30 p.m.   Language-Specific Workshops
            • French
            • Spanish
            • German
            • Japanese
5:00 p.m.   Friday's Workshop Concludes
6:15 p.m.   Visit to downtown Memphis and Beale Street (Optional)

Saturday, February 19
8:30 a.m.   *Business and Language: The Student's Perspective*
10:30 a.m. *The Business Language Class Within a Degree Program*
            Michael Doyle, UNC- Charlotte
12:00 p.m. Lunch
1:30 p.m.   Language-Specific Workshops
5:00 p.m.   Conclusion of Workshop

Sponsored by
UNCFSP-Institute for International Public Policy
and
Centers for International Business Education and Research (CIBERs)
at
The University of Memphis
Georgia State University
Brigham Young University
Michigan State University
San Diego State University
Georgia Institute of Technology
The University of South Carolina

BUSINESS LANGUAGE WORKSHOPS:
SPANISH, FRENCH, GERMAN, JAPANESE

CIBER SPONSORS 1993- 2011

Brigham Young University
Georgia Institute of Technology
Georgia State University
Michigan State University

San Diego State University
University of Memphis
University of South Carolina

UNCFSP-Institute for International Public Policy

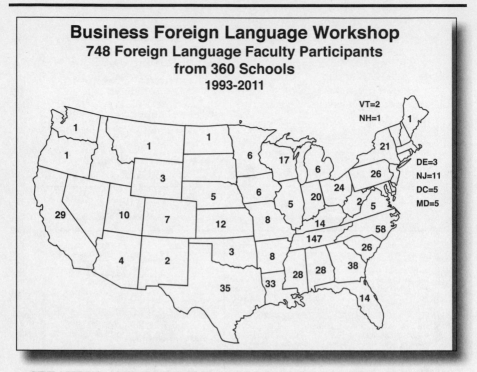

Business Foreign Language Workshop
748 Foreign Language Faculty Participants
from 360 Schools
1993-2011

SPEAKERS AND BUSINESS WORKSHOP LEADERS 1993-2011

GERMAN BUSINESS LANGUAGE WORKSHOP

Bettina Cothran, Georgia Institute of Technology
Monika Nenon, University of Memphis

SPANISH BUSINESS LANGUAGE WORKSHOP

Michael Doyle, University of North Carolina-Charlotte
Bruce Fryer, University of South Carolina
Felipe Lapuente, University of Memphis

FRENCH BUSINESS LANGUAGE WORKSHOP

Alvord G. Branan, San Diego State University
Steven J. Loughrin-Sacco, San Diego State University
James Schorr, San Diego State University
Will Thompson, University of Memphis

JAPANESE BUSINESS LANGUAGE WORKSHOP

Yuki Matsuda, University of Memphis
Robert Russell, Brigham Young University

ACAD. FOR SCIENCE AND FOREIGN LANG.
    Sara Meister
ADELPHI UNIVERSITY
    Marie Louise Vazquez
ALABAMA A&M UNIVERSITY
    Larry McDaniel
ALABAMA STATE UNIVERSITY
    Pamela Gay
    Gordon Sumner
ALBION COLLEGE
    Lisa Nowak
ALBUQUERQUE TECH-VOC. INST.
    Marvin Lozano
ALCORN STATE UNIVERSITY
    Belinda Griffith
    Cynthia Scurria
    Judy Smith
ALFRED UNIVERSITY
    Hiber Conteris
ARIZONA STATE UNIVERSITY
    Miko Foard
    Tomoko Shimomura
AUBURN UNIVERSITY
    Traci O'Brien
    Iulia Pittman
AURORA UNIVERSITY
    Denise Hatcher
AUSTIN PEAY STATE UNIVERSITY
    Culley Carson-Grefe
    Norbert Puszkar
    Karen Sorenson
BAYLOR UNIVERSITY
    Manuel Ortuno
BELLARMINE COLLEGE
    Gabriele Bosley
    Elizabeth Curry
    Harold Koch
BELMONT UNIVERSITY
    Cheryl Brown Geer
    David Julseth
    Francesca Muccini
    Natalia Pelaz
    Regine Schwarzmeier
BERRY COLLEGE
    Jennifer Corry
BETHANY COLLEGE
    Joseph Lovano
    Anju Ramjee
BETHUNE-COOKMAN UNIVERSITY
    Warren Ashby
    Susanne Eules
    Luis Rojas Lagunas
    Ambar Saleh
    Williams Wallenberg

BRADLEY UNIVERSITY
    Deborah Kessler
Brigham Young University
    Joaquina Hoskisson
    Hans Kelling
    Yvon LeBras
BUFFALO STATE COLLEGE
    Deborah Hovland
BUTLER UNIVERSITY
    Fred Yaniga
CALIFORNIA STATE UNIVERSITY
    Liz Martin
CALIFORNIA STATE UNIV., CHICO
    Patricia Black
    Karen Sorsby
CASTATE U., FULLERTON
    Linda Andersen
    Ervie Pena
CA STATE.U., SAN BERNARDINO
    Ruth Burke
CALVIN COLLEGE
    Sandra Clevenger
    Vicki De Vries
CANISIUS COLLEGE
    Laverne Seales
    Julia Wescott
CAPILANO COLLEGE
    Kazuko Mito
CARNEGIE MELLON UNIVERSITY
    Yumiko Kono
CARROLL COLLEGE
    Anne Doremas
    Cheryl Sitzler
CARTHAGE COLLEGE
    Richard Sperber
CASPER COLLEGE
    Lora Hittle
CENTRAL MISSOURI STATE UNIV.
    Sandra Merrill
    Alex Thiltges
CENTRAL STATE UNIVERSITY
    Hua Zhang Jones
    Kwawiski Tekpetey
CHAMPLAIN COLLEGE
    Barbara Bloom
CHESTNUT HILL COLLEGE
    Jean Faustman
CHICAGO STATE UNIVERSITY
    Araceli Canalini
    Evelyne Delgado-Norris
CHRISTOPHER NEWPORT UNIV.
    Danielle Cahill
CINCINNATI STATE TECHNICAL & CC
    Rosa-Maria Moreno

CLARK ATLANTA UNIVERSITY
    Rosalind Arthur
COLBY COLLEGE
    Arne Koch
COLLEGE OF CHARLESTON
    Viviane Bekrou
    Stephen Della Lana (2)
    Luis Ocanto
    Godwin Uwah (3)
    Felix Vasquez
COLLEGE OF NEW PALTZ
    Wilma Feliciano
COLUMBIA UNIVERSITY
    Hideki Hamada
COLUMBUS STATE COM. COLLEGE
    Garry Fourman
COLUMBUS STATE UNIVERSITY
    Efrain Garza
CONCORDIA COLLEGE
    Stephen Grollman
    Willard Hiebert
    Gay Rawson
CONCORDIA COLLEGE
    Stephen Grollman
    Willard Hiebert
CONNECTICUT COLLEGE
    J. L.-Marron Covance
    Jose Rodriguez
DAVID LIPSCOMB UNIVERSITY
    Charles Mcvey, Jr.
DAYTONA STATE COLLEGE
    Emma Brombin
DELTA STATE UNIVERSITY
    Karen Bell
DEPAUW UNIVERSITY
    Reiko Itoh
DILLARD UNIVERSITY
    Aurea Diab
    Helma Kaldewey
    Randolph Peters (2)
DORDT COLLEGE
    Diana Gonzalez
DUKE UNIVERSITY
    Lynn Dowell
    Elizabeth Fisher
    Deb Reisinger
    Azusa Saito
EAST TENNESSEE STATE UNIV.
    Karen Harrington (2)
    Christa Hungate (2)
    Jerome Mwinyelle
    Haakayoo Zoggyie
EASTERN MICHIGAN UNIVERSITY
    Sayuri Kubota

ELIZABETH CITY ST. UNIVERSITY
    Jose Gil
ELMHURST COLLEGE
    Janette Bayles
ELON COLLEGE
    Ernest Lunsford
    Brian Nienhaus
    Donna Van Bodengraven
EMORY & HENRY COLLEGE
    Xiangyun Zhang
EMORY UNIVERSITY
    Marianne Lancaster
    Noriko Takeda
FAIRFIELD UNIVERSITY
    Katherine Kidd
    Kathleen Kimball
FAIRLEIGH DICKINSON UNIV.
    Dorothy Walensky
FAYETTEVILLE STATE UNIVERSITY
    Timothy Ajani
    Hilary Barnes
    Aurelie Capron
    Jose Franco
    Milena Hurtado
    Jane Peacock (2)
    Jane Tarr
FEDERAL EXPRESS
    Donna Price
FLORIDA A&M UNIVERSITY
    Mary B Diallo (2)
    Johanna Ramos
FLORIDA MEMORIAL UNIVERSITY
    Rita Koyame
    William Perry (2)
FRANKLIN PIERCE COLLEGE
    Jack Donnelly
FRESNO CITY COLLEGE
    Camilla Colby
FRIENDS UNIVERSITY
    Jerry Smartt
FROSTBURG STATE UNIVERSITY
    Natalia Ramirez
GEORGETOWN COLLEGE
    Patricia Cooper
    Mary Skemp
GEORGIA COLLEGE & ST. UNIV.
    Gael Guzman-Medrano
GEORGIA SOUTHERN UNIVERSITY
    Juan Serna
    Jorge Suazo
GEORGIA STATE UNIVERSITY
    Robin Huff
    D. Martinez-Conde (2)
    German Torres

GEORGIAN COURT COLLEGE
  Patricia Mcmahon
GOETHE INSTITUTE CHICAGO
  Hartmut Karottki
GOVERNORS STATE UNIVERSITY
  Laura Casal
GRAMBLING STATE UNIVERSITY
  Encarna Abella
  Chimegsaikhan Banzar
  Alethea Lindsay
  Nancy Reeves
GRAND VALLEY STATE UNIVERSITY
  Donovan Anderson
  Anne Caillaud
  Khedija Gadhoum
  Natalia Gomez
  Zulema Moret
  Mitchell Place
  Regina Smith
  Severine Ward
GUSTAVUS ADOLPHUS COLLEGE
  Paschal Kyoore
HAMLINE UNIVERSITY
  Tamara Root
HAMPDEN-SYDNEY COLLEGE
  Dieudonne Afatsawo
HAMPTON UNIVERSITY
  Olayemi Adeniyi
  April Burriss
  Jacques Digbeu
  Colette Fortin
  Kanata Jackson
  Vahwere Kavota
  Michele Lewis
  Nelly Mcrae (2)
  Sylvain Poosson
  Susanne Toney
HANOVER COLLEGE
  Ann Kirkland
  Susanne Taylor
HARDING UNIVERSITY
  Robert McCready
HARDIN-SIMMONS UNIVERSITY
  Teresia Taylor
HARRISBURG AREA COM. COL.
  Judy Dibert
HARRIS-STOWE STATE UNIV.
  Yolanda Diaz
HIGH POINT UNIVERSITY
  Barbara Mascali
HOWARD UNIVERSITY
  James Davis
  Esther Kahn
  Marilyn Sephocle

  Jean-Jacques Taty
ILLINOIS COLLEGE
  Carol Ryan
INDIANA ST. U., BLOOMINGTON
  Guillaume Ansart
INDIANA UNIVERSITY
  Vania Castro
  Silvana Falconi
  Nikole Langjahr
  Rosalie Vermette
INDIANA U., BLOOMINGTON
  Catherine Fraser
  Nikole Langjahr
  Nyusya Milman
INDIANA UNIVERSITY NORTHWEST
  Ada Azodo
IOWA STATE UNIVERSITY
  Brett Bowles
  Dawn Bratsch-Prince
  Chad Gasta
JAMES MADISON UNIVERSITY
  Donald Corbin
  Carlos Fernandez
  Alessandro Lagana
  Andrea Naranjo-Merino
JOHN CARROLL UNIVERSITY
  Raj Aggarwal
  Douglas Jackson (2)
  Julia Karolle
JOHNSON & WALES UNIVERSITY
  Gwenn Lavole
JOHNSON C. SMITH UNIVERSITY
  Melissa Knosp
KALAMAZOO COLLEGE
  Hardy Fuchs
KANSAS STATE UNIVERSITY
  Amy Hubbell
KENNESAW STATE UNIVERSITY
  William Griffin
KENT STATE UNIVERSITY
  Hildegard Rossoll
  Cynthia Trocchio
KENTUCKY WESLEYAN COLLEGE
  Martha Kosir-Widenbauer
KUTZTOWN U. OF PENNSYLVANIA
  Carolina Moctezuma
  Karen Rauch
LAFAYETTE COLLEGE
  Cris Reyns-Chikuma
LANGSTON UNIVERSITY
  Sheila Rodriguez
LANSING COMMUNITY COLLEGE
  Keith Phillips
LEBANON VALLEY COLLEGE
  Angel Tuninetti

LEHIGH UNIVERSITY
    Marie Chabut
    Antonio Prieto
    Lenora Wolfgang
LEMOYNE-OWEN COLLEGE
    Olusoji Akomolafe
    Anne Connell
LINCOLN UNIVERSITY
    Gabrielle Malfatti-Rachell
    Maribel Charle Poza
LONGWOOD COLLEGE
    Isabel Dulfano
    Catherine Kapi
LOUISIANA STATE UNIVERSITY
    Andrea Hulse
LOUISIANA STATE U. SHREVEPORT
    Megan Conway
    Charlotte King
LOYOLA UNIV., NEW ORLEANS
    Javier Cortes de Jorge
    Isabel Durocher
LYNCHBURG COLLEGE
    Robert White
LYON COLLEGE
    Mieko Peek
MACMURRAY COLLEGE
    Linda Yamnitz
MANHATTAN COLLEGE
    Joan Cammarata
MARQUETTE UNIVERSITY
    German Carillo
    Alan Lacy
    Steven Taylor
MARY WASHINGTON COLLEGE
    Andrea Purdy
MARYGROVE COLLEGE
    Martine Danan
MASSACHUSETTS INST. OF TECH.
    Ayumi Nagatomi
MEMPHIS BIO-TECH
    Beth Flanagan
MERCED COLLEGE
    Caroline Kreide
MERCER UNIVERSITY
    Jerry Winfield
MERCYHURST COLLEGE
    Douglas Boudreau
    Keiko Miller
MEREDITH COLLEGE
    Carrie Holland
MERRIMACK COLLEGE
    Deborah Litvin
    Lynn McGovern

MESSIAH COLLEGE
    Sheila Rodriguez
    Vanisa Sellers
MICHIGAN STATE UNIVERSITY
    Patricia Paulsell
    Marc Rathmann
    Sarah Singer
    C.Villegas-Castaneda
MIDDLE TENNESSEE STATE UNIVERSITY
    Priya Ananth
    Oscar Diaz-Ortiz
    Judith Rusciolelli
    Isabelle Sutty
MILLSAPS COLLEGE
    Eiko Tashiro
MINOT STATE UNIVERSITY
    Harold Smith
MISSISSIPPI COLLEGE
    Anita Gowin
    Debbie Pierce
MISSISSIPPI DELTA COM. COLLEGE
    Ellen Steeby
MISSISSIPPI STATE UNIVERSITY
    K. Robbins-Herring
    Emma Rodriguez
    Rosa Vozzo
MISSISSIPPI VALLEY STATE UNIVERSITY
    Aurora Fiengo-Varn (2)
    Maximo Gutierrez (2)
    Tadesse Mengistu
    Rajanikanth Naraseeyappa
    Olesya Ovchinnikova
MOLLOY COLLEGE
    James Fonseca
MONMOUTH UNIVERSITY
    Priscilla Gac-Artigas
    Alison Maginn
    Julia Riordan-Goncalves
MONTCLAIR STATE UNIVERSITY
    Aristides Escobar
    G. Torres-Baumgarten
MONTEREY INST. INT'L STUDIES
    Naoko Matsuo
    Vicki Porras
MOREHOUSE COLLEGE
    Wanda Sandle
    Rossie Vickery
MORRIS BROWN COLLEGE
    Earlene Frazier
    Willie Pounds
MOUNT MARY COLLEGE
    Toni Wulff
NEBRASKA WESLEYAN UNIVERSITY
    Jo Ann Fuess

Joyce Michaelis
Catherine Nelson-Weber
NEW COLLEGE OF FLORIDA
Wendy Sutherland
NEW MEXICO STATE UNIVERSITY
Ana Brewinton
NICHOLLS STATE UNIVERSITY
Dennis Durocher
Mabelle Illidge
NORFOLK STATE UNIVERSITY
Richard Cobb
Isabel Killough (2)
Vadim Krakovich
NO. CAROLINA A&T STATE UNIV.
Jose Bravo-de-Rueda
Sarah Carrig
Nita Dewberry
Donald McDowell
NO. CAROLINA CENTRAL UNIV.
Claudia Becker
Minnie Sangster
Reine Turcato
NORTH CAROLINA STATE UNIV.
Helga Braunbeck
NORTH HARRIS COLLEGE
M. Cordero
NORTHEAST LOUISIANA UNIVERSITY
Barbara Nell
NORTHEASTERN UNIVERSITY
Robert Modee
NORTHERN ILLINOIS UNIVERSITY
John Bentley
Lanhui Ryder
NORTHERN KENTUCKY UNIV.
Jeremy Goebel
NORTHWEST MISSOURI STATE UNIV.
Pamela Brakhage
Channing Horner
Louise Horner
Christel Ortmann
Sylvia Richards
NORWICH UNIVERSITY
David Ward
OAKLAND UNIVERSITY
Ronald Rapin
Pamela Tesch
OAKTON COMMUNITY COLLEGE
Guiller Bosqued
OBERLIN COLLEGE
Ikuko Kurasawa
OHIO STATE UNIVERSITY
Jenny Fourman
OHIO UNIVERSITY
Tori Rohl

OLD DOMINION UNIVERSITY
Peter Schulman
OSAKA UNIVERSITY, JAPAN
Osamu Iemoto
OTTERBEIN COLLEGE
James Carr (2)
PACE UNIVERSITY
Judith Gale
Andres Villagra
PEPPERDINE UNIVERSITY
Diane Davis
Philippe Degaillande
Mahi Lashgari
PIKEVILLE COLLEGE
Ella Smith
PITTSBURG STATE UNIVERSITY
Judy Berry-Bravo
Edmee Fernandez
Myriam Krepps
Randi Polk
Mark West
PURDUE UNIVERSITY
Kristin Kvaalen
Claudia Schlee
RANDOLPH-MACON COLLEGE
Liliana Puppl-Redfern
RIVERSIDE COMMUNITY COLLEGE
Lisa Conyers
RHODES COLLEGE
Espi Ralston
ROLLINS COLLEGE
Nancy Decker
RUST COLLEGE
Carl Self
A. Turner
RUTGERS UNIVERSITY
Martine Benjamin
Otto Zitzelsberger
RUTGERS UNIVERSITY, NEWARK
Asela Laguna
SAINT JOSEPH'S UNIVERSITY
Thomas Buckley
SALEM COLLEGE
Norgard Klages
Ho Yoon
SALISBURY STATE UNIVERSITY
Gerry St. Martin
Brian Stiegler
Arlene White
SAM HOUSTON STATE UNIVERSITY
Ray Renteria
Yuki Waugh
SAMFORD UNIVERSITY
Barbara Crider

Thomas Hines
SAN DIEGO STATE UNIVERSITY
    Tamara Dunn
    David Earwicker
    Yoshiko Higurashi
    Kristin Lovrien-Meuwese
    James Schorr
SAVANNAH STATE UNIVERSITY
    Boniface Kawasha
    Irina Tedrick
SEATTLE PACIFIC UNIVERSITY
    Robert Baah
SHIPPENSBURG UNIVERSITY
    Agnes Ragone
SKIDMORE COLLEGE
    Charlene Grant
SONOMA STATE UNIVERSITY
    Christine Renaudin
SOUTH CAROLINA STATE UNIV.
    Gisela Carreras
    Rosemarie Doucette (2)
    Ruben Silvestry
    Chris Thornburg
SOUTHERN ADVENTIST UNIVERSITY
    Carmen Jimenez
SO. ILLINOIS U., EDWARDSVILLE
    Julian Bueno
    B. Carstens-Wickham
    Elizabeth Fonseca
    J. Mann
    Frederick Morrison
    G. Pallemans
    V. Zaytzeff
SOUTHERN NAZARENE UNIVERSITY
    Frank Johnson
SOUTHERN UNIVERSITY A&M COLLEGE
    Warner Anderson
    Sybil Carter
    Irma Cobb
    Linda Lassiter (2)
    Thomas Miller
    Mazie Movassaghi
SW MISSISSIPPI COM.M. COLLEGE
    Elaine Coney
SOUTHWEST MISSOURI ST. UNIV.
    Larry George
    M. Hargess
    Mary Hoak
    Madeleine Kernen
    Pedro Koo
    Judith Martin
    Walt Nelson
    Lyle Polly
SOUTHWEST TEXAS STATE UNIV.
    Lucy Harney

SPELMAN COLLEGE
    Estelle Archibold
    Jacqueline Edwards
ST. AMBROSE UNIVERSITY
    Scot Heisdorffer
ST. AUGUSTINE COLLEGE
    Olivia E Jones (2)
    Vanita Sehgal
ST. JOHN'S UNIVERSITY
    Zoi Petropoulou
    Annalisa Sacca
    Esperanza Saludes
STATE U. OF NEW YORK, NEW PALTZ
    Mercedes Rooney
    Louis Saraceno
    Giancarlo Traverso
STATE UNIVERSITY OF NY, OSWEGO
    Ana Djukicco
    Jesus Freire
    George Koenig
STATE UNIV. OF NY, PLATTSBURG
    Oscar Flores (2)
    Irene Lee
    Margaret Quequiner
STATE UNIVERSITY. OF NY, POTSDAM
    John Cross
SUP DE CO, LA ROCHELLE, FRANCE
    Judith Lambert
TALLADEGA COLLEGE
    James Shepard
    Michael Taku
TARLETON STATE UNIVERSITY
    Maria Bohm
    Burton Smith
TN FOREIGN LANGUAGE INSTITUTE
    Martin Deschenes
TENNESSEE STATE UNIVERSITY
    Robin Lee
    Ana Isabel Rueda-Garcia
TENNESSEE TECHNOLOGY UNIV.
    Eston Evans
    Heidemarie Weidner
TEXAS A & M UNIVERSITY
    Tiio Laane
TEXAS SOUTHERN UNIVERSITY
    Marylise Caussinus
    Tommy Erwin (3)
TEXAS TECH UNIVERSITY
    Lorum Stratton
THE CITADEL
    Zane Segle
THE COLLEGE OF NEW JERSEY
    Deborah Compte
    Ariane Pfenninger

THE UNIV. OF MARY WASHINGTON
  Scott Powers
THOMAS MOORE COLLEGE
  Maria Garriga
  Jacqueline Van Houten
THUNDERBIRD SCH. OF GLOBAL MGMT.
  Kay Mittnik
TREZVANT CAREER ACADEMY
  Bobbi Warren
TRINITY CHRISTIAN COLLEGE
  Paul Roggendorff (2)
TRUMAN STATE UNIVERSITY
  Gregg Siewert (2)
TUSKEGEE UNIVERSITY
  Carolina Marquez-Serrano
UNION UNIVERSITY
  Julie Glosson
  Jean Marie Walls (2)
UNIVERSITY OF ALABAMA
  Margaret Bond
  Maria Jesus Centeno
  Krista Chambless
  Judith Kirkpatrick
  Michael Schnepf
UNIV. OF ALABAMA, BIRMINGHAM
  Beth Cobb
  Belita Faki
  Karoline Kirst
UNIV. OF ALABAMA, HUNTSVILLE
  Sharron Abernathy
  Jacqueline Diot
  Kwaku Gyasi
  Taeko Horwitz
  Peter Meister (2)
UNIVERSITY OF ARIZONA
  Kathrin Maurer
  Kamakshi Murti
UNIVERSITY OF ARKANSAS
  Judith Ricker
UNIV. OF ARKANSAS, FAYETTEVILLE
  Jon Hassel
UNIV. OF ARKANSAS, LITTLE ROCK
  Jeanette Clausen
  Susanne Wagner
UNIV. OF ARKANSAS, PINE BLUFF
  Antony Hobbs
  Peter Wui
UNIVERSITY OF BRAZIL
  Joao Sedycias
UNIVERSITY OF CALIFORNIA
  Y-H Tohsaku
  Eiko Ushida
UNIVERSITY OF CALIFORNIA, DAVIS
  Miyo Uchida

UNIVERSITY OF CENTRAL ARKANSAS
  Phillip Bailey
  Dwight Langston
  Jose Martinez
UNIVERSITY OF CINCINNATI
  Noriko Fujioka-ito
  Isabel Parra
  Susan Sadlier
UNIV. OF COLORADO, BOULDER
  Hideko Shimizu (2)
UNIVERSITY OF COLORADO, DENVER
  Diane Dansereau
  Ted Wedelin
UNIVERSITY OF DAYTON
  Percio De Castro
  Elke Hatch
UNIVERSITY OF DENVER
  Michiko Croft
  Gabi Kathofer
  Terri Woellner
U. OF THE DISTRICT OF COLUMBIA
  Marie Racine
  Ibrahim Sakaji
UNIVERSITY OF EVANSVILLE
  Arcea Zapata de Aston
  Catherine Fraley
  Lesley Pleasant
UNIVERSITY OF FLORIDA
  Britta Herdegen
  Greg Moreland
  Ann Wehmeyer
UNIVERSITY OF ILLINOIS
  Jotaro Arimori
  Misumi Sadler
UNIV. OF ILLINOIS, SPRINGFIELD
  Anna Brawn
UNIVERSITY OF KANSAS
  Evelyn Allgeier
  William Blue
  Edma Delgado
  Diane Fourny
  Junko Maekawa-Young
  Jim Morrison
UNIVERSITY OF KENTUCKY
  Jeannine Blackwell
  Luisa Perez
  Inmaculada Pertusa
  Christina Wegel
UNIVERSITY OF LOUISIANA, MONROE
  Christian Rubio
UNIVERSITY OF MARY WASHINGTON
  Marcel Rotter
  Jose Sainz

UNIVERSITY OF MARYLAND
- Jo Ann Hinshaw
- Laura Kurz

UNIVERSITY OF MEMPHIS
- Kazuko Adcock
- Analdo Analdo-Gonzales
- Rebekah Anderson
- Daniel Bradford
- Meredith Broadhead
- Fernando Burgos
- Erin Czarra
- Marie-Lisa Charue
- Patricia Duggar
- Jay Durbin
- Lourdes Gabikagojeaskoa
- Cosetta Gaudenzi
- D. Anzaldo-Gonzalez
- Brigitte Guimond
- Michael Halper
- Michael Hartmann
- John Hasselle
- Nele Hempel
- David King
- Kelly Horgan
- Cedric Kolter
- Monicque Larocque
- Michael Lyons
- Rick Marcus
- Carla Martinez
- L. Marques-Rodrigues
- Kim McFadden-Effinger
- Sara McWilliams
- Leiah Miller
- Kathryn Newell
- Miho Ponnath
- Brad Pope
- Rika Rubin
- Michelle Scatton-Tessier
- Sanford Shefsky
- Susan Silver
- Elisabeth Silverman
- Scott Smith
- Akemi Sommer
- De-an Swihart
- Clay Tanner
- Keiko Teruyama
- Chris Thompson
- Junko Tokuda
- Ashley Troy
- Nik Turner
- Jose Velazquez
- Francisco Vivar
- Ashley Wallace
- Eric Wooten
- Josh Wright

UNIVERSITY OF MICHIGAN
- Shubhangi Dabak

UNIV. OF MICHIGAN, ANN ARBOR
- Dolores Pons
- Elizabeth Landers

UNIVERSITY OF MICHIGAN, FLINT
- Imane Hakam
- Stephanie Throne

UNIVERSITY OF MINNESOTA
- Patricia Mougel

UNIVERSITY OF MISSISSIPPI
- Hanna Albertson
- John Gutierrez
- Eva-Maria Metcalf
- Kaoru Ochiai
- Corina Petrescu
- Anne Quinney
- Christopher Sapp

UNIVERSITY OF MISSOURI, ST. LOUIS
- Anne-Sophie Blank (2)
- Elizabeth Eckelkamp
- Kimberley Sallee

UNIVERSITY OF MONTANA
- Yuka Tachibana

UNIVERSITY OF NEBRASKA, OMAHA
- Tej Adidam
- Elvira Garcia

UNIVERSITY OF NEW ORLEANS
- Jean Cranmer

UNIVERSITY OF NORTH ALABAMA
- Max Gartman
- Keith Lindley
- Claudia Vance

UNIVERSITY OF NC, CHAPEL HILL
- Sandra Summers

UNIVERSITY OF NC, CHARLOTTE
- Marie-Therse Noiset
- C. Vance

UNIVERSITY OF NC, GREENSBORO
- Karin Baumgartner
- Margo Bender
- Mary Ann Horley
- Wendy Jones-Worden

UNIVERSITY OF NC, WILMINGTON
- Susan Crampton
- Yoko Kano

UNIVERSITY OF NORTH FLORIDA
- Renee Scott

UNIVERSITY OF NOTRE DAME
- Lisa Caponigri
- Odette Menyard
- Setsuko Shiga

UNIVERSITY OF OKLAHOMA
- Logan Whalen

UNIVERSITY OF PENNSYLVANIA
  Betty Slowinski
UNIVERSITY OF PITTSBURGH
  Grisela Hoechel-Alden
  Charles-L. M. Metivier
  Sophie Queuniet
  Sabine Von Dirke
  Brett Wells
UNIVERSITY OF PORTLAND
  Kathleen Regan
UNIVERSITY OF SCRANTON
  Jaime Meilan
UNIVERSITY OF SOUTH CALIFORNIA
  Yuka Kumagai
UNIVERSITY OF SOUTH CAROLINA
  Oliver Debure
  Victor Duran
  Ursula Engelbrecht
  Natalie Hintz
U. OF SOUTH CAROLINA, BEAUFORT
  Juanita Alvarez
U. OF SOUTH CAROLINA, COLUMBIA
  Carla Grimes
U. OF SO. CAROLINA, SPARTANBURG
  Sharon Cherry
  Jay Coffman
  Regis Robe
UNIVERSITY OF ST. THOMAS
  Debra Andrist (2)
  Elizabeth Coscio
  Timothy Hagerty
  Oscar Hernandez
  Jean Lanskin
  Alvaro Rodriguez (2)
U. OF ST. THOMAS, MINNESOTA
  Ted Baenziger
U. OF TENNESSEE, KNOXVILLE
  Constancio Nakuma
  Stefanie Ohnesorg
  John Romeiser
  Yulan Washburn
  Dolly Young
UNIVERSITY OF TENNESSEE, MARTIN
  Ingrid Padial
UNIV. OF TEXAS-PAN AMERICAN
  Nalda Baez
UNIVERSITY OF VIRGIN ISLANDS
  Solomon Kabuka
  Kimmora Solomon
UNIVERSITY OF TOLEDO
  Linda Rouillard
  Debra Stoudt
UNIVERSITY OF TORONTO
  Michael Hager

UNIVERSITY OF VIRGINIA
  Beth Bjorklund
  Suzanne Houyoux
UNIVERSITY OF WEST GEORGIA
  Ioanna Chatzidimitriou
UNIVERSITY OF WISCONSIN
  Atsuko Borgmann
  Kristine Butler
  Tomomi Kakegawa
  Johannes Strohschank
  M.-France Strohschank
  Kazuhide Takeuchi
UNIV. OF WISCONSIN, EAU CLAIRE
  Juan Chaves
U. OF WISCONSIN, STEVENS POINT
  Renee Craig-Odders
UNIV. OF WISCONSIN, WHITEWATER
  Peter Hoff
  Manuel Ossers
  Kevin Rottet
UNIVERSITY OF WYOMING
  Sonia Hicks-Rodriguez
  Dorly Piske
VANDERBILT UNIVERSITY
  Peggy Setje-Eilers
  Todd Hughes
VA POLYTECHNIC INST. & ST. UNIV.
  Heide Witthoft
VIRGINIA STATE UNIVERSITY
  Mohamed Saidu Kabia
VIRGINIA WESLEYAN COLLEGE
  Mavel Velasco
WAKE FOREST UNIVERSITY
  Byron Wells
WASHBURN UNIVERSITY
  Gabi Lunte
WASHINGTON & JEFFERSON COL.
  Katrine Pflanze
  Sharon Taylor
WASHINGTON UNIVERSITY
  Lynn Breakstone
WAYNE STATE UNIVERSITY
  Salim Khaldieh
WEBER STATE UNIVERSITY
  Erika Daines
WEBSTER UNIVERSITY
  Graciela Corvalan
WESLEYAN COLLEGE
  Saralyn Desmet
WEST TEXAS A & M UNIVERSITY
  Lee Durbin
WEST VIRGINIA UNIVERSITY
  Jeffrey Bruner
  Twyla Meding

WESTERN CAROLINA UNIVERSITY
    Ronald Morgan
WESTERN KENTUCKY UNIVERSITY
    Laura Jackson
    Nathan Love
    Melissa Stewart
WESTMINSTER COLLEGE
    Joel Postema
WHEATON COLLEGE
    Samuel Zadi
WICHITA STATE UNIVERSITY
    Yumi Foster
WILLIAM WOODS UNIVERSITY
    Habiba Deming
WINGATE UNIVERSITY
    Ann Moncayo
WINSTON-SALEM STATE UNIVERSITY
    Michael Brookshaw (2)
    Leonard Muaka
    Bonaventure B. Omgba
WINTHROP UNIVERSITY
    Patrick Gallagher
WOFFORD COLLEGE
    Elisa Pollack
WRIGHT STATE UNIVERSITY
    Nancy Broughton
    Elfe Dona
    Mari O'Brien
XAVIER UNIVERSITY
    Susan Spillman
XAVIER UNIV. OF LOUISIANA
    Masako Dorrill
    Herman Johnson
YORK UNIVERSITY
    Pilar Ford
YOUNGSTOWN STATE UNIVERSITY
    Herve Corbe

HIGH SCHOOL FOREIGN LANGUAGE FACULTY PARTICIPANTS

ARLINGTON HIGH SCHOOL
    Andrew Reese
BARTLETT HIGH SCHOOL
    Robert Beger
    Mary McCullar
CENTRAL HIGH SCHOOL
    Brittany Camp
    Anne Holzemer
CHRISTIAN BROTHERS HIGH SCHOOL
    Grady Harbor
CORDOVA HIGH SCHOOL
    Carolina L-Harbor
CRAIGMONT HIGH SCHOOL
    Jody Janovetz
    Jaime Thomas
EAST HIGH SCHOOL
    Albert Jean Louis (2)
    Paul Reed
EVANGELICAL CHRISTIAN SCHOOL
    Lark Torti (3)
FRAYSER HIGH SCHOOL
    Marilyn Gaines
HOUSTON HIGH SCHOOL
    Rachel Markovitz
    Doreen Penrod
    Gail Ryan
KIRBY HIGH SCHOOL
    Barry Flippo
    Martha Sandoval
LAUSANNE COLLEGIATE SCHOOL
    Marcia Planchon
M. B. LAMAR HIGH SCHOOL
    Rob Bittle
    Yvette Heno
    Mary Lile
    Sylvia Wagman
MEMPHIS CITY SCHOOLS
    Joseph Dummitt
    Gebriele George
    Seiko Igarashi
    Maggie Lee
    Alyssa Villarreal
MEMPHIS UNIVERSITY SCHOOL
    Reginald Dalle
    Jose Hernandez
    Beba Heros
MILLINGTON CENTRAL HIGH SCH.
    Jason Davenport

NORTH ALLEGHENY SENIOR HIGH SCH.
    Barbara Zaun (2)
OVERTON HIGH SCHOOL
    Tina McBee
PAGE HIGH SCHOOL
    Terry Alexander
RIDGEWAY HIGH SCHOOL
    Albert Jean-Louis
    Rachel Markowitz
    Isabel Swearingin
SAINT AGNES ACADEMY
    Anita Kay
SHELBY COUNTY SCHOOLS
    Steven Baade
    Michael Halliburton
    Lisa Hoelmer
    Shannon Pryoe
    Andre Suffren
SNOWDEN SCHOOL
    Myra Govea-Dearce

SOUTHWIND HIGH SCHOOL
    Lisa Hoelmer
    Kandice Lee
ST. GEORGE'S INDEPENDENT SCHOOL
    Kathy Scruggs
WHITE STATION HIGH SCHOOL
    Carlos Espinosa
    Christiane Gilbert
    Cindy Ridgway
    Mark Sturgis
WHITEHAVEN HIGH SCHOOL
    Mary Antone
    Alix Morales

TOTAL LANGUAGE FACULTY PARTICIPANTS = 748

SCHOOLS = 360

GLOBALIZING BUSINESS SCHOOL (GBS) PROGRAM
FOR HBCU INSTITUTIONS

The GBS project is designed to raise awareness of the importance of international and interdisciplinary business education by equipping faculty with the pedagogical tools, knowledge, and experiences to incorporate international content into existing business courses and/or develop new courses. A major component of the program is one-on-one assistance provided by the sponsoring CIBERs to their respective HBCU in facilitating the implementation of international business education programs and in acquiring federal grant funds to support these efforts.

Summary Report: 2002-2006

The Globalizing Business School (GBS) Program for HBCU institutions has been one of the most interesting, enjoyable, and challenging projects conducted by the University of Memphis CIBER and Michigan State University African Studies Center during the 2002-06 grant cycle. The success of this program would not have been possible without the GBS partners — the Institute for International Public Policy (IIPP) of the United Negro College Fund — and the CIBERs at the University of Florida, Georgia Institute of Technology, Indiana University, University of Connecticut, University of Kansas, Michigan State University, Texas A&M University, and University of Wisconsin.

Michael Taku, Talladega College, and Mark Chichester, former Exec. Director, IIPP

Solomon Kabuka, Univ. of Virgin Islands, greeted by Ben Kedia, Univ. of Memphis

Ralph Hines, Director of the U.S. Department of Education's International Education and Graduate Programs Office said, "it's among the most sweeping efforts to help predominantly African American schools sharpen their competitive edge in an increasingly global economy" (The Commercial Appeal, April 27, 20002).

To accomplish the program's goals, a number of activities were provided (e.g., grant writing workshops, business foreign language workshops, faculty development programs in international business, area studies seminars on South Africa, and international study abroad tours).

The Memphis CIBER recently conducted an intensive effort to obtain summary evaluation data by sending an evaluation instrument to more than 150 faculty who participated in one or more components of the GBS program. The responses received represented almost all of the HBCU institutions. More importantly, the responses totally validated the value of this program and its impact on HBCU participants.

It is worthy of note that all respondents ranked the collaboration between the HBCU and their respective CIBER partners as **'Most Important'** to the success of the program.

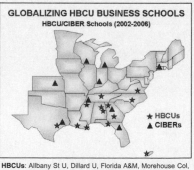
GLOBALIZING HBCU BUSINESS SCHOOLS
HBCU/CIBER Schools (2002-2006)

★ HBCUs
▲ CIBERs

HBCUs: Allbany St U, Dillard U, Florida A&M, Morehouse Col, Norfolk St U, Prairie View A&M, Rust Col, Southern U, St. Augustine's, Talladega Col, Tennessee St U, Tuskegee U, U of Virgin Islands. **CIBERs** at U of Florida, U of Kansas, Georgia Tech, Texas A&M, U of Connecticut, U of Wisconsin, Indiana U, U of Memphis and Michigan State U.

GLOBALIZING BUSINESS SCHOOLS PROGRAM FOR HBCUs
2002 - 2006

A Collaborative Project of Historically Black Colleges & Universities (HBCU), United Negro College Fund Special Programs' Institute for International Public Policy (UNCFSP-IIPP), Centers for International Business Education and Research (CIBER), and the United States Department of Education (USDOE)

ALBANY STATE UNIVERSITY
Alireza Dorestani
Jonathan Elimimian
Yousef Jahmani
Bingguang Li
DILLARD UNIVERSITY
Richard P Baucum
Courtney Blair (2)
Edgar Chase
Aurea Diab
Christian Fugar (2)
Richard S Igwike
Susan Kadlec
Helma Kaldewey
Tadesse Mengistu
Randolph R Peters (2)
Anthony Pinder
FLORIDA A & M UNIVERSITY
Mary B. Diallo (2)
Joycelynn Finley-Hervey
Roscoe Hightower
Aretha Hill
Angela Murphy
Johanna Ramos
Daaim Shabazz (3)
Sheryl Shivers-Blackwell (2)
Annette Singleton
J. Scott Sutterfield
MOREHOUSE COLLEGE
Siavaxh Abghari (2)
Cheryl Allen
Dr. Ross Glenwood
Keith Hollingsworth
Emmanuel Onifade
Mona Ray (2)
Glenwood Ross (2)
Wanda Sandle
Teloca Sistrunk (2)
Rossie Vickery
NORFOLK STATE UNIVERSITY
Jim Chen (2)
Richard Cobb
V Reddy Dondeti
Melinda Harris (2)
Isabel Killough (2)
Vadim Krakovich
Bidhu Mohanty
Christopher Ngassam
Bhagaban Panigrahi
Denise-Margaret Thompson
Allan Unseth
Mohamed Youssef
Enrique Zapatero (4)

PRAIRIE VIEW A & M UNIVERSITY
Henri L Bailey, III (2)
Gin Chong
Omprakash Gupta (2)
Kishwar Joonas
Emmanuel Opara
Rahim Quazi
Munir Quddus
Sudhir Tandon
Fred Wallace (2)
Jian Yang
RUST COLLEGE
Sheela Bhagat
Richard Frederick
Himanshu Mishra
Chigbo Ofong
Carl C. Self
Sujata Bose Sinha
A. June Turner
SOUTHERN UNIVERSITY A&M
Katrece Albert
Warner Anderson (2)
Donald R. Andrews (3)
Sybil Carter
Irma Cobb
SOUTHERN UNIVERSITY A&M
Mary Darby (3)
Ghirmay S. Ghebreyesus (2)
Stephen Jaros (2)
Linda Lassiter (2)
Earl Marcelle
Thomas Miller (2)
Mazie Movassaghi
Andrew Muhammad (2)
Sung No
Jose Noguera
Saviour Nwachukwu (2)
Joseph Omonuk
Mysore Ramaswamy
Gregory Spann (2)
Ashagre Yigletu (2)
ST. AUGUSTINE'S COLLEGE
Joyce Blackwell-Johnson
Olivia E Metzger Jones
James Allen Kendrick (3)
Marcel Ngambi
Vanita Sehgal
TALLADEGA COLLEGE
Kadhim Al-alwan (2)
Bernard Bray
Emmanuel Chijioke
Jennifer Richelle Cope
James Shepard (3)
Dr. Michael Taku (4)

TENNESSEE STATE UNIVERSITY
 Dharmendra Dhakal
 Galen Hull (2)
 Joel K. Jolayemi
 David (D) King (2)
 Robin Lee
 Xiaoming Li
 Vaidotas Lukosius (3)
 Nelson C. Modeste
 Francisca Norales
 Ana Isabel Rueda-Garcia
 Jeffrey Siekpe
TUSKEGEE UNIVERSITY
 Jerome Duncan
 Mark Freeman
 Elaine Fuller
 Alicia Jackson (2)
 Carolina Marquez-Serrano
 Benjamin Newhouse
 Earnell Seay
 Lee Simmons
 Jingyo Suh
 Leo Upchurch (3)

UNIVERSITY OF VIRGIN ISLANDS
 Aurelia Donald (2)
 Marie Hermann (2)
 Lonnie Hudspeth (2)
 Solomon Kabuka (3)
 Benon Kisuule
 Sharon Simmons
 Kimmora Solomon
 Aubrey Washington (3)

**TOTAL HBCU FACULTY
PARTICIPANTS = 215**

GLOBALIZING HBCU BUSINESS SCHOOLS (GBS) PROGRAM

A COLLABORATIVE PROJECT OF HBCUs, UNCFSP-IIPP, CIBERs AND USDOE*

The GBS Program is designed to infuse understanding and the importance of international and interdisciplinary business education by equipping faculty with the pedagogical tools, knowledge, and experiences to incorporate international content into existing business courses and/or develop new courses. An integral component of the program is one-on-one assistance provided by the sponsoring CIBERs to their respective HBCU in facilitating the implementation of international business education programs on their campuses and in acquiring federal grant funds to support these efforts.

GBS SUMMARY REPORT: 2006-2010

Following the USDOE's announcement of the 2006-2010 CIBER grant awards, the University of Memphis and Michigan State University CIBERs began to recruit potential HBCUs for the next four-year GBS Program. By the end of August 2006, UNCFSP—IIPP, 14 HBCUs and 14 CIBERs were enthusiastically committed to participating in the 2006-2010 GBS Program!

In September 2006, an Orientation and Grants Meeting launched the new four-year GBS program. Forty-six (46) representatives from participating HBCUs, UNCFSP—IIPP and CIBER co-sponsors attended. Presentations were made by Alabama A&M, Bowie State, IIPP-UNCFSP, and CIBERs at the University of Florida, University of Memphis and Texas A&M.

As a member of the GBS Program, each HBCU receives two scholarships each year covering the registration fees for language faculty to attend the annual **Business Language Workshop**. During the four-year GBS program (2006-2010), **a total of forty-nine (49) HBCU Language Faculty** attended either the Business Spanish, Business French, or Business German workshop. **Eighteen attended in 2007; seven attended in 2008; eleven in 2009; and thirteen in 2010.** (See page 3 for a listing of HBCU participants by school.)

February 2010 Business Language Workshop

HBCU Successes in the GBS Program (2006-2010)

GBS Orientation .... 29 HBCU Faculty	New Undergraduate IB Courses 44
Business Language Wrksp ... 49 HBCU Faculty	New Graduate IB Courses 8
BIE-HBCU Workshop .... 30 HBCU Faculty	Int'l Content Added to Bus. Courses 44
FDIB-Globalization Seminars .. 110 HBCU Faculty	Students Attended Study Abroad 152
BIE Proposals Submitted .... 14 HBCUs	Faculty Attended Study Abroad 54
BIE Grant Awards (7 HBCUs)................. $1.2 M	Int'l Research (Pres. & Publ.)................ 141
Alabama St. U. (twice), Bowie St. U.,	New IB Minors 4
Hampton U., North Carolina Central U.,	Int'l Business Collaborations 7
South Carolina St. U., Winston Salem St. U.	Int'l Academic Collaborations 33

*A Collaborative Project of Historically Black Colleges & Universities (HBCUs), United Negro College Fund Special Programs' Institute for International Public Policy (UNCFSP-IIPP), Centers for International Business Education and Research (CIBERs), and the United States Department of Education (USDOE).

GLOBALIZING BUSINESS SCHOOLS PROGRAM FOR HBCUs
2006 - 2010

A Collaborative Project of Historically Black Colleges & Universities (HBCU), United Negro College Fund Special Programs' Institute for International Public Policy (UNCFSP-IIPP), Centers for International Business Education and Research (CIBER), and the United States Department of Education (USDOE)

GBS SUMMARY REPORT: 2006-2010

In June 2007, thirty (30) HBCU faculty attended a BIE-HBCU workshop. BIE grant recipients from Tuskegee, Florida A&M, Prairie View and Alabama State presented topics such as: defining the focus of the grant application, proposing international initiatives based on their school's and community's needs, and lessons learned. Special guest **Tanyelle Richardson, BIE Grant Program Manager**, offered her expertise on "What To Do and What Not To Do" when applying for a BIE grant. **Blair Alexander, Acting Director, IIPP**, introduced an exceptional opportunity for sophomore students interested in public policy/international affairs.

As a member of the GBS Program, each HBCU receives three scholarships each year covering the program fees for business faculty to attend the annual FDIB-Globalization Seminars. To date **110 HBCU business faculty have participated in**

June 210 FDIB-Globalization Seminars

one of the five FDIB-Globalization Seminars offered: Introduction to International Business, International Finance, International Marketing, International Management, or Global Supply Chain Management, including workshops on Teaching, Research or Grant Opportunities. (**Thirty-three HBCU business faculty attended in 2007; 27 in 2008; 27 in 2009; and 23 in 2010).** (See page 3 for the list of HBCU faculty participants by school.)

Twelve (12) HBCU Faculty attended the Short-Term Study Abroad Conference coordinated by the University of TX-Austin CIBER in 2008, Brigham Young University CIBER in 2009, and Michigan State University CIBER in 2010. During the last two years of the GBS Program, each HBCU had the opportunity to select two business faculty who had been an active participants in the GBS Program, to participate in a study abroad program. **Twenty-four (24) HBCU faculty participated in CIBER Faculty Overseas Programs.** Three HBCU faculty attended the FDIB-India programs. Two faculty participated in each of the FDIB-Vietnam, FDIB-China, and FDIB-Eastern Europe programs. One HBCU faculty attended the FDIB-Turkey program. Seven faculty participated in the FDIB-Africa; four attended the FDIB-Mercosur; and three attended the FDIB-EU programs.

An integral component of the four-year GBS Program was the **HBCU-CIBER partnership.** The CIBER partner provided consultation for developing an International Plan for the HBCU's Business School and for the planning/preparation of a BIE grant proposal. **Fourteen BIE grant proposals were submitted. Seven HBCUs received USDOE BIE Grant Awards during 2007-2010!**

HBCU-CIBER PARTNERS: 2006-2010

	HBCU Institutions		CIBER Institutions
1	Alabama A & M University	1	Georgia Tech
2	Alabama State University	2	University of Connecticut
3	Bethune-Cookman College	3	University of Florida
4	Bowie State University	4	University of Maryland
5	Fayetteville State University	5	University of Pittsburgh
6	Florida Memorial University	6	Florida International University
7	Grambling State University	7	University of Memphis
8	Hampton University	8	Duke University
9	Mississippi Valley State University	9	Michigan State University
10	North Carolina Central University	10	University of North Carolina
11	South Carolina State University	11	University of South Carolina
12	Texas Southern University	12	Texas A&M University
13	University of Maryland Eastern Shore	13	University of Wisconsin
14	Winston-Salem State University	14	University of Pennsylvania

GLOBALIZING BUSINESS SCHOOLS PROGRAM FOR HBCUs
2006 - 2010 *(continued)*

ALABAMA A & M UNIVERSITY
  Augustine Dike
  Chris Enyinda
  Marasha Griffin
  Rohit Jain
  Barbara Jones (3)
  Larry McDaniel
  Halima Qureshi
  M. Robbani (2)
  Andrea Tillman (2)
ALABAMA STATE UNIVERSITY
  Brenda Autry
  Le-Quita Booth (2)
  Xueyu Cheng
  Sun Gi Chun
  Susan Coleman
  Pamela Gay
  Charlie Hardy
  Janel Bell Haynes
  Kamal Hingorani (2)
  Gow-Cheng Huang
  Robert McNeal
  Walter Montgomery
  Tammy Prater
  La'Shaun Seay
  Kim Smith
  Jerald Tharpe
  Percy Vaughn Jr. (2)
  Jiin Wang
  Don Woodard
BETHUNE-COOKMAN UNIVERSITY
  Warren Ashby
  Sussan Aysar
  Susan Baxter
  Gina Beckles
  Susanne Eules
  Luis Rojas Lagunas
  Aubrey Long
  Robin Rance
  Ambar Saleh
  Michael Santonino
  George Stapleton
  Aysar Sussan
  W. Wallenberg (2)
BOWIE STATE UNIVERSITY
  James Dixon, Sr.
  Fiseha Eshete (3)
  Jongdoo Lee
  Granville Sawyer (3)
  Regina Tawah
FAYETTEVILLE STATE UNIVERSITY
  Boris Abbey
  Keshia Abraham
  Timothy Ajani

  Hilary Barnes
  Aurelie Capron
  Khalid Dubas
  Jose Franco
  Lewis Hershey
  Milena Hurtado
  Pamela Jackson (3)
  Baeyong Lee
  Fazlul Miah
  S. Muhammed
  Donatus Okhomina
  Jane Peacock (2)
  Christine Powell
  Assad Tavakoli
  Dothang Truong
  Thomas Williams (2)
  Craig Wishart (2)
FLORIDA MEMORIAL UNIVERSITY
  Abbas Entessari (4)
  Rita Koyame
  Robert Labadie
  Cheulho Lee
  William Lucky
  Debra Perkins (3)
  William Perry (2)
GRAMBLING STATE UNIVERSITY
  Encarna Abella
  C. Banzar
  Semere Haile (2)
  Ghebre Keleta
  Anthony Nelson
  Obonnaya Nwoha (5)
  Gary Poe (5)
HAMPTON UNIVERSITY
  Priscilla Aaltonen
  Olayemi Adeniyi
  Piradee Aimjirakul
  Jack Chirch (2)
  Jacques Digbeu
  Kanata Jackson (4)
  Vahwere Kavota
  Terri Kirchner
  Michele Lewis
  Nicoleta Maghear
  Edwin Makamson (2)
  Nellie McRae (2)
  Sylvain Poosson
  Natalie Robertson
  Patrick Simanjuntak
  Susanne Toney (2)
  Lida Zarrabi
MISSISSIPPI VALLEY STATE UNIV.
  Curressia M. Brown
  Farhad Chowdhury (2)

Ina Freeman
Aurora Fiengo-Varn (2)
Tadesse Mengistu (4)
R. Naraseeyappa (3)
N. Rajanikanth
NORTH CAROLINA CENTRAL UNIV.
Claudia Becker
Deirdre Guion
Raj Iyengar
Javad Kargar (2)
Robert Moffie
Mark Rosso
Bijoy K. Sahoo
Minnie Sangster
M. Sundararajan (2)
Reine Turcato
SOUTH CAROLINA STATE UNIVERSITY
Hanas Abdul Cader
Gisela Carreras
R. Doucette
Keli Feng
David Jamison (4)
Jaejoo Lim
Guohua Ma
Kathy Quinn (2)
Ruben Silvestry
Renu Singh
Chris Thornburg
TEXAS SOUTHERN UNIVERSITY
Donald Bond
K. Ofori-Brobbey
Marylise Caussinus
Claudius Claiborne
Mayur Desai

Tommy G. Erwin (3)
David Hansen
Burke Mathes (3)
Lucy Ojode (2)
K. Ofori-Brobbey
Kiz. Ramaswamy
Marion Smith
UNIV. MARYLAND EASTERN SHORE
Emmanuel Acquah
Ayodele J. Alade
Nagy Habib
Dandeson Panda (3)
WINSTON-SALEM STATE UNIVERSITY
Michael Brookshaw (2)
Monica Cain
William Carden
Moula Cherikh
Suresh Gopalan
Robert Herring
N. Karagiannis
Alican Kavas
Leonard Muaka (2)
B. Balla Omgba
Notis Pagiavlas
Z. Madjd-Sadjadi
Beth Schneider
Swapan Sen (3)
Kathy Stitts
Edward Zajicek (2)

**TOTAL HBCU FACULTY
PARTICIPANTS = 224**

GLOBALIZING HBCU BUSINESS SCHOOLS (GBS) PROGRAM
A COLLABORATIVE PROJECT OF HBCUs, UNCFSP-IIPP, CIBERs AND USDOE*

The GBS Program is designed to infuse understanding and the importance of international and interdisciplinary business education by equipping faculty with the pedagogical tools, knowledge, and experiences to incorporate international content into existing business courses and/or develop new courses. An integral component of the program is one-on-one assistance provided by the sponsoring CIBERs to their respective HBCU in facilitating the implementation of international business education programs on their campuses and in acquiring federal grant funds to support these efforts. Established in 2002, the Globalizing Business Schools (GBS) Program is an exemplary and highly successful program for internationalizing business education at HBCUs.

GBS PROGRESS REPORT: 2010-2011 (YEAR ONE)

To provide a springboard for HBCU and CIBER collaboration during the 2010-2014 grant period, the **HBCU Globalizing Business Schools Conference** hosted by the University of Memphis CIBER was held on May 23-24, 2010. Seventeen (17) HBCU Business Deans and one business faculty member at each HBCU were invited to the Conference as guests of the CIBER conference sponsors. The Conference provided the opportunity for HBCU Deans and business faculty to learn more about: (1) The importance of international and interdisciplinary business education for their faculty and students; (2) Equipping HBCU faculty with the knowledge to incorporate international content into existing business courses and/or develop new courses, pedagogical tools, and research; (3) Assistance provided by sponsoring CIBERs to facilitate and implement an international business education program on their campus; (4) Tools and techniques for acquiring Federal grant funds (especially a BIE) to support internationalization efforts on campus; (5) Opportunities to gain first-hand experience through Faculty Study Abroad programs; and (6) The purpose of the GBS Program for HBCU institutions which is to build capacity at HBCUs in the area of international business through systemic FDIB program participation during the next four years (October 2010 - September 2014).

HBCU Globalizing Business Schools Conference, May 23-24, 2010

Michael L. Ducker, COO and President of International at FedEx Express Corp., gave the keynote presentation on "Globalization and the Future of Business." Nicholas M. Bassey, Director, UNCFSP-IIPP, and Tanyelle Richardson, Senior Program Manager, USDOE, International Studies Branch provided information about student programs and grant opportunities available through their organizations. Four representatives from HBCUs who participated in the previous 2006-2010 GBS Program — Hampton U., Florida Memorial U., Alabama State U., and Bethune Cookman U. — gave a panel presentation on the "Impact of the GBS Program" on their campus. The Conference concluded with dinner and a guided tour of the National Civil Rights Museum.

GLOBALIZING BUSINESS SCHOOLS PROGRAM FOR HBCUs
2010 - 2014

A Collaborative Project of Historically Black Colleges & Universities (HBCU), United Negro College Fund Special Programs' Institute for International Public Policy (UNCFSP-IIPP), Centers for International Business Education and Research (CIBER), and the United States Department of Education (USDOE)

GBS PROGRESS REPORT: 2010-2011 (YEAR ONE)

By October 2010, **twenty (20) HBCUs** had submitted Letters of Commitment signed by the HBCU President, Business Dean, and GBS Program Leader indicating their sincere interest in actively participating in the four-year GBS Program. **Twenty-one CIBERs** each agreed to partner with an HBCU as a sponsor of the 2010-2014 GBS Program. The one-on-one HBCU-CIBER partnership is a vital component to the success of the GBS Program.

In February 2011, participating HBCUs were invited to send two language faculty to the Business Language Workshop. **Twenty-seven (27) HBCU Language Faculty** participated in one of four workshops—Business Spanish, Business German, Business Japanese, or Business French. In June 2011, each HBCU was invited to send three business faculty to the FDIB-Globalization Seminars. **Fifty-three HBCU Business Faculty** participated in one of six two-day seminars—Intro to IB, Int'l Accounting, Int'l Management, Int'l Marketing, Int'l Finance or Global Supply Chain Management, plus a half-day workshop focusing on Grant Opportunities, Pedagogy, or Research.

2010-2014 HBCU-CIBER PARTNERS

1.	Alcorn State University	U Memphis CIBER
2.	U. of Arkansas at Pine Bluff	U Colorado at Denver CIBER
3.	Central State University	U Pittsburgh CIBER
4.	Clark Atlanta University	Georgia St U CIBER
5.	Chicago State University	U Wisconsin CIBER
6.	Delaware State University	George Washington University
7.	U. of District of Columbia	Florida Int'l U CIBER
8.	Elizabeth City State U.	Michigan St U CIBER
9.	Governors State U.	Indiana U CIBER
10.	Harris-Stowe State U.	U Maryland CIBER
11.	Howard University	U Pennsylvania CIBER
12.	Jackson State University	Brigham Young U CIBER
13.	Johnson C Smith U.	Duke U CIBER
14.	Langston University	TX A&M / U TX-Austin (consortium)
15.	Lincoln University	Temple U CIBER
16.	North Carolina A&T U.	U North Carolina at Chapel Hill CIBER
17.	Savannah State U.	Georgia Institute of Tech. CIBER
18.	Southern U. at New Orleans..	U Connecticut CIBER
19.	Virginia State U.	U South Carolina CIBER
20.	Xavier U. of Louisiana	U Miami CIBER

IMPORTANT NOTE: Due to severe budget cuts for the 2011-2012 CIBER grant year, the annual Business Language Workshop will be postponed until 2013.

FDIB-Globalization Seminars, June 2-5, 2011

HBCU Successes in the GBS Program 2010-2011 (Year One)

GBS Conference (May 2010)....32 HBCU Faculty	New Undergraduate IB Courses.................. 7
Business Language Wrksp....27 HBCU Faculty	New Graduate IB Courses 2
FDIB-Globalization Seminars.... 53 HBCU Faculty	Int'l Content Added to Bus. Courses.......... 32
BIE Proposals Submitted 5	Students Attended Study Abroad 49
(Note: BIE Grant Award Cancelled in 2011)	Faculty Attended Study Abroad 20
	Int'l Research (Pres. & Publ.)...................... 64

GLOBALIZING BUSINESS SCHOOLS PROGRAM FOR HBCUs
2010 - 2014 *(continued)*

ALCORN STATE UNIVERSITY
- Wille Anderson
- Marcharie Chambliss
- Lisa Micicih
- Clyde Posey
- Cynthia Scurria
- Judy Smith
- A. Benedict Udemgba

CENTRAL STATE UNIVERSITY
- Charles Anderson
- Firooz Ghavami
- Hua Zhang Jones
- Edwige Sery (2)
- Charles Showell
- Kwawiski Tekpetey

CHICAGO STATE UNIVERSITY
- Zafar Bokhari
- Linnae Bryant
- Araceli Canalini
- Evelyne Delgado-Norris
- Wolanyo Kpo (2)
- Roosevelt Martin (2)
- Vincent Osaghae

CLARK ATLANTA UNIVERSITY
- Rosalind Arthur
- Rajul Gokarn
- Siriyama Herath
- Vincent Osaghae
- Marlissa Phillips
- Zelealem Yiheyis
- John Young

DELAWARE STATE UNIVERSITY
- Bridget Anakwe
- Constant Beugre
- Nandita Das
- Young Kwak
- Nanda Viswanathan (2)

ELIZABETH CITY STATE UNIVERSITY
- Jose Gil
- Yan Jin
- Debjani Kanjilal
- Alex Ogwu
- Ngozi Ogwu
- Narendra Sharma
- Kungpo Tao

GOVERNORS STATE UNIVERSITY
- Anthony Andrews
- Laura Casal
- David Green
- Olumide Ijose
- Susan Ji
- Evelina Mengova
- Feng Tian

HARRIS-STOWE STATE UNIVERSITY
- Yolanda Diaz
- Joyce Eisel
- Robert Kamkwalala
- John David Kerr
- Peter Ndoma-Ogar
- Charles Sykes
- Fatemeh (Fara) Zakery

HOWARD UNIVERSITY
- Micah Crump
- Maru Etta
- Susan Harmeling
- Esther Kahn
- Masoud Kavoossi
- Youngho Lee
- Narendra Rustagi
- Marilyn Sephocle
- Jean-Jacques Taty

JOHNSON C. SMITH UNIVERSITY
- Melissa Knosp
- Sunday Ndoh
- James Nguyen
- Yvette Russell
- Alfred Smith
- Perumal Thirumurthy

LANGSTON UNIVERSITY
- Michael Hamilton (2)
- Hossein Sarjeh Payma
- Sheila Shoemake-Garcia
- Noopur Singh
- Solomon Smith

LINCOLN UNIVERSITY
- Robert Allen
- William Dadson
- Maribel Charle Poza
- Ganga Ramdas
- Oswald Richards (2)
- Harry Washington

NORTH CAROLINA A&T STATE UNIV.
- Jose Bravo-de-Rueda
- Sarah Carrig
- Linda Coley
- Kathryn Dobie
- Susan Houghton
- Brandis Phillips
- George Stone
- Danielle Winchester

SAVANNAH STATE UNIVERSITY
- Anshu Arora
- Boniface Kawasha
- Suman Niranjan
- Irina Tedrick
- Jun Wu

SOUTHERN UNIVERSITY AT NEW ORLEANS
David (Ghasem) Alijani
Marjorie Fox
Adrine Harrell-Carter
Frank Martin
Muhammed Miah
J. Steven Welsh

UNIV. OF ARKANSAS AT PINE BLUFF
Lawrence Awopetu
Serena Brenneman
Eddie Hand
Antony Hobbs
Carla Martin
Joon Park
Peter Wui (2)

UNIV. OF THE DISTRICT OF COLUMBIA
Paul Bachman
Jian Hua
Charlie Mahone
Marie Racine
Ibrahim Sakaji
William White

VIRGINIA STATE UNIVERSITY
Yao O. Amewokunu
Elin Cortijo-Doval
David Coss
Lynette Hammond
Steve Holeman
Mohamed Saidu Kabia
Junsang Lim
Bryan Menk

XAVIER UNIVERSITY OF LOUISIANA
James Bartkus
Cary Carol
Richard Peters
Masako Dorrill
Herman Johnson
Mark Quinn
Candice Roche
Shael Wolfson

**TOTAL HBCU FACULTY
PARTICIPANTS = 133**

1991-1992

Ralph Albanese: Conference on Language for Students of Business & Economics
T. Bettina Cornwell: International Faculty & Student Exchange Dev.
Irene Duhaime: Strategic Management Society Conference
George Lucas: American Marketing Association; Int'l Marketing Conf.

1992-1993

Irene Duhaime: Strategic Management Society Conference; SW Federation of
    Administrative Disciplines
O.C. Ferrell: Internationalizing Business Ethics
Ben Kedia: Academy of Int'l Business; Alliance of Univ. for Democracy
Nicholas Rokas: UCLA-CIBER Conference on Teachers of Modern Languages &
    International Business

1993-1994

Mohammad Amini: TIMS XXXII International Conference
Rabi Bhagat: International Congress of Applied Psychology
Martine Danan: Int'l Comparative Literature Association Congress
Linda Ferrell: Academy of Business Administration
Michael Gootzeit: History of Economics Society Meeting
Ben Kedia: Academy of Management
Thomas McInish: Pacific Basin Finance Conference
Ravinder Nath: 1994 Pan Pacific Conference

1994-1995

Emin Babakus: 4th Annual World Business Congress
Rabi Bhagat: Society of Industrial and Organizational Psychology
Quentin Chu: American Finance Association Meeting
T. Cornwell: 7th Bi-Annual World Marketing Congress
James Rakowski: Academy of Business Administration International
Mike Shields: Management Control System Conference

1995-1996

Ralph Albanese: Eastern Michigan University Conference on Languages and
    Communication for World Business and Professions
Mohammad Amini: Int'l Federation of Operational Res. Soc. 14th Triennial Conf.
Daniel Coldwell: 41st International Atlantic Economic Conference; ASSA Meeting
Michael Gootzeit: John Rae Bicentenary Conference at King's College
Satish Mehra: SWFAD Conference
Larry Moore: North Atlantic Regional Business Law Association
Monika Nenon: American Council on Teaching of Foreign Languages
Prashant Palvia: Information Resources Management Assoc. International Conf.;
    International Conference on Automation
C. Pyun: 7th Annual Asia Pacific Futures Symposium
James Rakowski: 41st International Atlantic Economic Conference
Ed Salas: American Council on Teaching Foreign Languages

1996-1997

Rabi Bhagat: 34th Annual Academy of Management Meeting
Quentin Chu: Pacific Basin Business Conference
T. Cornwell: Academy of International Business
Kenneth Holland: International Studies Assoc. & Japan Association for Int'l Relations
    Joint Convention; XVII World Congress of the Int'l Political Science Assoc.

Moon Kim: Guesthouse of the Dresder Bank, Koenigstein
Prashant Palvia: 1996 National Decision Sciences Institute Conference
James Rakowski: 43rd International Atlantic Economic Conference
Mike Shields: Comparative Management Accounting Conference
William Thompson: Modern Language Association Convention

1997-1998

Emin Babakus: Western Academy of Management Meeting
Rabi Bhagat: Academy of International Business Meeting
Kee Chung: Korea-America Finance Assoc. & Korean Finance Assoc.
Peter Davis: 1998 Academy of Management Meeting
Michael Gootzeit: European Society for the History of Economic Thought Conference
Ben Kedia: Babson-Kauffman Research Conf.; Best Papers Proceedings, 34th Academy
     of Management; Best Papers Proceedings, South Asia Conference
C. S. Pyun: 6th Annual East West Conference

1998-1999

Kee Chung: Korea-America Finance Assoc. & Korean Finance Assoc.
Daniel Coldwell: 47th International Atlantic Economic Conference
Peter Davis: 59th Annual Academy of Management Meeting
Detelin Elenkov: Conference on Eastern Europe Politics
Ben Kedia: Academy of International Business; American Society for Competitiveness
Albert Okunade: International Health Economics Association Conf.
C. Pyun: Asia Pacific Central Banking Conf. & Financial Management Assoc. Int'l
Satish Mehra: 6th Annual APICS E&R Foundation Workshop

1999-2000

Rabi Bhagat: Academy of Management; SE Academy of Management
Peter Davis: 1999 Academy of International Business
Detelin Elenkov: Leadership Strategies for the Economies in Transition
Michael Gootzeit: European Society for the History of Econ. Thought
Ben Kedia: AIEA Annual Conference
Loel Kim: Association for Business Communications Conference
C. Pyun: Korea-American Finance & Korean Finance Assoc. Meetings

2000-2001

Surendra Agrawal: Applied Business Research Conference; Int'l Business Education
     and Technology Conference
Rabi Bhagat: Academy of International Business Conference; International
     Association for Cross Cultural Psychology
Robert Blanton: International Studies Association Conference
Detelin Elenkov: Academy of International Business Conference
Michael Gootzeit: European Society for the History of Econ. Thought
Ben Kedia: Academy of Management Meeting
Loel Kim: CIBER 2000 Workshop for Language Faculty
Balaji Krishnan: Academy of International Business Conference
Satish Mehra: XVIII Annual Pan Pacific Conferences
Larry Moore: Nat'l Meeting of the Academy of Legal Studies in Business; SE Academy
     of Legal Studies in Business
Albert Okunade: Int'l Health Economics Assoc. & 13th Annual Biennial World Conf.
C. S. Pyun: Korea America Finance & Korean Finance Association

2001-2002

Surendra Agrawal: Asian Pacific Conf. of Int'l Accounting Issues
Rabi Bhagat: International Academy for Applied Psychology; International Association for Cross-Cultural Psychologists
Robert Blanton: 44th Annual International Studies Association Meeting
Lloyd Brooks: Global Information Technology Management Assoc.; Annual Global Information Technology Management
W. Chu: Asia/Pacific Business Outlook Conference
Michael Gootzeit: European Society for the History of Econ.Thought
Felipe Lapuente: Asociacion Internacional de Hispanistas
C. S. Pyun: Korea-American Economic
Bob Taylor: Applied Business Research Conference
William Thompson: American Assoc. of Teachers of French
Jerry Turner: International Symp. on Audit Research; NE Decision Sciences Inst.

2002-2003

Surendra Agrawal: Congress of the European Accounting Association
Demetrio Anzaldo-Gonzalez: Congress of Mexican Literature
Rabi Bhagat: SIOP Conference
Robert Blanton: Annual Conference of the International Studies Assoc.
Michael Gootzeit: Notre Contemporain? Économie, Administration et Gouvernement au Siècle des Lumières
Pankaj Jain: Eastern Finance Association's Thirty-ninth Annual Mtg.
Phillip Kolbe: African Real Estate Conference
Euntae Lee: Pan-Pacific Conference
Robert O'Halloran: Annual Conference in Halifax, Nova Scotia, Can.
J. Rakowksi: National Identities and Movements in European History
Tom Stafford: Annual Global Information Technology Mgmt. Conf.
William Thompson: American Assoc. Teachers of French Convention

2003-2004

Surendra Agrawal: 27th Annual Congress of the European Accounting Association; University of Geneva Managerial Accounting
Demetrio Anzaldo-Gonzalez: XIX Coloquio Intenacional de Literatura Mexicana e Hispanoamericana
Rabi Bhagat: Academy of Int'l Bus.; Int'l Acad. for Intercultural Res.
Robert Blanton: International Studies Association 2004
Luis Brunstein: Missouri Valley Economic Association
Fernando Burgos: 17th Annual Int'l Conference in Literature and the Visual Arts, including Cinema; South Atlantic Modern Language Assoc. Convention
Michael Gootzeit: European Society for the History of Econ.Thought
Pankaj Jain: American Finance Association's 2004 Annual Meeting
Christine Jiang: 2004 China International Conference in Finance
Phillip Kolbe: 16th Australasian Finance Conference
Cynthia O'Halloran: ASAC 2004
Robert O'Halloran: ASAC 2004
C. Pyun: Korea-America Finance Assoc. & Korea Finance Association

2004-2005

Surendra Agrawal: 28th Annual Congress of the European Accounting Assoc.; Catalan Congress on Accounting and Management

Rabi Bhagat: IAIR Conference
Volodymyr Lugovskyy: National Bureau of Economic Research Conference on
       International Trade and Investment
C. S. Pyun: Korea-America Finance Association & the Korean Finance and Korean
       Securities Associations Joint Conference
James Rakowski: TRANSCOMP 2005
Rose Rubin: International Health Economics Association (IHEA)
William Thompson: American Association of Teachers of French
Howard Tu: Academy of Management

2005-2006

Rabi Bhagat: IACCP and IAAP; IAB Conf.; Academy of Int'l Bus.; IAIR
Lloyd Brooks: Global Information Technology Management Assoc. World Conf.
Lourdes Gabikagojeaskoa: Lessons from the MBA Classroom: Business Concepts for
       Foreign Language Teachers and Professionals
Michael Gootzeit: European Society for the History of Econ. Thought
Christine Jiang: Conference in Shanghai
Volodymyr Lugovskyy: Nat'l Bue. of Econ. Research
C.S. Pyun: International Economic Symposium; Korea-American Finance Assoc.
Bill Smith: AEA Mtg.

2006-2007

Laura Anderson: Homeland Security and Canada-U.S. Border Trade: Implications for
       Public Policy and Business Strategy Conference
Rabi Bhagat: Academy of International Business; SIOP Conference
Michael Gootzeit: Italian Asso. for the History of Political Economy IV National
       Conference; Their Impact on Econonmic Thought During the 19th Centry
V. Lugovskyy: 10th Annual Conference on Global Economic Analysis; Domestic Prices
       in an Integrated World Economy Conference
Albert Okunade: International Health Economics Association's 6th Biennial Conf.; 6th
       Biennial Conference of the IHEA
C. S. Pyun: Business, Information and Management Academy
William T. Smith: Catholic University in Eichstaat, Germany

2007-2008

Rabi Bhagat: Academy of Int'l Business
Lourdes Gabikogojeaskoa: Teaching Spanish for Business: A Global Approach
Michael Gootzeit: Italian Society for the History of Economic Thought
Ted Lee: Pan-Pacific Int'l Conference
Robin Poston: Int'l Conf. on Information Systems
C. S. Pyun: Korea-America Finance Assoc.
Marla Stafford Royne: Hangzhou Dianzi University
William Thompson: CIBER Business Language Conference; American Association of
       Teachers of French,
Rezaee Zabihollah: 15th Annual Global Finance Conference

2008-2009

Michael Gootzeit: Italian Association for the History of Political Economy
Volodymyr Lugovskyy: Domestic Prices in an Integrated World Economy
Yuki Matsuda: CIBER Business Language Conference
Robin Poston: International Simulation & Gaming Association

Rose Rubin: Int'l Trade & Finance Association
Marla Stafford: American Academy of Advertising

2009-2010

Rabi Bhagat: Academy of International Business Conference
Lourdes Gabikagojeaskoa: Eran sonadores de paraisos
Michael Gootzeit: STOREP Conference
Ted Lee: Pan-Pacific Business Association
Yuki Matsuda: CIBER Business Language Conf.; Annual Conference of Asian Society
Sandra Mortal: EFA
Alex Nikolsko-Rzhevskyy: National Bureau of Economic Research (NBER)
Robin Poston: AMCIS
C. S. Pyun: KAFA joint conference with Allied Korean Finance Associations
Marla Stafford: American Academy of Advertising Conference
William Thompson: CIBER Business Language Conference
Tina Wakolbinger: POMS Conference

2010-2011

David Allen: International Workshop on Human Resource Management
Michael Gootzeit: Storep: Economic Dev. & Social Cohesion: Converging Goals
Shana Hong: European Accounting Association Congress
Yuki Matsuda: Association of Teachers of Japanese
Sandra Mortal: European Financial Management Association
A. Nikolsko-Rzhevskyy: National Bureau of Economic Research; Assoc. Conf.
C.S. Pyun: Korea Institute of Public Finance
William Thompson: CIBER Business Language Conference
Zabi Rezaee: Forensic Investigative Accounting Conference

2011-2012

Rebecca Laumann: NAFSA Conference
Yuki Matsuda: CIBER Business Language Conference
C.S. Pyun: Korea-America Finance Association
Lan Zhang: International Conference on Business Chinese Teaching

SUMMER RESEARCH AWARDS FOR
U of M FOGELMAN COLLEGE FACULTY

2003	Dr. Mitzi Pitts		Dr. Michael Gootzeit
	Dr. C. S. Pyun		Dr. C. S. Pyun
	Dr. Tom Stafford	2007	Dr. Robin Poston
	Dr. Qiang (Richard) Zhang		Dr. Radhika Jain
2004	Dr. Emin Babakus		Dr. Judy Simon
	Dr. Christine Jiang		Dr. Volodymyr Lugovskyy
2005	Dr. Pinaki Bose	2008	Dr. Robin Poston
	Dr. P. K. Jain		Dr. P. K. Jain
	Dr. Robert Thieme	2009	Dr. Rabi Bhagat
	Dr. Jerry Turner		Dr. C. S. Pyun
2006	Dr. Rabi Bhagat	2010	Dr. P. K. Jain
	Dr. Pinaki Bose		Dr. Tom Stafford

1991

T. Bettina Cornwell: Faculty Dev. in Int'l Marketing (U. of South Carolina CIBER)
John Gnuschke: Faculty Study Abroad in Lille, France (U. of Memphis CIBER)
Mathew Jewett: Faculty Study Abroad in Lille, France (U. of Memphis CIBER)
Jim King: Faculty Dev. in Int'l Accounting (U. of South Carolina CIBER)
Peter Tat: Faculty Study Abroad in Lille, France (U. of Memphis CIBER)
Pochara Theerathorn: Faculty Dev. in Int'l Business (U. of South Carolina CIBER)

1992

David H. Ciscel: Faculty Study Abroad in Grenoble, France (U. of Memphis CIBER)
Peter S. Davis: Faculty Study Abroad in Grenoble, France (U. of Memphis CIBER)
George Lucas: Faculty Study Abroad in Grenoble, France (U. of Memphis CIBER)
Tom Schwartz: Faculty Dev. in Int'l Finance (U. of South Carolina CIBER)
David Spiceland: Faculty Study Abroad in Grenoble, Fr. (U. of Memphis CIBER)
Charles Stubbart: Faculty Dev. in Int'l Management (U. of South Carolina CIBER)
Peter Tat: Faculty Dev. in Int'l Marketing (U. of South Carolina CIBER)
Howard Tu: Faculty Dev. in Int'l Management (U. of South Carolina CIBER)

1994

Ken Austin: Faculty Dev. in Int'l Accounting (U. of South Carolina CIBER)
Emin Babakus: Faculty Dev. in Int'l Marketing (U. of South Carolina CIBER)
Rabi Bhagat: Faculty Dev. in Int'l Management (U. of South Carolina CIBER)
William Carpenter: Faculty Study Abroad in Antwerp (U. of Memphis CIBER)
Irene Duhaime: Faculty Study Abroad in Antwerp (U. of Memphis CIBER)
Satish Mehra: Faculty Study Abroad in Antwerp (U. of Memphis CIBER)
Raymonde Neil: CIBER Language Conference (U. of CA, Los Angeles CIBER)
James Rakowski: Faculty Study Abroad in Antwerp (U. of Memphis CIBER)

1995

Delano Black: Faculty Study Abroad in Antwerp (U. of Memphis CIBER)
Ken Holland: Faculty Dev. in Int'l Business, Mexico (Texas A&M CIBER)
Sidney McPhee: Faculty Study Abroad in Antwerp (U. of Memphis CIBER)
Rose Rubin: Faculty Study Abroad in Antwerp (U. of Memphis CIBER)
William T. Smith: Faculty Study Abroad in Antwerp (U. of Memphis CIBER)
Yiumin Tse: Faculty Dev. in Int'l Finance (U. of South Carolina CIBER)

1996

Surrendra Agrawal: Faculty Dev. in Int'l Accounting (U. of South Carolina CIBER)
Carol Danehower: Faculty Dev. in Int'l HR Mgmt. (U. Colorado Denver CIBER)
Thomas O. Depperschmidt: Faculty Study Abr. in Antwerp (U. of Memphis CIBER)
Theodore Mealor: Faculty Study Abroad in Antwerp (U. of Memphis CIBER)
Monika Nenon: Foreign Language & Culture for Bus. & Economics (UCLA CIBER)
Robert V. Smythe: Faculty Study Abroad in Antwerp (U. of Memphis CIBER)
Robert R. Taylor: Faculty Study Abroad in Antwerp (U. of Memphis CIBER)

1997

Clifton V. Dixon: Faculty Study Abroad in Antwerp (U. of Memphis CIBER)
Philip T. Kolbe: Faculty Study Abroad in Antwerp (U. of Memphis CIBER)
Jeffrey Krug: Faculty Dev. in Int'l Management (U. of South Carolina CIBER)
Ksiang-te Kung: Faculty Study Abroad in Antwerp (U. of Memphis CIBER)
C. S. Pyun: Faculty Study Abroad in Antwerp (U. of Memphis CIBER)
Francisco Vivar: Business Language Conference (San Diego St U. CIBER)

1998

Robert Berl: Faculty Dev. in Marketing (U. of South Carolina CIBER)
Carol Danehower: Faculty Study Abroad Mercosur (Florida International U. CIBER)
Peter Davis: Faculty Dev. in Int'l Management (U. of South Carolina CIBER)
Coy Jones: Faculty Dev. in Int'l HR Mgmt. (U. Colorado Denver CIBER)
Felipe Lapuente: Business Language Conference, (U. of Illinois CIBER)
Monika Nenon: Business Language Conference, (U. of Illinois CIBER)
Bob Taylor: Faculty Dev. in Int'l Management (U. of South Carolina CIBER)

1999

Neil Southern: Faculty Dev. in Int'l Business (U. of South Carolina CIBER)

2000

Carol Beinstock: Faculty Study Abroad EU in Antwerp (U. of Memphis CIBER)
Charles Hall: Faculty Study Abroad EU in Antwerp (U. of Memphis CIBER)
Loel Kim: Workshop for Language Faculty (U. of Ohio CIBER)
Balaji Krishnan: Faculty Dev. in Int'l Marketing (U. of South Carolina CIBER)
Hsiang-te Kung: Faculty Study Abroad EU in Antwerp (U. of Memphis CIBER)
James Lukawitz: Faculty Study Abroad Mercosur (Florida International U. CIBER)
Monica Nenon: Workshop for Language Faculty (Ohio St. U. CIBER)

2001

David Allen: Fac. Dev. in Human Resource Mgmt. (U. of Colorado-Denver CIBER)
Rabi Bhagat: Faculty Study Abroad Mercosur (Florida International U. CIBER)
Robert Blanton: Faculty Study Abroad EU in Antwerp (U. of Memphis CIBER)
Peter Davis: Faculty Dev. in Int'l Business (U. of South Carolina CIBER)
Larry Moore: Faculty Study Abroad Mercosur (Florida International U. CIBER)
William Thompson: Business Language Conference, (U. of Illinois CIBER)

2002

Marla Stafford: Faculty Dev. in Int'l Business (U. of South Carolina CIBER)
Barbara Davis: Faculty Study Abroad EU in Antwerp (U. of Memphis CIBER)

2003

Carol Danehower: Faculty Study Abroad in India (U. of Connecticut CIBER)
Cynthia Deale: Faculty Study Abroad in India (U. of Connecticut CIBER)
P. K. Jain: Faculty Dev. in Int'l Business (U. of South Carolina CIBER)
Craig Langstraat: Faculty Study Abroad in Eastern Europe (U. of Pittsburgh CIBER)
C. S. Pyun: Faculty Study Abroad Mercosur (Florida International U. CIBER)
James Rakowski: Faculty Study Abroad Mercosur (Florida IInternational U. CIBER)

2004

Lloyd Brooks: Faculty Study Abroad in India (U. of Connecticut CIBER)
Balaji Krishnan: Faculty Study Abroad Mercosur (Florida International U. CIBER)
K. K. Fung: Faculty Study Abroad Mercosur (Florida International U. CIBER)
Monica Nenon: Workshop for Language Faculty (Ohio St. U. CIBER)
Katrina Savitskie: Faculty Study Abroad in India (U. of Connecticut CIBER)
zracy Smith: Faculty Study Abroad EU in Antwerp (U. of Memphis CIBER)

2005

Lourdes Gabikagojeaskoa: Workshop for Language Faculty (Ohio St. U. CIBER)
Balaji Krishnan: Faculty Study Abroad in Eastern Europe (U. of Pittsburgh CIBER)

Craig Langstraat: Faculty Study Abroad Mercosur (Florida International U. CIBER)
Yuki Matsuda: Business Language Workshop (Brigham Young U. CIBER)
Robert O'Halloran: Faculty Study Abroad in India (U. of Connecticut CIBER)
Rose Rubin: Faculty Study Abroad in India (U. of Connecticut CIBER)
Katrina Savitskie: Faculty Study Abroad Mercosur (Florida International U. CIBER)
William Thompson: Workshop for Language Faculty (Ohio St. U. CIBER)
WilliliamThompson: Business Language Workshop (Brigham Young U. CIBER)

2006
Lloyd Brooks: Faculty Study Abroad Mercosur (Florida International U. CIBER)
Balaji Krishnan: Faculty Study Abroad in China (U. of Colorado-Denver CIBER)
Yuki Matsuda: Business Language Workshop (Georgia Tech CIBER)
James Lukawitz: Faculty Study Abroad in Eastern Europe (U. of Pittsburgh CIBER)
John Malloy: Faculty Study Abroad EU in Antwerp (U. of Memphis CIBER)
Robert O'Halloran: Faculty Study Abroad EU in Antwerp (U. of Memphis CIBER)
Robin Poston: Faculty Study Abroad in Eastern Europe (U. of Pittsburgh CIBER)
William Thompson: Business Language Workshop (Georgia Tech CIBER)

2007
Eric Brey: Faculty Study Abroad in India (U. of Connecticut CIBER)
Lloyd Brooks: Faculty Study Abroad in China (U. of Colorado-Denver CIBER)
Robin Poston: Faculty Study Abr. in Eastern Europe (U. of Pittsburgh CIBER)

2008
Rabi Bhagat: Faculty Study Abroad EU in Strasbourg (U of Memphis CIBER)
Carol Danehower: Faculty Dev. in Int'l Business (U. of Memphis CIBER)
James Lukawitz: Faculty Study Abroad in China (U. of Colorado-Denver CIBER)
Yuki Matsuda: Business Language Workshop (U. of Florida CIBER)
Robin Poston: Faculty Study Abroad in India (U. of Connecticut CIBER)
William Thompson: Business Language Workshop (U. of Florida CIBER)

2009
Quentin Chu: Faculty Study Abroad EU in Strasbourg (U of Memphis CIBER)
Tom Meservy: Faculty Study Abroad Mercosur (Florida International U. CIBER)
Sandra Mortal: Faculty Study Abroad Mercosur (Florida International U. CIBER)
Tom Stafford: Faculty Study Abroad EU in Strasbourg (U of Memphis CIBER)
Terry Umbreit: Faculty Study Abroad EU in Strasbourg (U of Memphis CIBER)

2010
Laura Alderson: Faculty Study Abroad in Turkey (U. of Kansas CIBER)
Jasbir Dhaliwal: Faculty Study Abroad Mercosur (Florida International U. CIBER)

2011
Emin Babakus: Faculty Study Abr. EU in Brussels (U Memphis & U. Pittsburgh CIBERs)

2012
David Allen: Faculty Study Abroad Mercosur (Florida International U. CIBER)
Robin Poston: Faculty Study Abroad Mercosur (Florida International U. CIBER)
Yuki Matsuda: CIBER Business Language Conference (UNC, Chapel Hill CIBER)

Ackerman, David: After the Coup; Doing Business in Germany; International
  Negotiating; Research Support
Aïssaoui, Rachida: Academy of Management ; ESOC (EGOS-Sage-OMT-CJBS)
Beaver, Freddie: Business Information Technology Conference
Billing, Tejinder: Academy of Int'l Business
Busija, Edie: Seven Revolutions Seminar; Research Support
Chen, Yu: American Accounting Association, International Accounting Sec.
Clampit, Jack: Academy of International Business; EUCE and CIBER Doctoral
  Consortium; AIB-SE; Academy of Manaagement
Desai, Ashay B. American Society for Competitiveness
Dibrell, Clay: American Society of Competitiveness; South Asia Conference;
  Academy of International Business
Ding, David: Dissertation Research Award
Elliottt, David: Research Support
Farber, Vanina: First European Meeting of Latinoamericanists
Fenwick, Mary: Doing Business in Mexico
Ferrell, Linda: Research Support
Francis, J. D.: Academy of Management; American Society for Competitiveness;
  East-West Conference; Research Support
Gaffney, Nolan: Academy of International Business; Internationalizing Doctoral
  Education in Business Conference; Southern Management Assoc
Gondo, Marie: Internationalizing Doctoral Educ. in Business: A PhD Conf.
Harveston, Paula: Academy of Management; Southern Management Assoc.;
  American Society for Competitiveness Conference; Babson-Kauffman
  Research Conference; International Conf. of the Strategic Management
  Society; South Asia Conference; Western Academy of Management;
  Southwest Business Symposium; Big Emerging Markets Conference;
  East-West Conference
Hoffman, Joyce: Decision Sciences Institute National Conference
Hu, Tao: Americas Conf. on Infor. Systems; Data Collection for Dissertation
Huseynw, Fariz: Internationalizing Doctoral Educ. in Business: A PhD Conf.
Imahe, Hisashi: Database Support
Jain, Archana: Financial Mgmt. Assoc. International; So. Finance Assoc.
Jain, Chinmay: Southern Finance Assoc.; Academy of International Bus.
Jain, Pawan: World Business Congress; Northern Finance Association; Eastern
  Finance Assoc.; Southern Finance Association; CMIE-Prowess and the
  China Financial Databases for Research
Jetter, Michael: Canadian Economics Assoc.; Finance & Economics Conf.
Kamau, Edward M.: Academy of International Business
Kanjilal, Debjani: American Society of Health Economists
Keillor, Bruce: Dissertation Research Award
Kim, Seun Yong: Internationalizing Doctoral Educ. in Business Workshop
Kumar, Anil: Information Resources Management Association
Lado, Augustine: Dissertation Research Award
Lahiri, Som: Everything New is Old Again; FDIB-Globalization Seminars;
  Academy of International Business; Western Hemispheric Development

Challenges in the Global Context; Academy of International Business; Dissertation Research in India

Lebo, J. : Impact of NAFTA on Higher Educ. Policy in Canada, Mexico, U.S.

Liu, Wei: Academy of International Business; China Conference; International Business With China: Opportunities and Challenges; Midwest Academy of Management

Ma, Rong: Academy of International Business

Maignan, Isabelle: Data Collection for Dissertation

Mao, En: IRMA Conference; Decision Sciences Institute

Mahadevan, Lakshman: Americas Conference on Information Systems

Mooty, Scott: Internationalizing Doctoral Education in Business Conference; Southern Management Association; Tilburg Conference on Innovation; Enhancing U.S. Competitiveness for Innovation

Moustafa, Karen: Internationalizing Doctoral Education in Business Sem.

Mukherji, Ananda: American Society for Competitiveness; Strategic Management Society Conference; Southern Management Association; Small Bus. Institute Directors' Association; Academy of International Bus.- SE

Mukherji, Jyotsna: East-West Conference

Mukherjee, Deb: FDIB-Globalization Seminars; Seven Futures; Academy of International Business; Western Hemispheric Development Challenges in the Global Context; Southern Management Association; Research Conference & Workshop on Offshoring

Myers, Susan: Doctoral Internationalization Consortium in Marketing

Nikolsko-Rzhevskyy, Alex: Southern Economic Association Conference

Nordtvedt, Rick: Internationalizing Doctoral Educ. in Business Workshop

Onita, Colin Gabriel: Americas Conference on Information Systems

Parikh, Bhavik: European Financial Mgmt. Assoc.; Global Finance Conf.

Perez, Liliana: Academy of Management; Internationalizing Doctoral Education in Business Workshop; Academy of International Business; Teaching International Strategies Workshop; Dissertation Research

Peterson, Robert M.: Academy of International Business; East-West Conference; American Society for Competitiveness

Prakash, Amarnath: Information Resources Management Conference

Reddy, Rama: Academy of International Business; Academy of Management

Sawyer, Eric: After the Coup; Arthur Andersen Symposium; Research Support

Soebetki, Sukono: Disertation Research Award

Steverson, Pam: World Congress on Intellectual Capital; Seven Revolutions Sem.

Tiller, David: NAFTA Conference

Vann, Carol: International Financial Reporting Standards Conference

Wamwara-Mbugua, L. Wakiuru: Dissertation Res.; Acad. of International Bus.

Wongchoti, U.: Collect PACAP Data

Wu, Yue: Internationalizing Doctoral Education in Business: A PhD Conf.

Xingya, Lin: Chinese Business Law course.

Zhang, Xihui (Paul): Americas Conf. on Information Systems

63 PH.D. STUDENTS ATTENDED 107 CONFERENCES